shed: Salem, Massachusetts, 1915
ealogical Publishing Co., Inc.
, 1980
ress Catalogue Card Number 74-29148
andard Book Number 0-8063-0660-2
ited States of America

AN INDEX OF PIO[NEERS FROM]

MASSACHU[SETTS]

TO THE

WES[T]

ESPECIALLY T[HE STATE]
OF MICHI[GAN]

COMPILED B[Y]

CHARLES A. [

This list includes many sons [of]
Bay State families who [settled in New]
York and states of the [

Originally pu[blished
Reprinted: G[
Baltimore, 19[
Library of Co[ngress
International [
Made in the U[nited States

Baltimor[e]

GENEALOGICAL PUBLI[SHING]

1980

INTRODUCTION

It may fairly be said that American genealogists are fortunate in the matter of publications prepared for their especial use. From the first appearance of "Durrie" down to the recent completion of the splendid "Index to persons" for the first fifty volumes of the "New England historical and genealogical register" there has been no lack of handbooks, indexes, guides, bibliographies and reference lists making available the wealth of material in print.

Yet much remains to be done. Where is the family historian who has not worried over and vainly sought for the sons and daughters of our old New England families who left the homes between 1780 and 1850, leaving no trace beyond the tradition that they went "West"? Prior to the discovery of gold in California and the later development of the Mountain and Pacific states following the completion of the transcontinental railroad, the term "West" to be sure was comparatively restricted in meaning, though from a New England standpoint it might signify anything from Central New York to the Mississippi Valley.

The emigrant pioneers were too busily engaged in establishing themselves and building new communities to maintain long their relations with the old homes or to preserve the raw materials of history. The New England element, however mindful at home of the value of local records, formed but a fraction of the new commonwealths; vital statistics were not matter of public care, and even under the enactments of later times, scarcely anything has been transmitted to print.

To be sure pioneer societies sprang up everywhere during the later years of the first generation, but they have published or preserved very little for us. Historical societies, such as the "Michigan Pioneer and Historical Society" have done much to perpetuate the memory of the pioneers, as have also a few notable periodicals, but the field is far too broad for such agencies. It seems clear that he who would investigate the lives of the pioneers must find the most of his material between the covers of the quarto and folio county histories and nowhere else.

(i)

This class of books, bulky, expensive and much maligned, first began to appear in the late "seventies" principally the production of a few men who went into the publishing business in Chicago, Philadelphia and elsewhere seeing a chance to reap a golden harvest from the country folk by publishing sketches and portraits of such as would subscribe at exorbitant figures. The works were of slight value historically; in fact it was almost impossible to get a writer of any repute to lend his name to such an undertaking. About a decade later (1885–95) came another like movement, only the output now bore some such title as "Portrait and biographical album" and omitted the historical part altogether. And since 1900 there have been a number published, but more diversified in form and character and of a considerable higher degree of excellence. Certain common points are noted: publication by subscription, quarto or folio size, heavy paper, numerous portraits usually of poor quality, leather binding, the earlier ones almost invariably beginning with extended lives of the presidents and governors of the state; and indexes, when found at all, most pitifully insufficient.

Let it be understood that the foregoing characterization does not apply to all county histories of this period: some works of this class have been produced by real historians and issued by ordinary publishers, while there is another group of modest little works by local writers, usually printed at home and containing little or no biographical material. These last are useless for our present purpose however.

But after making all due allowance for the unsatisfactory character of these histories; nearly every sketch in them contains genealogical material and oftentimes an extended family record in several ancestral lines. Inadequate as may be the sketch of an emigrant ancestor, the descendants of the present generation are almost invariably located, thus furnishing clues for further investigation.

The present is the first serious attempt, as far as known, to make available for genealogists a portion of this material—Massachusetts emigrants as found in the county histories of Michigan. It would have been easy to enlarge the list by including such works as the various general biographical histories of the state, the collections of the "Michigan Pioneer and Historical Society," etc., but it seems best to restrict our researches to the fairly homogeneous class of county histories and a few other works of similar character.

It should be borne in mind that the following is not merely a list of Massachusetts pioneers in Michigan. In fact a large number of the persons named never saw Michigan, the intention being to index the name of every native of the Bay State who emigrated, whether the subject of the biographic sketch or one of his near or remote ancestors.

Very few of the volumes listed are available in the great libraries of Massachusetts. The Berkshire Athenæum of Pittsfield, the Essex Institute of Salem and the Public Library of Worcester have none at all; the State Library at Boston one volume only and the Public Library and the New England Historic-Genealogical Society of Boston, two each. There may be a few more in other collections in the state but probably no considerable number. Among other libraries comparatively near are the New York State Library at Albany with 17 volumes and the Lenox branch of the Public Library of New York City with 18. Of the total of 73 works listed, the Library of Congress has 54.

In a way, the very inaccessibility of the material is an added reason for indexing it, as it certainly exists in print and if the index reveals nothing for our use, it can simply be eliminated from consideration, while with an exact reference given one knows just what he wants to consult and where it can be seen.

The purpose has been to give name, date and town of birth, and date of removal and *state* in which pioneer settled. When dates are not found, they are often supplied with a ?, which means "approximately" or as near as can be ascertained from the context. It has seemed better to do this even with a possibility of 15 or 20 years miscalculation in extreme cases, rather than leave names entirely indeterminate with respect to time.

No notice has been taken of the considerable number of pioneers who were simply "from New England" though a part of them must belong to us.

The work has been hastily done and it is too much to hope that it will be found free from errors and omissions. We trust it may be useful to inquirers and result in the restoration of many a lost branch to its proper place in the ancestral tree.

WORKS INDEXED

List of Michigan county histories, giving the abbreviations used in this work and libraries reporting the books in their collections. B = Boston Public Library; D = Detroit Public Library; L = New York Public Library (Lenox branch); L. C. = Library of Congress; Mass. = Mass. State Library, Boston; Mich. = Michigan State Library, Lansing; N. Y. S. = New York State Library, Albany; New Eng. = New England Historic Genealogical Society, Boston; Univ. M. = University of Michigan, Ann Arbor.

Of the 83 counties in the state no less than 69 are represented in the list, several of them two or more times.

Alcona County, see *Lake Huron.*

Alger County, see *Northern M.; Northern P.; Upper P.*

Allegan Hist. History of Allegan and Barry counties. Philadelphia, D. W. Ensign & co., 1880. 521 p. (L. C., Mich., N. Y. S.)

Allegan Twent. A twentieth century history of Allegan County . . . Compiled under the editorial supervision of Dr. Henry F. Thomas. Chicago, The Lewis pub. co., 1907. 655 p. (Allegan Township Library, Allegan, Mich.)

Allegan County, see also *Kalamazoo Port.*

Alpena County, see *Lake Huron.*

Antrim County, see *Traverse.*

Baraga County, see *Houghton; Northern M.; Northern P.; Upper P.*

Barry County, see *Allegan Hist.*

Bay Gansser History of Bay County, Michigan and representative citizens... By A. H. Gansser. Chicago, Richmond & Arnold, 1905. 726 p. (L., L. C., Mich.)

Bay Hist. History of Bay County, Michigan, with illustrations and biographical sketches of some of its prominent men and pioneers. Chicago, H. R. Page & co., 1883. 281 p. (D.)
Substantially the same as History of the Lake Huron shore, the two works being identical for more than half their pages, and differing elsewhere chiefly in arrangement.

Bay County, see also *Lake Huron; Saginaw Port.*

Benzie County, see *Traverse.*

Bean Creek The Bean Creek Valley. Incidents of its early settlement. Collected from the memories of its earliest settlers now living . . . By James J. Hogaboam. Hudson, Mich., J. M. Scarritt, 1876. 140 p. (L. C.)

Berrien Hist. History of Berrien and Van Buren counties. Philadelphia, D. W. Ensign & co., 1880. 548 p. (L. C.; Mich.; N. Y. S.)

Berrien Port. Portrait and biographical record of Berrien and Cass counties. Chicago, Biographical pub. co., 1893. 922 p. (L. C.)

Berrien Twent. A twentieth century history of Berrien County. Judge Orville W. Coolidge, author and editor. Chicago, Lewis pub. co., 1906. 1007 p. (D.)

Branch Hist. History of Branch County. Philadelphia, Everts & Abbot, 1879 347 p. (L. C., Mich.)

Branch Port. Portrait and biographical album of Branch County. Chicago, Chapman bros., 1888. 648 p. (L. C.)

Branch Twent. A twentieth century history and biographical record of Branch County, Michigan. Rev. Henry P. Collin, M. A., author and editor. New York, Lewis pub. co., 1906. 879 p. (L. C.)

Calhoun History of Calhoun County. Philadelphia, L. H. Everts & co., 1877. 212 p. (D., L. C., Mich., N. Y. S.)

Calhoun County, see also *Homer.*

Cass Hist. History of Cass County. Chicago, Waterman, Watkins & co., 1882. 432 p. (L. C.)

Cass Rogers History of Cass County, from 1825 to 1875. By Howard S. Rogers Cassopolis, Mich., W. H. Mansfield, 1875. 406 p. (Univ. M.)

Cass Twent. A twentieth century history of Cass County, Michigan. L. H. Glover . . . editor. Chicago, Lewis pub. co., 1906. 782 p (L. C.)

Cass County, see also *Berrien Port.*

Charlevoix County, see *Traverse.*

Cheboygan County, see *Traverse.*

Chippewa County, see *Northern M.; Northern P.; Upper P.*

Clinton Past   Past and present of Clinton County, Michigan by Judge S. B. Daboll, assisted by D. W. Kelley; together with biographical sketches... Chicago, The S. J. Clarke pub. co., 1906.   575 p.
Only copy located is in possession of its publishers, 358 Dearborn st., Chicago.

Clinton Port.   Portrait and biographical album of Clinton and Shiawassee counties... Chicago, Chapman bros., 1891. 1001 p. (L., Mich.)

Clinton County, see also *Shiawassee.*

Delta County, see *Northern M.; Northern P.; Upper P.*

Detroit   History of Detroit and Wayne County.   By Silas Farmer. 3d, or Township and biographical edition. Detroit, S. Farmer & co., 1890. 2 volumes (D., L. C.)
The 2d or Biographical edition 1889 contains nearly the same material, but page references do not apply exactly; the 1st edition, 1884 is in one volume; general history without biographies.

Dickinson County, see *Northern M.; Northern P.; Upper P.*

Eaton County, see *Ingham Hist.*

Emmet County, see *Traverse.*

Genesee Hist.   History of Genesee County. With illustrations and biographical sketches. [By Franklin Ellis.] Philadelphia, Everts and Abbott, 1879. 446 p. (B., L., L. C., N. Y. S.)

Genesee Port.   Portrait and biographical record of Genesee, Lapeer and Tuscola counties. Chicago. Chapman bros , 1892. 1056 p. (L. C.)

Gogebic County, see *Northern M.; Northern P.; Upper P.*

Grand Rapids City   The city of Grand Rapids and Kent County, Mich., up to date, containing biographical sketches of prominent and representative citizens. [Logansport, Ind.] A. W. Bowen & co., 1900. 1105 p. (L.)

Grand Rapids Hist.   History of Grand Rapids and its industries.   By Dwight Goss. Chicago, C. F. Cooper & co., 1906. 2 vols. (L. C., Mich.)
Paged continuously: v. 1, p. 1–682; v. 2, p. 683–1312.

Grand Rapids Lowell   History of the city of Grand Rapids, Michigan. (With an appendix—History of Lowell, Michigan), by Albert Baxter.

New York, Munsell & co., 1891. 854 p. (L. C., Mich.)

Grand River   Memorials of the Grand River Valley, by Franklin Everett. Chicago, The Chicago legal news company, 1878.   545 + 74 p. (Univ. M.)

Grand Traverse County, see *Traverse.*

Gratiot   Portrait and biographical album of Gratiot County. Chicago, Chapman bros., 1884. 820 p. (L. C., Mich.)

Hillsdale Hist.   History of Hillsdale County, Michigan, with illustrations and biographical sketches. Philadelphia, Everts & Abbott, 1879. 334 p. (L. C., N. Y. S.)

Hillsdale Port.   Portrait and biographical album of Hillsdale County. Chicago, Chapman bros., 1888. 1004 p. (L., L. C.)

Hillsdale County, see also *Bear Creek.*

Homer   Homer and its pioneers, and its business men of today.   By William A. Lane. Homer, Mich., P. W. Chase, 1883.   146 p. (L. C.)

Houghton   Biographical record; this volume contains biographical sketches of leading citizens of Houghton, Baraga and Marquette counties. Chicago, Biographical pub. co., 1903.   410 p. (D., L., L. C., Mich.)

Houghton County, see also *Northern M.; Northern P., Upper P.*

Huron   Portrait and biographical album of Huron County. Chicago, Chapman bros., 1884.   500 p. (L. C.)

Ingham Hist.   History of Ingham and Eaton counties, Michigan, with illustrations and biographical sketches of their prominent men and pioneers. By S. W. Durant.   Philadelphia, D. W. Ensign & co., 1880.   586 p. (B., D., L. C., N. Y. S.)

Ingham Port.   Portrait and biographical album of Ingham and Livingston counties.   Chicago, Chapman bros., 1891.   871 p. (L. C., Mich.)

Ingham County, see also *Lansing.*

Ionia Hist.   History of Ionia and Montcalm counties, Michigan, with illustrations and biographical sketches... By John S. Schenck. Philadelphia, D. W. Ensign & co., 1881.   502 p. (N. Y. S.)

Ionia Port. Portrait and biographical album of Ionia and Montcalm counties... Chicago, Chapman bros., 1891. 846 p. (D., Mich.)

Ionia County, see also *Grand River.*

Iosco County, see *Lake Huron.*

Iron County, see *Northern M.; Northern P.; Upper P.*

Isabella Portrait and biographical album of Isabella County. Chicago, Chapman bros., 1884. 589 p. (L. C.)

Jackson Hist. History of Jackson County, Michigan, together with . . . porttraits of prominent persons and biographies of representative citizens. Chicago, Inter-state pub. co., 1881. 1156 p. (D., L., L. C., Mich., N.Y.S.)

Jackson Port. Portrait and biographical album of Jackson County, Michigan. Containing... biographical sketches of prominent and representative citizens . . . Chicago, Chapman bros., 1890. 881 p. (Mich.)

Kalamazoo Hist. History of Kalamazoo County, Michigan. With illustrations and biographical sketches of its prominent men and pioneers. [By S. W. Durant.] Philadelphia, Everts & Abbott, 1880. 552 p. (D., L. C., N. Y. S.)

Kalamazoo Port. Portrait and biographical record of Kalamazoo, Allegan and Van Buren counties. Chicago, Chapman bros., 1892. 986 p. (L.C.)

Kalkaska County, see *Traverse.*

Kent History of Kent County, Michigan; together with . . . portraits of prominent persons, and biographies of representative citizens. Chicago, C. C. Chapman & co., 1881. 1426 p. (D., L., L. C., N. Y. S.)

Kent County, see also *Grand Rapids; Grand River.*

Keweenaw County, see *Northern M.; Northern P.; Upper P.*

Lake Huron History of the Lake Huron shore. With illustrations and biographical sketches of some of its prominent men and pioneers. Chicago, H. R. Page & co., 1883. 280 p. (D.)

Substantially the same as "History of Bay County" 1883; the two works being identical for more than half their pages and differing elsewhere chiefly in arrangement.

Lansing Past and present of the city of Lansing and Ingham County, Michigan by Albert E. Cowles, historically, together with biographical sketches . . . Lansing, Mich., The Michigan historical publishing association [1904]. 583 p. (Mich.)

Lapeer County, see *Genesee Port.*

Leelanaw County, see *Traverse.*

Lenawee Hist. Historical and biographical record of Lenawee County. . . By W. A. Whitney & R. I. Bonner. Adrian, Mich., 1879–80. 2 v. (L. C.; New Eng. has v. I only.)

Lenawee Illus. Illustrated history and biographical record of Lenawee County... By J. I. Knapp and R. I. Bonner. Adrian, Mich., 1903. 511 p. (D., L., L. C.)

Lenawee Port. Portrait and biographical album of Lenawee County. Chicago, Chapman bros., 1888. 1217 p. (L.)

Lenawee County, see also *Bear Creek.*

Livingston County, see *Ingham Port.*

Luce County, see *Northern M.; Northern P.; Upper P.*

Mackinac County, see *Northern M.; Northern P.; Upper P.*

Macomb Hist. History of Macomb County Michigan, containing . . . biographical sketches, portraits of prominent men and early settlers. Chicago, M. A. Leeson & co., 1882. 924 p. (D., L., L. C., Mass., Mich., N. Y. S.)

Macomb Past Past and present of Macomb County, Michigan. By Robert F. Eldredge; together with biographical sketches of many of its leading and prominent citizens and illustrious dead. Chicago, The S. J. Clarke pub. co., 1905. 712 p. (L.)

Marquette County, see *Houghton; Northern M.; Northern P.; Upper P.)*

Mecosta Portrait and biographical album of Mecosta County. Chicago, Chapman bros., 1883. 654 p. (D., L., L. C.)

Menominee County, see *Northern M.; Northern P.; Upper P.*

Midland Portrait and biographical album of Midland County. Chicago, Chapman bros., 1884. 433 p. (D., L., L. C., Mich.)

Monroe History of Monroe County. T. E. Wing, editor. New York, Munsell & co., 1890. 606+53 p. (D., L. C.)

Montcalm County, see *Ionia Hist.; Ionia Port.*

Muskegon Hist. Histoiy of Muskegon County, Michigan. with illustrations and biographical sketches of some of its prominent men and pioneers. Chicago, H. R. Page & co., 1882. 151 p. (L. C., Mich.) Appended is History of Ottawa County. 1882. 133 p.

Muskegon Port. Portrait and biographical record of Muskegon and Ottawa counties. Chicago, Biographical pub. co., 1893. 577 p. (D., L., L. C.)

Muskegon County, see also *Grand River.*

Newaygo Portrait and biographical album of Newayco[!] County. Chicago, Chapman bros., 1884. 572 p. (L. C.)

Northern M. Portrait and biographical record of Northern Michigan. Chicago, Record pub. co., 1895. 551 p. (D., L. C.)

Northern P. Memorial record of the Northern Peninsula of Michigan. Chicago, The Lewis pub. co., 1895. 642 p. (D., L. C., Mich.)

Northern Peninsula, see also *Northern M., Upper P.*

Oakland Biog. Biographical record; this volume contains biographical sketches of leading citizens of Oakland County. Chicago, Biographical pub. co., 1903. 681 p. (D., L., L. C.)

Oakland Hist. History of Oakland County [By S. W. Durant.] Philadelphia, L. H. Everts & co., 1877. 334 p. (D., L. C., Mich., N. Y. S.)

Oakland Port. Portrait and biographical album of Oakland County. Chicago, Chapman bros., 1891. 959 p. (D., L. C.)

Oceana Oceana County pioneers and business men of today. By L. M. Hartwick. Pentwater, Mich., 1890. 432 p. (L. C.)

Ontonagon County, see *Northern M.; Northern P.; Upper P.*

Osceola Portrait and biographical album of Osceola County. Chicago, Chapman bros., 1884. 422 p. (L., L.C., Mich.)

Ottawa Hist., see *Muskegon Hist.*

Ottawa County, see also *Grand River; Muskegon Port.*

Saginaw Hist. History of Saginaw County, Michigan; together with . . . portraits of prominent persons and biographies of representative citizens. [By M. A. Leeson and D. Clarke]. Chicago, C. C. Chapman & co., 1881. 960 p. (L. C., N.Y.S.)

Saginaw Port. Portrait and biographical record of Saginaw and Bay counties. Chicago, Biographical pub. co., 1892. 1044 p. (L. C.)

St. Clair History of St. Clair County, Michigan, containing . . . biographical sketches. Chicago, A. T. Andreas & co., 1883. 790 p. (D., L., L. C., N. Y. S.)

St. Joseph History of St. Joseph County. Philadelphia, L. H. Everts & co., 1877. 232 p. (D., L. C., N. Y. S.)

Sanilac Portrait and biographical album of Sanilac County. Chicago, Chapman bros., 1884. 546 p. (L. C.)

Schoolcraft County, see *Northern M.; Northern P.; Upper P.*

Shiawassee History of Shiawassee and Clinton counties, Michigan with illustrations and biographical sketches of their prominent men and pioneers. Philadelphia, D. W. Ensign & co., 1880. 541 p. (D., L. C., Mich.)

Shiawassee County, see also *Clinton Port.*

Traverse The Traverse region, historical and descriptive with . . . portraits and biographical sketches . . . Chicago, H. R. Page & co., 1884. 369 p. (Mich.)

Tuscola County, see *Genesee Port.*

Upper P. History of the Upper Peninsula of Michigan . . . Chicago, The Western historical co., 1883. 549 p. (D., Mich., N. Y. S.)

Upper Peninsula, see also *Northern M.; Northern P.*

Van Buren County, see *Berrien Hist.; Kalamazoo Port.*

Washtenaw Hist. History of Washtenaw County, Michigan; together with . . . portraits of prominent persons and biographies of representative citizens. Chicago, C. C. Chapman & co., 1881. 1452 p. (D., L., L. C., Mich., N. Y. S.)

Washtenaw Past Past and present of Washtenaw County, Michigan by Samuel W. Beakes, together with biographical sketches of many of its prominent and leading citizens and illustrious dead. Chicago, The S. J. Clarke pub. co., 1906. 823 p. (Univ. M.)

Washtenaw Port. Portrait and biographical album of Washtenaw County, Michigan, containing biographical sketches of prominent and representative citizens . . . Chicago, Biographical publishing co., 1891. 639 p. (Univ. M.)

Wayne Chron. Wayne County historical and pioneer society. Chronography of notable events in the history of the Northwest Territory and Wayne County . . . Compiled by Fred Carlisle. Detroit, 1890. 484 p. (D., L. C.)

Wayne Land. Landmarks of Wayne County and Detroit by R. B. Ross and G. B. Catlin. Revised by C. W. Burton. Detroit, 1898. 872+320 p. (D., L. C., N. Y. S., Mich., New Eng.)

Wayne County, see also *Detroit.*

Wexford County, see *Traverse.*

The 14 counties not represented lie in the northern part of the Lower Peninsula and nearly all in its eastern portion—a section which was of late development and must have received comparatively few New England pioneers. They have no histories as far as known, and are :

Arenac	taken from Bay County 1883			
Clare	laid out 1840,	not organized till	1871	
Crawford	"	"	first census taken	1880
Gladwin	"	1831,	not organized till	1875
Lake	"	1840,	"	1871
Manistee	"	"	"	1855
Mason	"	"	"	1855
Missaukee	"	"	"	1871
Montmorency	"	"	first census taken	1884
Ogemaw	"	"	not organized till	1875
Oscoda	"	"	first census taken	1880
Otsego	"	"	not organized till	1875
Presque Isle	"	"	"	1871
Roscommon	"	"	"	1875

PIONEERS FROM MASSACHUSETTS

In addit on to the abbreviat ons of book titles, (explained on pages 1–5) the following are used: b. for born; d. for died; m. for married; set. for settled in.

ABBE, Theodore C., set. Mich., 1832. Berrien Hist., 306.

ABBEY, Shubal, b. Granby, 1793; set. O., 1815. Midland, 333.

ABBOTT, Aaron, of New Braintree, set. N. Y., 1803. Lenawee Hist. II, 252.

—— Maria, b. 1797; m. 1814 Daniel Walker of Vt., Pa. and Mich. Jackson Port., 787; Jackson Hist., 873.

—— Naomi, m. 1815? Samuel French of N. Y. Northern P., 456.

—— William, set. Vt., 1815? N. H., N. Y., Mich. Lansing, 304.

ADAMS, Charles, set. Vt., 1834? Washtenaw Hist., 959.

—— Charles F., b. Salisbury, 1827, set. Canada, 1829, Ill., 1859, Mich., 1863. Lake Huron, 150.

—— Daniel, b. Cambridge, 1768; set. N. H. Berrien Port., 915.

—— Ebenezer, b. Quincy, 1760? set. N. Y. Macomb Hist., 787.

—— George W., b. Lenox, 1832; set. Mich., 1874. Jackson Hist., 787.

—— Isaac, set. N. Y., 1810? Macomb Hist., 489.

—— Isaac O., b. Newburyport; set. Mich., 1836. Berrien Hist., 272, 275.

—— James, set. Mich., 1840. Clinton Past, 266.

—— John, set. N. H., 1805? Macomb Hist., 687.

—— Margaret, m. 1800? Anson Waring of N. Y. Detroit, 1233.

—— Mary, b. Shutesbury, 1805? m. 1824. Joseph Davis of N. Y. Branch Twent., 830.

—— Prudence, m. 1810? Eliab Ellison of N. Y. Ionia Port., 263.

—— Rev. S. C., set. N. Y., 1835? Mich. Cass Twent., 441.

ADAMS, Sylvia, b. Barre, 1812; m. Henry Foster of Vt., N. Y. and Mich. Jackson Hist., 628.

—— Wales, b. Medway, 1804; set. Mich. Branch Hist., 221, 228; Branch Twent., 240.

AIKEN, Hannah, m. 1822 Amasa D. Chapman of N. Y. Oakland Biog., 433.

ALBEE, Zattue, set. Vt., O., 1826. Grand Rapids City, 502.

ALDEN, Elisha, set. N. Y., 1810? Kent, 647.

—— Hiram, b. Ashfield, 1792; set. N. Y. Mich., 1824. Branch Port., 596, 618.

—— Pliny, b. Ashfield, 1787; set. N. Y. Branch Port., 600.

ALDRICH, Abram, Sr., b. Upton, 1775; set. N. Y., Mich., 1832. Branch Port., 360; Branch Twent., 674.

—— Chad, b. 1768: set. N. Y. Lenawee Hist. II, 85, 167.

—— Daniel, set. Mich., 1833. Calhoun, 163.

—— Deborah, b. 1775; m. Arthur Power of N. Y. Oakland Port., 891.

—— Eunice, m. 1795? John Morton of N. Y. and Mich. Lenawee Port., 580.

—— Hosea, of Uxbridge; set. N. Y., 1800? Hillsdale Hist., 238.

—— Jabez, b. Northbridge, 1795? set. N.Y., 1807, Mich., 1833. Lenawee Hist. II, 269.

—— Leonard, set. N. Y., 1800? Genesee Port., 714.

—— Mercy A., b. Cheshire, 1808; m. 1831 William Dunbar of Mich. Monroe, 355.

—— Savel, set. N. Y., Mich., 1835. Clinton Past, 300.

—— Seth, b. Berkshire Co., 1804; set. Mich., 1833. Macomb Hist., 688.

ALDRIDGE, Eunice, m. 1810? John Morton of N. Y. and Mich. Hillsdale Port., 655.

ALGER, Benajah, set. N. Y., Mich., 1842. Genesee Port., 282.

—— Josiah, b. 1782; set. N. Y., 1793, Mich. 1823. Genesee Hist., facing 282.

ALLARD, John P., set. Mich., 1836. Kalamazoo Hist., 960.

ALLEN, Artemus, b. 1800; set. N. Y., 1813, Mich., 1836. Branch Port., 289.

—— Damarius, set. Mich., 1835. Cass Twent., 364.

—— David P., b. 1810; set. N. Y., 1835, Mich., 1867. Isabella, 188; Saginaw Hist., 916 and Saginaw Port., 684.

—— E. W., b. Salem, 1853; set. Mich., 1880. Upper P., 427.

—— George W., set. Mich., 1832. Lenawee Port., 230.

—— Sally, of Cheshire; m. 1812 Charles Pratt of Mass., N. Y. and Mich. Lenawee Hist. II, 483.

—— William S., b. 1856; set. Mich., 1878. Upper P., 375.

ALLIS, Edward P., b. Franklin Co., 1819; set. Mich., 1844. Lenawee Port., 330.

—— Lucius, b. 1817; set. O., Mich., 1865. Hillsdale Port, 552.

—— Thomas W., b. Conway, 1798; set. N. Y., 1823, Mich., 1856. Lenawee Hist. II, 355.

ALMY, Peleg, b. Westport, 1781; set. N. Y., Kent, 1391.

ALVORD, Josiah, set. N. Y., 1815, Mich., 1834. Ionia Port., 457.

—— Justus, set. N. Y., O.; d. 1868. Isabella, 382.

—— N. C., set. Mich., 1835. Wayne Chron., 75.

AMES, —— b. near Petersham, 1794; set. N. H., Mich., 1837. Lenawee Port., 583.

—— Charles, b. Petersham, 1799; set. Ala., N. Y., Mich., 1833. Lenawee Port., 986.

—— Ezra, b. Petersham, 1813; set. Mich., 1833. Lenawee Port., 1015.

—— Jotham, b. Framingham, 1756; set. N. H. Lenawee Hist. I, 450.

—— Louisa, b. Petersham, 1796; m. 1819, Alpheus Pratt of N. Y. and Mich. Lenawee Hist. I, 406.

—— Mason, set. O., 1850? Kent, 1304.

—— Philena, m. 1825? Otis Mallory of N. Y. Genesee Port., 441.

AMES, William B., b. Petersham, 1808; set. N. H., 1816, N. Y., 1831, Mich., 1833. Lenawee Hist. I, 449.

AMSDEN, Anna, b. 1784; m. Ami Whitney of N. Y. Hillsdale Port., 193.

—— Isaac, set. N. Y., 1800? Washtenaw Past, 182.

—— Philena, m. 1820? Loren Moore of N. Y. and Mich. Washtenaw Hist., 1021.

—— Polly, b. Conway, 1792; m. George Brockway of N. Y. Hillsdale Port., 858.

—— Timothy, b. Dover, 1808; set. Mich., 1837. Washtenaw Hist., 493.

ANDERSON, Anna, m. 1825? John Webb, Jr. of N. Y. Genesee Port., 899.

—— Elizabeth, of Deerfield; m. 1813 Dennis Cooley of Mich. Macomb Hist.,817.

—— James, b. Blandford, 1790; set. N. Y., Mich. Hillsdale Port., 295, 548.

—— Rachel, m. 1810? Jacob Pratt of N. Y. O. and Mich. Ionia Port., 547.

ANDRESS, Betsey, b. Essex Co.; m. William Knowlton of Vt. and O. Branch Port., 470.

ANDREWS, Ebenezer, set. N. Y., 1820? Ionia Port, 718.

ANDRUS, Sally, m. 1791 James Hazzard of Mass. and N. Y. St. Joseph, 107.

ANGELL, Crawford, b. 1827; set. Mich., 1845. Kent, 94.

—— Horace, b. New Ashford, 1815; set. Mich., 1835. St. Clair, 119.

APTHORP, Alden, set. O., 1840. Mecosta, 349.

ARCHER, Betsey, b. Springfield, 1780; m. Henry Beebe of N. Y. Macomb Hist., 787.

ARMES, Lydia, m. 1800? John Bush of Vt. Newaygo, 285.

ARMS, Clarissa, (Mrs. James B) b. Palmer, 1802. Washtenaw Hist., 689.

—— Eliza, b. Conway, m. 1st, 1830? Ichabod S. Nelson; m. 2d, Rulef D. Cregs. Cass Twent., 609.

—— Israel, set. Mich., 1827. Washtenaw Past, 805.

—— James B., b. S. Deerfield, 1801; set. Mich., 1834. Washtenaw Hist., 493, 689, 1451.

ARMS, Christopher, set. N. Y., 1810? Mich., 1823. Oakland Port., 671.

ARMSTRONG, Nathaniel A., set. Mich., 1841. Cass Twent., 454.

ARNOLD, George, b. 1812; set. Mich., 1835. Berrien Port., 531.

—— Henry,b. Sheffield. 1807; set. O.,1828 Mich., 1835. Cass Twent., 54, 614.

—— Phebe, b. Norton, 1796; m. 1812 Turner Crane of N. H., N. Y., and Mich. Hillsdale Port., 845; Lenawee Hist. II, 483; Lenawee Illus., 87; Lenawee Port., 569.

ASHLEY, Anson, set. O., 1830? Upper P., 444.

—— Patience, b. Taunton; d. 1873; m. Benjamin McLouth of N. Y. and Mich. Branch Port., 273.

—— Robert, of Fowlerville, set. N. Y., 1804. Genesee Port., 787.

ATHERTON, Adonijah, b. Hampshire Co., 1750; set. N. Y. Genesee Hist., 348.

—— Adonijah, Jr., b. 1783; set. N. Y. and Mich. Genesee Hist., 348.

—— Perus, b. 1795? set. N. Y. and Mich. Genesee Hist., 348.

—— Shubael, of Shelburne; b. 1788; set. N. Y., 1808, Mich., 1825. Genesee Hist., 349; Genesee Port., 815.

ATWATER, Sarah, b. 1785?; m. Stephen S. Virgil of N. Y. Genesee Port., 703.

ATWOOD, Alvina, m. 1815? Doctor Millard of Mass., N. Y., and Mich. Ionia Port., 660, 670.

—— Charles H. T., b. Boston, 1853; set. Me., Mich. Upper P., 340.

—— Eliza, b. New Bedford, 1808; m. Joel Monroe of N. Y., O., and Mich. Kalamazoo Hist., 220.

—— Zenas, b. Franklin Co., 1791; set. N. Y., 1815, Mich., 1836. Ingham Port., 371.

AUSTIN, Catherine, m. 1845? George H. Rodgers of Mass. and Me. Grand Rapids City, 368.

—— Jonathan W., b. Salem; set. Vt., Mich., 1830. Lenawee Port., 424.

—— Sylvester, b. 1785; set. N. Y., 1816. Clinton Port., 397.

—— William S., b. 1793; set. N. Y. Branch Port., 542.

AVERILL, Samuel, set. Mich., 1818, Kansas. Oakland Port., 935.

AVERY, Sumner, b. 1814; set. O., Ia., 1852, Mich., 1865. * Clinton Past, 287.

AYLESWORTH, Henry, set. N. Y., 1820? Jackson Hist., 993.

AYRES, Joseph, b. 1804; set. N. Y., 1820? O., 1826, N. Y., 1830. Jackson Hist., 993; Jackson Port., 327.

BABBITT, Ezra, b. Franklin Co.; set.. N. Y, O., Ind., Ill., Mich.; d. 1880. Branch Port., 342.

—— Levi, b. 1805; set. N. Y., 1830? Jackson Port., 620.

—— Uri, set. Vt., 1800? Washtenaw Port., 299.

BABCOCK, James L., b. Goshen, 1840 or 45; set. Ill., Mich., 1860 or '71, Washtenaw Hist., 961; Washtenaw Past, 340; Washtenaw Port., 628.

—— Susan, m. 1825? Asa Crandall of N.Y. Newaygo, 393.

—— William, b. Pittsfield, 1783; set. N.Y., Mich., 1836. Grand River, appendix 4.

BACHELOR, Catherine, b. 1776; m. Stephen Bathrick of N. Y. Berrien Hist., 388.

—— Consider, b. Ashfield; set. N. Y., 1825? Oakland Port., 220.

—— Hannah, m. 1830? Thomas Hosner of N. Y. and Mich. Oakland Port., 220.

—— Lucy, m. 1825? Addison Ingles of N. Y. and O. Berrien Twent., 769.

BACKUS, Anson, Sr., b. Lee, 1782; set. N.Y. 1805? Lenawee Port., 1213.

BACON, Asaph, b. Northampton; set. N.Y., Wis., Mich., 1845. Hillsdale Port., 555.

—— Catherine, of Bedford; m. 1833 John M. Fitch of Mich. Clinton Port., 263.

—— Joel W., b. Pittsfield; set. N. Y., 1815? St. Clair, 720.

—— Nancy, b. 1780; m. 1st,—— Mathewson; m. 2d, 1817 Daniel S. Judd of Mich. Oakland Port., 305.

—— Nancy, m. 1830? Bradley Adams of Vt., N. Y. and Mich. Gratiot, 355.

—— Susan, m. 1805? Jotham Dyer of Vt., N. Y. and Mich. Jackson Hist., 621.

BADGER, Stephen, b. 1760? set. N. H., 1800? Clinton Port., 788.

BAGG, Abner, of Lanesboro; set. N. Y., 1810? Wayne Chron., 357.

—— Joseph, b. Lanesboro, 1797; set. N.Y., 1810? O., 1836, Mich., 1838. Wayne Chron., 357.

BAGLEY, Amasa, of Norfolk Co.; set. Mich., 1819. Oakland Hist., 319.

BAILEY, Dana, b. 1790? set. Vt., 1800. Kalamazoo Port., 200.

—— Joseph, Revolutionary soldier; set. N. Y. Hillsdale Port., 299.

—— Joseph S., b. Chesterfield, 1797; set. N. Y., Mich. Kent, 1294.

—— Mehitable, m. 1800? Ralph Bailey of N.Y. Hillsdale Port., 299.

—— Polly, of Bridgewater; m. 1820? Daniel Camp of N. Y. and Mich. Lenawee Port., 1194.

—— Ralph, b. Bridgewater, 1782; set. N. Y., 1822, Mich., 1830. Hillsdale Hist., 314, 326; Hillsdale Port., 299.

BAIRD, John A., b. 1827; set. O., 1841, Mich., 1856. Kalamazoo Port., 702.

—— Robert H., b. 1794; set. O. Kalamazoo Port., 702.

BAKER, Abel, of Barnstable; set. N. Y., 1800? Northern P., 191.

—— Appolos, set. N. Y.; d. 1823. Lenawee Port., 594.

—— David, b. Adams, 1779; set. N. Y., 1800? Lenawee Hist. II, 168.

—— David W., b. 1799; set. N. Y., 1820? Mich., 1833. Lenawee Illus., 148.

—— Harvey N., b. 1803; set. Canada, 1820? Mich., 1836. Allegan Twent., 308; Kalamazoo Port., 496.

—— Jesse, set. Mich., 1847. Monroe, appendix 49.

—— John b. Adams, 1798; set. N. Y., 1800, Mich.,1832. Lenawee Hist. I, 152; Lenawee Illus., 142.

—— John, b. Westhampton, 1814; set. Mich., 1839. St. Clair. 122.

—— Joseph M., b. Adams, 1780; set. Vt., 1790? N. Y., 1800, Mich., 1833. Lenawee Hist. I, 425, 465; Lenawee Hist. II, 267; Lenawee Illus., 256; Lenawee Port., 303, 957.

—— Moses, b. Dartmouth, 1776; lived in Adams; set. N. Y., 1800? Mich., 1832. Lenawee Hist. I, 152, 165; Lenawee Illus., 142, 148.

—— Samantha, m. 1835? Henry Turner of Mich. Midland, 294.

—— Sarah, m. 1800? —— Eddy of Mass. and N. Y. Lenawee Port., 659.

—— William, b. Berkshire Co., 1784; set. N. Y. Lenawee Port., 931.

BALCOM, Henry, b. 1742; set. Vt., 1775? N. Y., 1785? Detroit, 1186.

—— Mercy J., m. 1840? Z. S. W. Richardson of Canada and O. Northern P., 441.

BALDWIN, Charles M., b. Windsor, 1806; set. Mich., 1833. Lenawee Illus., 342.

—— Esther E., b. Windsor, 1807; m. 1834 Noah K. Green of Mass. and Mich. Lenawee Hist. I, 268; Lenawee Illus., 412; Lenawee Port, 914.

—— George W., set. Wis., 1852; d. 1854. Berrien Port., 842.

—— John, b. Palmer, 1770; set. R. I. Wayne Chron., 339.

—— Mercy, m. 1860 Charles W. Stocum of Mich. Lenawee Port., 602.

—— Millicent C., b. Windsor, 1804; m. 1830 Simon D. Wilson of Conn. and Mich. Lenawee Hist. I, 339; Lenawee Port., 568.

—— Ozro A. E., b. New Marlborough, 1849; set. Mich., 1865. Berrien Port., 842; Berrien Twent., 995.

—— Samuel C., b. Windsor, 1829; set. Mich, 1835. Lenawee Illus., 133.

BALL, Charles, W. b. Goshen, 1849; set. Mich., 1867. Osceola, 242.

—— George F., b. 1819; set. Mich., 1834? Clinton Port., 545.

—— Lydia, m. 1805? Josiah Newton of Vt. Oakland Port., 935.

—— Nathan, b. 1765? set. Vt., N. Y.; d. 1826. Lenawee Port., 986.

—— Sawyer, set. Mich., 1860. Berrien Port., 759.

—— William H., b. Huntington, 1858; set. Mich., 1860. Berrien Port., 758.

BALLARD, Asa N., set. Mich., 1828; d. 1844. Washtenaw Port., 266.

—— Daniel, soldier of 1812; set. N. Y. Berrien Port., 356.

—— James, b. Charlemont, 1805; set. Vt., Mich., 1838. Grand Rapids Hist., 186; Grand Rapids Lowell, 113; Kent, 206, 261.

—— Nancy, b. Roxbury, 1788; m. James Day of Conn. Lenawee Hist. I, 269.

BALLOU, —— set. N. Y., O., Mich.; d. 1860. Kalamazoo Port., 478.

BANCROFT, Joseph, b. Salem, 1781; set. N. Y., 1815? Mich., 1824. Oakland Biog., 112.

BANCROFT, Julia A., b. 1824; m. 1843? George F. Ball of Mich. Clinton Port., 545.

—— Neley, b. Auburn, 1799, set. N. Y., 1827, Mich., 1835. Lenawee Hist. II, 260; Lenawee Port., 738.

—— Sally A., m. 1815? Solomon Davis of N. Y. Hillsdale Port., 959.

BANGS, Joshua, b. Hingham, 1764; set. N. Y. Berrien Hist., 392.

—— Nathaniel, b. 1789; set. Vt., N. Y. Berrien Hist., 392.

BANKS, DR. F. A., b. 1854; set. Mich., 1877. Upper P., 242.

BANNISTER, Clarissa, m. 1825? John Cranson of N. Y. and Mich. Clinton Port., 987.

BARBER, John, b. Worcester Co., 1775; set. N. Y., 1791. Lenawee Hist. II, 191.

BARDEN, Sally, m. 1810? John A. Johnson of N. Y. Midland, 243.

BARDWELL, Jonathan, set. N. Y., 1815. Washtenaw Hist., 625.

BARKER, George W., b. Deerfield, 1815; set. N. Y., 1835? Osceola, 214.

—— Lucius B., b. 1801; set. N. Y., Mich., 1836. Kalamazoo Port., 456.

—— Margaret, m. 1810? Israel Allen of Conn., Pa. and Mich. Lenawee Port., 222.

—— Mason, set. N. Y., 1815? Detroit, 1044.

—— Paul, set. N. Y., 1790? Clinton Port., 752.

—— Russel, set. N. Y., 1810? Kalamazoo Port., 456.

BARLOW, Obed, set. N. Y., 1820? Ionia Port., 544.

BARNABY, Abigail B. M., b. 1812; m. 1836 Thorndike P. Saunders of N. Y. and Mich. Washtenaw Past, 79.

BARNARD, Uriah, b. Nantucket, 1761; set, O. Berrien Port., 217.

BARNES, Brigham, b. Hardwick, 1835; set. Mich., 1868. Ionia Port., 603.

—— Charlotte, m. 1820? Jonathan H. Crosby of N. Y. and Mich. Jackson Hist., 969.

—— John B., b. Lowell; graduate of Amherst college; set. Mich., 1842. Shiawassee, 135.

—— Lucy, b. 1797; m. William S. Austen, of N. Y. Branch Port., 542.

BARNES, Mary, b. W. Stockbridge; m. 1810? Silas Runyan of N. Y. and O. Gratiot, 381.

—— N. H., b. Grafton, 1816; set. Mich. Jackson Hist., 788.

BARNEY, Aaron, b. 1785; set. N. Y., Mich. Berrien Hist., opposite 467.

—— Milton, b. New Marlborough, 1796; set. N. Y., Mich., 1832. Homer, 44.

BARR, Lewis, b. 1792; set. Mich. Washtenaw Hist., 592.

BARRETT, Alexander, set. Mich., 1832. Ionia Port., 461.

—— Benjamin, b. 1784; set. Vt. Lenawee Hist. I, 175.

—— Emma, b. Barrington, 1808; m. 1st, 1828 Granville Jones of Mass.; m. 2d, 1845 Sam Hungerford of Mich. Detroit, 1437.

—— Erastus B., b. Hampden Co., 1836; set. Mich., 1865. Sanilac, 404.

—— Seymour, b. Williamstown, 1815; set. Vt., 1818, Mich., 1832. Lenawee Hist. I, 175; Lenawee Port., 584.

BARROWS, David, set. N. Y, 1820? Wis. Macomb Hist., 690.

BARTHOLOMEW, Almeda, m. 1805? Ebenezer Ranney of N. Y. Kalamazoo Port., 609.

BARTLETT, Azel E., b. Hinsdale, 1827; set. Mich. Kalamazoo Port., 829.

—— Delphia C., m. 1846 John L. Andrews of Mich. Oakland Port., 888.

—— Frances J., m. 1836 Hiram Graham of N. Y. and Mich. Hillsdale Port., 521.

—— Martha, m. 1825? John Brodish of N.Y. Kent, 568.

—— Priscilla, m. 1795? Asa Parks of Mass. and N. Y. Washtenaw Hist., 1309.

—— W. W., b. 1834; set. N. Y., 1836, Pa., 1842, Mich., 1864. Traverse, 92.

—— William L., set. N. Y., 1810? Berrien Hist., 531.

BARTLEY, George, b. Chelsea, 1835; set. N. Y. Northern P., 149.

—— George B., set. Mich., 1865? Northern P., 67.

BARTON, Hannah, m. 1825? Philetus Sweatland of O. Gratiot, 423.

—— Lucretia, of Charlton; b. 1800; m. 1825? Harvey Dodge of Mass. and Mich. Clinton Past, 365.

BELL, George S., b. Chester, 1812; set. O., 1821, Mich., 1854. Gratiot, 682.

—— Harmony, b. 1814; m. David Converse of O. Berrien Port., 854.

—— John C., b. 1783; set. O., 1821. Gratiot, 682.

—— Julia A., m. 1825? Chauncey Knapp of Mich. Washtenaw Hist., 1085.

BELLOWS, Elizabeth, m. Bowman Dennis of Mass. and Mich. Clinton Port., 506.

BEMENT, Edwin, b. Westfield, 1811; set. O., 1820, Mich., 1869. Ingham Hist., 189.

BEMIS, Amariah, b. 1785; set. Conn. Oakland Port., 348.

—— Charles L., b. Hampden Co., 1850; set. Mich., 1863. Ionia Port., 787.

—— Marquis D., set. Mich., 1863. Ionia Port., 787.

—— Mary J., b. Springfield; m. 1858 George Newberry of Mich. Oakland Biog., 83.

—— Wallace C., b. Hampden Co., 1852; set. O., 1860? Mich., 1863. Ionia Port. 796.

BENEDICT, Aaron, b. Salem? Revolutionary soldier; set. N. Y. Ionia Hist., 189.

—— Ruth, b. 1807; m. Elijah Carrier of Conn. and N. Y. Hillsdale Port., 582.

—— Washburn, b. 1824; set. Mich., 1846. Cass Hist., 145; Cass Twent., 355.

BENJAMIN, Cynthia, b. Martha's Vineyard, 1793; m. John Bassett of N. Y. Branch Port., 191.

—— Eli, b. 1823; set. Mich., 1854. Cass Hist., 146; Cass Twent., 358.

—— Harvey, set. N. Y. 1830? Saginaw Hist., 764.

—— Sally, m. 1815? Daniel Childs of N. Y. Hillsdale Port., 266.

—— Samuel, b. Watertown, 1753; set. Me. Grand Rapids Lowell, 436.

BENNETT, Arabella, b. Worcester Co., 1799; m. 1824 Robert Shankland of Mich. Washtenaw Hist., 626.

—— Jonas, b. Worcester Co., set. N. Y., 1817. Branch Port., 310.

—— Luther, set. N. Y., Mich., 1830. Macomb Past, 440.

BENTON, Eli, b. 1800; set. Mich., 1827. Washtenaw Hist., 494.

—— Elijah, set. N. Y., 1840, Mich., 1848. Washtenaw Port., 396.

BENTON, Ezra E., b. Pittsfield, 1798; set. N.Y. Branch Port., 561.

BERRICK, Francis H., b. Middlesex, 1823; set. Mich., 1869. Berrien Port., 308.

BERRY, Anna, b. Salem, 1801; m. Lewis Buckingham of N. Y. and Mich. Genesee Port., 702.

—— William, of Salem; set. N. Y., 1810? Mich. Genesee Port., 702.

BEST, Sally, m. 1810? David Wells of Vt. Washtenaw Hist., 1353.

BIBEAU, Eva, m. 1879 A. Desjardins of Mich. Upper P., 458.

BICKFORD, Dearborn, set. N. Y., 1810? Genesee Port., 677.

BICKNELL, C. C., b. 1831; set. Mich., 1865. Kent, 1255.

—— Lucy A., b. Berkshire Co.; m. 1857 Charles Oldfield of Ia. and Mich. Kent, 1223.

BIDWELL, Lydia, b. 1804; m. John B. Peebles of N. Y., O. and Mich. Lenawee Port., 637.

BIGELOW, Abel, set. Mich., 1825; d. 1848. Ingham Port., 813.

—— Betsey, b. Waltham, 1783; m. 1806 Simeon Dewey of N. H., N. Y. and Mich. Lenawee Hist. I, 375, 496; Lenawee Port., 1102.

—— Margaret, m. 1800? Alexander Phelps of Conn. Washtenaw Hist., 864.

—— Marlin, b. 1800; set. O. Kalamazoo Port., 851.

BILL, Isaac, b. 1776; set. N. Y., 1800. Saginaw Port., 811.

BILLINGS, Phebe, m. 1830? Sullivan Jones of N. Y. Newaygo, 193.

—— William J., set. Vt., 1812. Jackson Port., 343.

BILLS, Lydia, b. Berkshire Co., 1795? m. Charles Bow of N. Y. and Mich. Hillsdale Port., 539.

BINGHAM, Origen S., b. Shelburne, 1824; set. Mich, 1831. Branch Port., 424; Branch Twent., 241.

BIRCHARD, Matthew W., b. Becket, 1788; set. Vt., 1789, Mich., 1839. Wayne Chron., 337.

BIRD, Gardner, b. 1802; set. N. Y., Mich., 1831. Oakland Port., 613.

—— Melzer, b. Windsor? 1805; set. N. Y., Mich., 1833. Ingham Port., 769.

BIRD, Rowland, b. 1793; set. N. Y., Mich., 1832. Bean Creek, 126; Hillsdale Hist., 285.

BISBEE, Clarissa, b. Plainfield, 1788; m. William Mitchell of Mass. and Mich. Lenawee Port., 285.

—— Julia A., m. 1835? Joshua N. Robinson of O. Gratiot, 378.

BISHOP, ISAAC, b. 1758; Revolutionary soldier; set. N. Y. Cass Twent., 747.

—— Levi, b. Russell, 1815; set. Mich., 1835. Detroit, 1112; St. Clair, 119; Wayne Chron., 253.

—— Luther, set. N. Y., 1815? Ionia Port., 322.

—— William, of Hampden Co.? set. N. Y., 1840? Detroit, 1284.

BISSELL, Blodget, set. O., 1810. Kalamazoo Port., 522.

—— Justus, set. O., 1804. Kalamazoo Port., 707.

BIXBY, David, b. Sutton, 1783; set. N. Y., 1815, Mich., 1827. Lenawee Hist. I, 91; Lenawee, Port., 1021.

BLACK, George H., b. Ashburnham, 1853; set. Mich., 1859. Berrien Twent., 341.

—— Hattie M., m. 1862 James L. McKie of Mich. Berrien Twent., 802.

BLACKMAN, Ansel, set. O., 1825? d. 1855, Gratiot, 390.

—— Elizabeth, m. 1820? Shubael Goodspeed of N. Y. and Mich. Washtenaw Hist., 1084.

—— John H., b. 1783; set. O., 1808, Mich., 1841. Kalamazoo Port., 470.

—— Martha, m. 1800? James Tracy of N. Y. Jackson Hist., 873.

BLACKMAR, Charles, b. 1784; set. N. Y., 1810? Mich., 1829. Lenawee Hist. I, 434, 453.

BLACKMER, Charles M., b. 1844; set. Mich., 1856. Washtenaw Hist., 1424.

—— David, b. Hampshire Co., 1803; set. Mich., 1856. Monroe, appendix, 35.

BLAIR, Alfred, set. O., 1820? Newaygo, 183.

BLAISDELL, Joseph S., set. Vt., 1825? Mich., 1835. Kent, 1212.

BLANCHARD, Washington Z., b. Andover; set. N. Y., 1820? Ionia Port., 774.

BLISS, ——, of Springfield; m. 1825? Samuel Brass of Mich. Clinton Past, 407.

BLISS, Elizabeth, b. Berkshire Co., 1795; m. 1815? Smith Slocum of N. Y. Hillsdale Hist., 199.

—— Hervey, b. Royalston, 1779 or 1789; set. O., 1814, Mich., 1816. Lenawee Hist. II, 483; Lenawee Illus., 207; Monroe, 125.

—— Israel, of Royalston; set. Mich., 1816; d. 1819. Monroe, 125.

—— Obediah, of Savoy; set. N. Y., 1820? O. Grand Rapids Hist., 211; Grand Rapids Lowell, 699.

—— Rebecca, b. 1802; m. George Walker of Mass. and Mich. Ingham Port., 454.

—— Silvanus, of Royalston; set. Mich., 1814. Monroe, 125.

—— Thomas, of Salem; set. Mich., 1836. Kalamazoo Port., 509.

BLIVEN, Albert H., b. Lee, 1825; set. Mich. Lenawee Hist. I, 193.

—— George W., b. Great Barrington, 1821; set. O., Mich., 1833. Lenawee Hist. I, 193; Lenawee Port., 785, 789.

—— Joseph F., b. Great Barrington, 1823; set. Mich. Lenawee Hist. I, 193; Lenawee Port., 789.

BLODGETT, Ludim, Revolutionary soldier; set. N. Y. Branch Port., 412.

BLOOD, Anna, b. 1798; m. 1818 Eleazer E. Calkins of N. Y. and Mich. Oakland Port., 278.

—— O. T., b. Middlesex Co., set. Mich., 1860? Traverse, 165.

BLY, Lucinda, m. 1820? Lucius B. Barker of N. Y. and Mich. Kalamazoo Port., 456.

BODFISH, Oliver, of New Bedford; set. N. Y.; d. 1883. Gratiot, 305.

BOICE, Judson A., b. 1825; set. O., Mich., 1857. Ionia Port., 744.

BOIES, John K., b. Blandford, 1828; set. Mich., 1845. Lenawee Hist. I, 364; Lenawee Illus., 206; Lenawee Port., 750; St. Clair, 120.

BOLLES, Amelia, m. 1820? G. W. Peters of N. Y. and Mich. Washtenaw Hist., 863.

BOLTWOOD, George S., b. Amherst, 1861; set. Mich., 1885. Grand Rapids City, 64.

—— Lucius, of Hampshire Co.; bought land in Mich., 1836. Allegan Hist., 220.

—— Lucius, b. Amherst, 1862; set. Mich., 1887. Grand Rapids City, 65; Grand Rapids Hist., 762.

BOND, Augustus, b. Lanesboro, 1812 or 1821; set. Mich., 1836. Washtenaw Hist., 494, 1390.

—— George, set. Mich., 1838. Lansing. 308.

—— Jonas, of Conway; set. N. Y., 1800. Lenawee Illus., 104.

—— Jonas, b. Berkshire Co., 1810; set. N. Y., 1823, Mich., 1835. Washtenaw Hist., 1390.

—— Josiah, b. Conway, 1799; set. N. Y., 1800, Mich., 1848. Lenawee Illus., 103.

—— Samuel, b. Worcester, Apr., 1784; set. Mich., 1836. Washtenaw Hits 1390.

—— Samuel, b. Worcester County, Aug., 1784; set. N. Y., 1823, Mich., 1836, Washtenaw Hist., 1390.

—— Theodosia, m. 1825? Luther Boyden of Mich. Washtenaw Hist., 691.

BONNEY, Tryphosa, b. Chesterfield, m. 1810? Ariel Murdock of N. Y. Berrien Hist., 521.

—— Walter E., set. Mich.? Newaygo, 365.

BOODY, Nathan, b. Taunton, 1819; set. Mich., 1834. Lenawee Hist. II, 336.

—— Sylvester, of Taunton; b. 1787; set. Mich., 1834. Lenawee Hist. II, 336.

BORDWELL, Medad, b. Shelburne, 1790; set. N. Y., Mich., 1835. Calhoun, 136

BOUGHTON, Guy C., b. Stockbridge; set. O., 1818. Lenawee Port., 1140.

—— Selleck C., b. W. Stockbridge, 1796; set. Pa., 1822, Mich., 1831. Lenawee Hist. I, 84.

BOURN, Seth, b. Berkshire Co., 1833; set. Mich., 1862. Bay Hist., 199.

BOW, Charles, b. Berkshire Co., 1794; set. N. Y., Mich. Hillsdale Port., 539.

BOWEN, Daniel W., b. Cheshire. 1810; set. N. Y., Mich., 1854. Washtenaw Port., 638.

—— Eliza, b. Boston, 1800? m. Isaac Lewis of N. Y. Berrien Port., 136.

—— Henry, set. N. Y., 1815? Washtenaw Port., 638.

—— Henry, 3d, b. Cheshire, 1807; set. N. Y., 1814, Mich., 1849. Lenawee Hist. II, 195.

—— Martin, of Stafford; set. N. Y., 1810. Washtenaw Hist., 1396.

BOWEN, Nancy, m. 1810? Lemuel S. Scott of Mass. and Mich. Washtenaw Hist., 735.

—— Sylvanus, b. Rehoboth, 1780; set. R. I., N. Y., 1812. Lenawee Hist. I, 339.

BOWERMAN, Benjamin, set. N. Y., 1825. Jackson Hist., 884.

—— Dorothy, of Berkshire Co.; m. 1810? James Hathaway of Mass. and Mich. Lenawee Port., 657.

—— Emeline, b. Barnstable Co.; m. 1825? Ira B. Weeks 'of N. Y., O. and Mich. Jackson Port., 432.

—— Moses, set. N. Y., 1810? Lenawee Port., 323.

BOWMAN, Peace, m. 1795? John Burton of Me. Midland, 215.

BOYCE, Anna, m. 1854 Joseph S. Graves of Mich. Berrien Port., 345.

BOYD, Rachel F., m. 1835? George Taylor of Maine. Muskegon Port., 253.

—— William A., b. Richmond, 1785; set. N. Y. Monroe, 163.

BOYDEN, E. L., set. Mich., 1850? Washtenaw Hist., 698.

—— Jonathan, set. N. H., 1800. Saginaw Hist., 832.

—— Luther, of Conway; b. 1788; set. Mich., 1826. Washtenaw Hist., 691; Washtenaw Past, 803.

—— Nancy, b. Medfield? 1796; m. Isaac Wellman of Mass., Vt., N. Y. and Mich. Grand Rapids City, 1074.

BOYINGTON, L. Permelia, b. Paxton, 1815? m. Israel B. Estey of N. H. and Vt. Clinton Port., 227.

BOYNTON, Nehemiah, b. Medford, 1857; set. Mich., 1896. Wayne Land., appendix 16.

BRACKETT, William H., b. Lynn, 1841; set. Vt., 1857, Mich., 1871. Monroe, appendix, 44.

BRADFORD, Moses, set. Mich., 1830? Kent, 1331.

—— Polly, m. 1790? John B. Simonson of N. Y. Oakland Port., 511.

BRADISH, Calvin, b. Cummington, 1773; set. N. Y., 1793; Mich., 1831. Lenawee Hist. I, 339; Lenawee Port., 310.

—— Chloe, b. Hardwick, 1775; m. 1800? Gain Robinson of Mass. and N. Y. Lenawee Hist. I, 524; Lenawee Port. 1103.

BRADISH, Rowene, b Cummington, 1786; m. 1801 John Comstock of N. Y. and Mich. Lenawee Hist. I, 499; Lenawee Port., 648.

BRADLEY, Addiniram, b. Sandisfield, 1799; set. N. Y., Mich. Branch Twent., 768.

—— Eunice J., of Lanesboro; m. 1833 Daniel A. Loomis of Mich. Lenawee Hist. I, 123.

BRADLEY, H. M., b. Lee, 1824; set. O., 1835, Mich., 1855. Bay Hist., 136.

—— Nathan B., b. Lee, 1831; set. O., 1835; Mich., 1852. Bay Gansser, 371; Bay Hist., 83; Lake Huron, 83.

—— William, set. O., 1835. Lake Huron, 83.

BRAGG, Sarah W., of Assonet; m. 1830 Humphrey Shaw of Mich. Saginaw Port., 564.

BRALEY, Amos, b. 1820; set. N. Y., 1823, Mich. Midland, 194.

—— Ephraim, set. N. Y., 1823. Midland, 194.

—— Phineas D., b. Berkshire Co., 1811; set. Mich., 1823. Saginaw Hist., 652.

BRAMAN, Thomas, b. 1799; set. Mich., 1833. Washtenaw Hist., 1425.

BRANCH, Abigail, b. Benson? 1807; m. 1827 George Wallace of Mass. and Mich. Clinton Port., 259.

—— Elizabeth, m. 1845? W. H. Gardner of O. Northern P., 542.

—— Nathan C., of Worthington; set. O., Mich., 1846. Ingham Hist., 335, 347.

BRANT, Simeon, set. N. Y., 1790? Berrien Hist., 224.

BRASS, Samuel, b. Boston, 1802; set. Mich. Clinton Past, 407.

BREED, Nathaniel, b. Cape Cod; set. N. H., 1800? Kalamazoo Port., 911.

BREWSTER, Elizabeth M., of Worthington, b. 1808; m. Andrew T. McReynolds of Mich. Grand Rapids City, 309.

BRIDGE, Abba G., of Boston; m. 1839. James M. Nelson of Mich. Kent, 1090.

BRIDGES, Polly, of Berkshire Co., m. 1810? Ira R. Paddock of N. Y. and Mich. Branch Port., 454.

BRIDGMAN, Charles, b. Northampton, 1815? set. O. Genesee Port., 643.

—— George W., set. Mich., 1876. Berrien Hist., 147.

BRIGGS, Abigail, m. 1855? Sylvanus Kinney of Mich. Lenawee Port., 223.

BRIGGS, Andreas, b 1795; set. O. Sanilac, 252.

—— Daniel B., b. Adams, 1829; set. Mich., 1854. Macomb Hist., 648; St. Clair, 125.

—— Ebenezer, set. Mich., 1850? Saginaw Port., 701.

—— Elizabeth V., of Adams; m. 1864 J. M. Potter of Mich. Ingham Port., 828.

—— Enoch, set. N. Y., 1821. Clinton Port., 721.

—— Hiram C., b. Mansfield, 1819; set. N. Y., 1821, Mich., 1839. Clinton Port., 721.

—— Isaac S., b. Plymouth, 1807; graduate of Harvard, 1829; set. N. Y. Northern P., 341.

—— Nathan H., set. Mich., 1835. Grand Rapids Hist., 704; Grand Rapids Lowell, 594.

—— Nathaniel W., of Taunton; set. Ind., 1872? d. 1877. Washtenaw Hist., 774.

—— Susan N., b. Middleboro; m. 1867 William J. Loveland of Mich. Saginaw Port., 701.

BRIGHAM, Barna L., b. Prescott, 1813; set. Mich., 1836. Kalamazoo Hist., facing 461; Kalamazoo Port., 798.

—— Curtis, b. Franklin Co., 1793; set. Mich., 1834. Allegan Hist., 478; Kalamazoo Port., 361.

—— David, set. N. Y., 1795. Bay Hist., 201.

—— John W., b. Boston, 1822; set. Mich., 1834. Kalamazoo Port., 361.

—— Louise, b. Princeton; m. 1815? John Proctor of Vt. Kent, 665.

—— Lydia, b. 1820; m. William Y. Gilkey of Mich. Kalamazoo Port., 406.

—— Sallie, m. 1815? Benjamin Eager of Vt. and N. Y. Kalamazoo Port., 586.

BRIGHTMAN, Emeline, b. Fall River, 1826; m. Uri Blodgett of N. Y. and Mich. Branch Port., 413.

—— Samuel, b. near Fall River, 1794; set. N. Y., Mich. 1844. Lenawee Port., 1121.

BRINTON, Samuel, b. 1794; set. Conn., 1820? Mich. Branch Twent., 447.

BROKELBANK, Mary, m. 1800? James Eaton of N. Y. and Mich. Lenawee Port., 472.

BRONSON, Daniel, of Berkshire Co.; set. N. Y., 1794, Mich., 1818. Oakland Hist., 131.

—— William, b. Berkshire Co., 1793; set. N. Y., 1794, Mich., 1818. Oakland Hist., 131.

BROOKS, Abijah E., b. Wendell, 1842; set. Mich., 1873. Kent, 959.

—— Ebenezer, b. Worcester Co., set. Vt., 1805. Macomb Hist., 691.

—— George, b. Townsend, 1823; set. N.H. Mich., 1869. St. Clair, 560.

—— John, set. O., 1812. Gratiot, 598.

BROOKS, Martha, m. 1805? Rufus Cody of N. Y. Hillsdale Port., 715.

BROSS, Maria, m. 1835? Reuben Gilmore of Mass. and Mich. Jackson Port., 700.

BROWN, C. S., b. Hadley, 1821; set. N. Y., Mich., 1848. Northern P., 502.

—— Caroline, b. Charlemont, 1817; m. 1838 Perley Bills of Mich. Lenawee Port., 1160.

—— Catharine, m. 1800? Darius Kimball of N. H., Pa., N. Y. and Mich. Lenawee Port., 779.

—— Charles B., b. Brimfield, 1844; set. Mich., 1864. Kalamazoo Port., 701.

—— Clara, m. 1830? Casper Bartley of Mass. and Wis. Northern P., 149.

—— Clara, b. Warwick; m. 1852 James Farrar of N. H. and Mich. Lenawee Illus., 300; Lenawee Port., 260.

—— Clarissa, m. 1820? James DeLong of N. Y. and Mich. Ionia Port., 326.

—— Cynthia, b. Cheshire, 1802; m. 1823 Ezekiel Angell of N. Y. Lenawee Illus., 339; Lenawee Port., 393.

—— Daniel, set. Vt., 1800? N. Y. Washtenaw Hist., 969. Washtenaw Port., 255.

—— Daniel, set. O., 1825? Muskegon Port., 347.

—— David, set. Mich., d. 1858. Muskegon Port., 422.

—— E. Gertrude, of Boston; m. 1890 George W. Webber of Mich. Ionia Port., 192.

—— Elijah, set. N. Y., 1825? Mecosta, 272.

—— Essuck, b. Cheshire; set. N. Y., 1810? Lenawee Illus., 340.

—— Ethan, b. Stockbridge, 1791; set. N. Y. Mecosta, 528.

BROWN, Frederick, set. N.Y., 1825? Grand Rapids City, 569.

—— Frederick E., b. Boston, 1850; set. N. Y., Mich., 1869. Bay Hist., 149.

—— Genet, of Worcester; set. Mich., 1835. Ingham Hist., 453.

—— George R., b. 1829; set. Mich., 1840? Bay Gansser, 624.

—— Harriet A., of Concord; m. 1832 Jeremiah A. Robinson of Mass., O. and Mich. Jackson Hist., 701.

—— Henry B., b. Lee, 1836; set. Mich. 1859. Wayne Chron., 413.

—— Hepsibah, b. 1776; m. Elijah Hill of N. Y. Oakland Port., 429.

—— Israel P., set. Vt., 1800? Kalamazoo Port., 895.

—— Joel, set. Vt., 1812 soldier. Muskegon Port., 122.

—— John, set. N. Y.; Revolutionary soldier. Ionia Port., 483.

—— John, set. N. Y., 1815. Washtenaw Port., 457.

—— Jonas, b. Heath, 1795; set. Mich., 1836. Monroe, 505.

—— Jonas, set. Mich., 1840? Bay Gansser, 624.

—— Joseph, b. Heath, 1785; set. N. Y., 1810. Hillsdale Hist., 291.

—— Lemuel D., b. Hadley, 1805; set. N. Y., 1825, Mich., 1839. Hillsdale Hist., 233; Hillsdale Port., 537.

—— Lorah R., b. 1785? set. N. Y. Hillsdale Port., 457.

—— Luther, b. Windsor; 1812 soldier; set. N. Y. Berrien Port., 697.

—— Mary H., m. 1825? David H. Daniels of Mich. Kalamazoo Port., 630.

—— Matilda, of Rowe; b. 1777; m. 1793 Nathaniel Gleason of Mass., N. Y. and Mich. Lenawee Hist. I, 303.

—— Nancy, m. 1800? Samuel Cook of Vt. and N. Y. Calhoun, 75.

—— Nicholas, b. 1777? set. N. Y. Branch Hist., 193.

—— Noah, set. N. Y., 1825? Calhoun, 131.

—— Otis, b. Worcester, 1787; set. Mich., 1839. Hillsdale Port., 537.

—— Polly, of Lunenburg; m. 1805? Moses Fitch of Mass. and Mich. Clinton Port., 263.

—— Samuel, b. Brimfield, 1778; set. Mich., 1831. Kalamazoo Hist., 460, 482.

BROWN, Solomon, set. N. Y., Mich., 1852. Lenawee Port., 780.

—— Susanna, b. 1793; m. Jacob Rogers of Pa. Lenawee Port., 1178.

—— Timothy, b. Leyden; set. N. Y., 1805? d. 1853. Ionia Port., 483.

—— W. Symington, of Stoneham; Jackson Hist., 659.

—— William, set. N. Y., 1819, Pa., 1837. Gratiot, 324.

—— William F., b. 1818; set. N. Y., Mich., 1863. Gratiot, 324.

—— William H., of Middlesex Co; set. Va., O., Mich., 1866. Mecosta, 553.

BROWNELL, P. T., b. Fairhaven, 1855; set. Mich., 1876. Upper P., 344.

—— Susan A., b. N. Adams, 1823; m. 1840 Porter Beal of Mich. Lenawee Hist. II, 175.

—— Thomas, b. 1804; set. Mich., 1825, Kan. Lenawee Hist. II, 175.

BROWNING, Betsey, m. 1790? William Greene of N. Y. Jackson Port., 840.

BRUNSON, Flavius J., b. 1786; set. N. Y., 1815? Clinton Port., 706; Shiawassee, 516.

BRYAN, Richard, of Cheshire; b. 1786; set. Mich., 1838. Hillsdale Hist., 330; Hillsdale Port., 410.

—— William, b. Cheshire, 1816; set. Mich., 1837. Hillsdale Port., 410.

BRYANT, Elizabeth, b. Fitchburg; m. 1885 Frank H. Milham of Mich. Kalamazoo Port., 288.

—— Nathaniel, set. Vt., 1817. Hillsdale Port., 512.

—— Nathaniel, b. 1810; set. Mich. Hillsdale Port., 512.

—— Otis B., b. Hingham, 1860; set. Mich., 1880. Upper P., 344.

—— Samuel, of Northampton; set. N. Y., 1820? Ionia Hist., 440.

—— Susan, b. Cheshire, 1820; m. 1837 William Bryan of Mich. Hillsdale Port., 410.

BUCK, Aseneth, m, 1815? Joseph B. Leonard of N. Y. Branch Twent., 779.

—— Levi, b. 1786; set. N. Y.; d. 1816. Hillsdale Hist., 249; Hillsdale Port., 553.

—— Lucretia, b. western Mass., 1787; set. N. Y., 1807; m. 1st Peter Lake of N. Y.; m. 2d 1819, Israel Waggoner. Lenawee Hist. I, 483.

BUCK, Reuben, set. N. Y., 1803? Mich. Lenawee Hist. II, 287.

BULL, A. E., of Sheffield; b. 1808; set. Mich., 1836. Allegan Hist., facing 480.

BULLARD, Amos, b. Athol, 1809; set. Mich., 1830. Washtenaw Hist., 1307; Washtenaw Port., 456.

—— Fisher, b. Franklin; set. N. H., 1820? Kent, 1392.

—— Henry, set. Ind., 1830, Ill., 1868. Berrien Twent., 319.

BULLEN, Reuben R., b. Charlton, 1806; set. N. Y., 1824, Pa., 1828, Mich., 1836. Ingham Hist., 224; Lansing, 552.

BULLOCK, Esther, m. 1810? Allen Dryer of N. Y. Ingham Port., 345.

—— George W., b. Savoy, 1809; set. Mich., 1836. Saginaw Hist., 213.

BULLOCK, Shubael, b. Cambridge, 1793; set. N. Y. Genesee Port., 811.

BUNCHER, Charles, b. Lowell, 1839; set. Mich, 1873. Wayne Land. 656.

BURBANK, Robert G., set. N. Y., 1840? Northern P., 546.

BURDEN, Nancy, b. Lanesboro, 1805? m. William Carpenter of N. Y. Hillsdale Port., 870.

BURLEIGH, John L., b. 1842; set. N. Y., Mich., 1874. Washtenaw Hist., 569.

BURLEY, Susan, of Salem; m. 1837 Cortland B. Stebbins of N. Y. and Mich. Lansing, 572.

BURLINGAME, Rachel, b. Berkshire Co., m. 1830? Seth Aldrich of Mich. Macomb Hist., 688.

BURNETT, Andrew J., set. N. Y., 1820? Mich., 1844. Allegan Twent., 440.

—— David, b. S. Hadley, 1808; set. Mich., 1836. Grand Rapids Hist., 176; Grand Rapids Lowell, 106; Grand River, appendix, 6; Kent, 200.

—— Lois, b. 1810; m. Caleb Myers of N. Y. and Mich. Allegan Twent., 440.

—— Mary, b. Chesterfield, 1782; m. 1802 Joseph Rice, Jr., of N. Y. and Mich. Lenawee Port., 598.

BURNHAM, Calvin, set. Mich., 1839. Monroe, 127.

—— Nancy, b. Montague; m. 1843 Jason Hemenway of Mich. Lenawee Port., 438.

BURNHAM, Olive C., b. Montague, 1821; m. 1840 Lysander Ormsby of Mich. Lenawee Port., 306.

BURNS, George T., b. Lowell, 1843; set· Wis., 1856, Mich., 1873. Upper P., 243·

BURPEE, Samuel S., b. Templeton, 1801; set. Mich., 1830. Calhoun, 76.

BURR, Robert, b. Great Barrington; set. N. Y., 1800? Calhoun, 145.

BURT, Alvin, set. N. Y., 1792. Macomb Hist., 241.
—— Daniel, set. O., 1825. Muskegon Port., 347.
—— Scammel, set. Vt., 1805? Saginaw Hist., 766.
—— William A., b. Petersham or Taunton, 1792; set. N. Y., 1799 or 1813, Mich., 1824. Detroit, 1179; Macomb Hist., 241; Macomb Past, 695; Northern P., 10; Upper P., 428.

BURTON, George, b. 1791; set. N. Y. Branch Twent., 582.

BUSH, Charles, b. Worcester, 1798; set. Mich., 1834. Allegan Twent., 404.
—— David, b. Pittsfield, set. N. Y., 1809, Mich., 1838. Washtenaw Hist., 1391.
—— John, set. Vt., 1811. Newaygo, 285.
—— Martha, of New Braintree; m. 1795? Aaron Abbott of Mass. and N. Y. Lenawee Hist. II, 252.
—— Orry, set. N. Y., 1820? Macomb Hist., 574.
—— Russell, b. Greenfield, 1803; set. Vt., 1811, Canada, Mich., 1856. Newaygo, 286.

BUSWELL, Jacob, set. N. Y., 1825? Muskeon, Port., 555.

BUTLER, Isaiah, b. 1806; set. N. Y., Mich. Genesee Port., 922.
—— Justin H., b. near Boston, 1803; set. N. Y., Mich., 1827. Oakland Port., 489.

BUTTON, Emily E., m. 1830? Warren Rundel of Conn., Pa. and Mich. Oakland Port., 200.

BUTTRICK, Rosamond, b. Hawley, 1809; m. 1st —— Humphrey; m. 2d, Ebenezer Jones of N. Y. Osceola, 257.

BYAM, Lucretia, m. 1815? Josiah Mansfield of N. Y. Mecosta, 308.

CALDWELL, James C., b. Worcester Co., 1824; set. Pa., Mich. Isabella, 213, 267.

CALDWELL, Moses, set. Pa., Mich., 1840. Isabella, 267.

CALKINS, Jonathan, b. 1760? Revolutionary soldier; set. Vt. 1783? N. Y. Oakland Biog., 340.

CALL, Eunice. b. Coleraine, 1802; m. 1824 Orlando B. Stillman of N. Y., O , & Mich. Ingham Hist., 217; Ingham Port., 495.
—— Joel, 1812 soldier; set. N. Y. Branch Port., 343.
—— Orlando B., set. N. Y., 1840? Mich., 1860. Ionia Port., 742.

CAMPBELL, Eliza E., m. 1850? Daniel E. Hull of Mass., O. & Mich. Lenawee Port., 487.
—— William, set. N.Y., 1820? Mich., 1848. Oakland Port., 256.

CAMPFIELD, Sarah, m. 1820? Oliver Tiffany of N. Y. and Mich. Jackson Port., 310.

CANFIELD, Celira, b. Tyringham, 1810; m. 1830 Edson Fuller of O. and Mich. Mecosta, 178; Newaygo, 180.
—— Lucy, b. Sandisfield; m. 1830? David Granger of N. Y. Kalamazoo Port., 917.

CANNON, John, b. Salem or New Salem, 1808; set. N. Y., Mich., 1831. Macomb Hist., 224, 725.
—— Pearl, b. Warwick, 1784; set. N. H., Vt., N. Y., Mich., 1833. Macomb Hist., 724, 725.

CARD, Charles M.. b. Stockbridge? 1825; set. N. Y., Mich., 1868. Midland. 365.
—— Laura A., b. Williamstown, 1827; m. William J. Baker, and Leonard Taylor of Mich. Branch Port., 332; Branch Twent., 508.

CARDY, David B., b. New Bedford, 1817; set. Canada, 1853, Mich., 1859. Bay Hist., 204.

CAREY, Rufus, set. N. Y., 1790? Hillsdale Port., 834.

CARLETON, Edmund, b Haverhill, 1734; set. N. H. Northern P., 79.

CARPENTER, Alanson, set. Mich., 1840? Jackson, Hist., 829.
—— Anna, m. 1820? Truman Walker of Mich. Calhoun, 115.
—— Esther, b. 1801; m. 1821 Andrew Coryell of Mich. Lenawee Hist. I, 189.
—— Ezra, b. Rehoboth, 1698; set. N. H. Lenawee Hist. I, 299; Lenawee Illus., 151.

CARPENTER, Ezra, b. Attleboro, 1776; set. N. Y., 1803, Mich., 1826. Lenawee Hist. I, 189; Washtenaw Hist., 1250; Washtenaw Port., 403.

—— Harriet, b. 1805; m. Elijah Kingsley of Mich. Berrien Port., 426.

—— John E., soldier of 1812; set. N. Y. Berrien Port., 512.

—— Josiah, b. Adams, 1801; set. N. Y., 1826, Mich., 1836. Lenawee Hist. II, 460; Lenawee Port., 612.

—— Julius, b. Worcester, 1836; set. Mich., 1836. Oakland Port., 628.

—— Powell, b. 1771; set. N. Y., 1800? Oakland Biog., 423.

—— R., b. 1806; set. Mich., 1844. Washtenaw Hist., 495.

—— Sidney, b. Worcester Co., 1810; set. N. Y., 1824, Mich., 1836. St. Joseph, 188.

—— William, b. Charlestown, 1752; set. N. H., N. Y., 1808. Lenawee Illus., 120; Lenawee Port., 1202.

CARRIER, Elijah, b. 1798; set Ct., N. Y. Hillsdale Port., 582.

CARROLL. Deborah of Rowe; m. 1845 Josiah Upton of Mass. and Mich. Clinton Past., 422.

CARRUTH, Thomas, b. Marlborough, 1849; set. Mich., 1883. Monroe, appendix 36.

CARTER, Ira F., set. Wis., 1840? Saginaw Hist., 840.

—— Nathaniel, b. Leominster, 1806; set. Mich., 1831. Macomb Hist., 226, 245, 691.

CARY, Martha A., m. 1869 T. C. Bishop of Mich. Jackson Hist., 1064.

—— Selden P., b. Williamstown, 1819; set. Mich., 1853. Detroit, 1453.

CASE, Ezekiel, b. Washington; set. N. Y., 1810? Mich. Hillsdale Port., 233.

—— James, set. N. Y., 1800? Oakland Port., 347.

—— Sarah B., b. 1831; set. Mich. Washtenaw Hist., 495.

CASEY, Samuel, b. Lanesboro, 1803; set. N. Y., Mich., 1826. Washtenaw Hist., 1075.

CASSADA, James, set. N. Y., d. 1836. Gratiot, 560

CASTLE, Melissa, m. 1825 Ashley Parks of N.Y. and Mich. Washtenaw Hist., 1310.

CASWELL, Solomon, b. Belchertown, 1796; set. N. Y., 1805, O., 1817. Mich., 1821. Oakland Hist., 286.

CATLIN, Jane, b. 1813; m. Daniel Hull of O. and Mich. Ionia Port., 318.

CAULKINS, Betsey, m. 1815? Horace Hovey of O. and Mich. Clinton Port., 480.

CAWKINS, Priscilla, m. 1825? Frederick Prior of Mass. and Mich. Oakland Biog., 577.

CAZAR, Jane, m. 1805? Elijah Moore of N.Y. Isabella, 477.

CHACE, Jonathan, b. Worcester Co., set. Vt., 1800? Saginaw Hist., 820.

CHADWICK, Benjamin F., set. N. Y., Mich. Berrien Hist., 479.

—— Lewis, b. 1799; set. Vt., 1800, Mich., 1834. St. Clair, 308.

CHALKER, Nathaniel, b. 1780; set. Vt., N. Y., Mich., 1837. Clinton Port., 890.

CHAMBERLAIN, Benjamin, set. N. Y., 1815? Kent, 702.

—— C. Cloa, of Dudley; m. 1805 Moses Curtis of N.Y. Kalamazoo Hist. facing 476.

—— Eliza M., b. Petersham, 1809; m. 1st, Jesse Rogers of Mass. and Mich., m. 2d, Robert J. Street of Mich. Lenawee Hist. I, 471.

—— Luther, b. Westford, 1795; set. Vt., N. Y., Mich., 1839. Kalamazoo Hist., 403.

—— Milton, set. Mich.; d 1859. Genesee Port., 511.

—— Moses, b. Hopkinton, 1757; set. N. H., Vt. Berrien Port., 885.

—— Nicholas, set. N. Y., 1790? Kalamazoo Port., 381.

—— Samuel, b. Chelsea. 1734; set. N. H., Vt. Berrien Port., 885.

CHAMBERLIN, Benjamin, b. Bedford, 1806; set. N. Y., Mich., 1836. Calhoun, 175.

—— John M., b. Springfield, 1809; set. N. Y., Mich., 1828. Oakland Port., 672.

—— Nancy, of Dalton, m. 1805? Harry Day of N. Y. Macomb Hist., 695.

—— Porter, set. Mich., 1829. St. Clair, 721.

—— Wells, set. N. Y., 1820? Washtenaw Port., 344.

CHANDLER, Jonathan, b. Concord? set. Vt., N. Y., Mich. Branch Port., 484.

CHANEY, Hannah, m. Nathaniel Parmeter of Mass. and N. Y. Newaygo, 328.

CHAPEL, Annis L., m. 1840? Luke L. Dennison of Mass. Midland, 197.

CHAPIN, Almno M., b. Chicopee, 1810; set. N. Y., Mich., 1843. Ingham Hist., 313, 316; St. Clair, 122.

—— Gad, set. Vt.; Revolutionary soldier; set. N. Y., 1879. Washtenaw Hist., 284.

—— Hannah, b Franklin Co.; d. 1833; m. Zadock Hale of Vt. Kalamazoo Port., 407.

—— Henry A., b. Leyden, 1813 or 14; set. Mich., 1836. Cass Hist., 146; Cass Twent., 60, 357.

—— James set. Mich., 1840? Mecosta, 479.

—— Jane. m. 1835? Joseph L. Beebe of N. Y. Jackson Hist., 587.

—— Joseph, b. Pamsa(?); set. N. Y., Pa., 1832. Kalamazoo Port., 824.

—— Levi, b. Chicopee, 1787; set. N. Y., 1818, Mich., 1844. Ingham Hist., 316.

—— Marshall, b. Bernardston, 1798; set. N. Y., Mich., 1819. Detroit, 1033; Wayne Chron., 202.

—— Noah J., b. 1814; set., N. Y. 1815? Mich., 1854. Traverse, 287.

—— Rachel, m. Paul Davis, Revolutionary soldier, of Mass. and N. Y. Branch Port., 459.

CHAPMAN, Alcott C., of Pittsfield, b. 1793; set. Mich., 1816? Monroe, 140.

—— Edmond, set. N. Y., 1810? Mich., 1836. Branch Twent., 500.

—— George W., b. Belchertown, 1815; set. Mich , 1841. Saginaw Hist., 816; Saginaw Port., 815.

—— Jane, m. 1830? Jarrah Sherman of N. Y. Jackson Port., 753.

—— Lucius W., b. Franklin Co., 1820; set. Mich., 1870. Saginaw Port., 251, 899.

—— Nina, m. 1840? Lyman West of O. and Mich. Clinton Past., 238.

—— Wellington, b. Hampshire Co., 1814; set. Mich., 1841. Saginaw Hist., 818; Saginaw Port., 855.

—— William H. H., b. Berkshire Co., 1841; set. Mich., 1841. Saginaw Port., 815.

CHAPPELL, William, set. N. Y., 1800? Clinton Past, 193.

CHASE, Alanson, b. 1806; set. Mich., 1830? Washtenaw Hist., 1076.

—— Benjamin, set. N. Y., 1815? Washtenaw Hist., 973.

——Clark, set. N. Y., 1800? d. 1821. Kalamazoo Hist., facing 423.

—— Mrs. J. M., b. 1822; set. Mich., 1847. Washtenaw Hist., 496.

CHESEBROUGH, Elisha, set. N. Y., 1820? Jackson Port., 697.

—— Maria, m. 1820? Milton Holmes of Mass. and N. Y. Jackson Port., 698.

—— Sarah, b. 1793; m. 1815? Warner I. Hodge of Mass. and Mich. Jackson Hist., 831; Jackson Port., 697.

CHILD, Alpha, b. Boston, 1836; set. Wis. Mich., 1872. Kent, 422.

CHILDS, Clarissa, b. 1790? m. 1810 Shubael Atherton of N. Y. and Mich. Genesee Hist., 348; Genesee Port., 815.

—— Daniel, b. 1779; set. N. Y., 1819. Hillsdale Port., 266.

—— Henry B., b. Shelburne, 1814; set. Mich., 1846. Grand Rapids City, 604; Kent, 263.

—— Sarah, m. 1819 Shubael Atherton of N. Y. Genesee Hist., 349.

—— Sophia, b. Pittsfield, 1789; m. 1816 Samuel Ledyard of N. Y. Branch Port., 615.

CHITTENDEN, Elizabeth, b. 1783; set. Mich. Washtenaw Hist., 590.

CHUBB, Franklin, set. Mich., 1830? Clinton Port., 335.

CHURCH, Chandler M., b. Berkshire Co., 1804; set. N. Y., Mich. Calhoun, 145.

—— Jesse, set. N. Y., 1807. Calhoun, 145.

—— Lucy, m. 1810? Appolos Baker of Mass. and N. Y. Lenawee Port., 594.

—— Nathan, b. 1847; set. Mich., 1869. Kent, 429.

—— Thomas B., b. Dighton, 1813 or 21; set. Mich., 1838. Grand Rapids Hist., 725; Grand Rapids Lowell, 753; Kent, 971.

CLAGHORN, Elizabeth, b. Williamsburg; m. 1800? Joseph Beal of N. Y. and Mich. Ionia Port., 457; Lenawee Hist. II, 175.

—— Sarah, b. Williamsburg, 1776; m. 1800 Ephraim Green of N. Y. Lenawee Hist. I, 484.

CLAPP, James H., set. N. Y., 1850, O. Grand Rapids City, 436.

CLAPP, Luther, b. Hampshire Co., set. O. 1840. Gratiot, 362.

—— Stephen, b. Northampton, 1750; set. N. Y., 1780. Lenawee Hist. I, 492.

CLARK, Albert, b. Northampton; set. O., Mich., 1863. Berrien Port., 583.

—— Aurilla, m. 1820? Justus Stiles of N.Y. and Mich. Muskegon Port., 322.

—— Calvin, b. Westhampton, 1805; set. Mich., 1835. St. Clair, 122.

—— Climene, b. Westhampton; m. 1839 Erastus Hopkins of Mich. Oakland Hist., 189.

—— Enos, set. N. Y., 1820? Mich., 1839. Allegan Twent., 455.

—— Ethan A., set. N. Y., 1820? Oakland Port., 269.

—— Hannah, of Greenwich, m. 1804 Bradford Newcomb of Vt. Lenawee Hist. I, 309.

—— James M., set. O., 1840? Osceola, 240.

—— Jason, b. 1791; set. N. Y., Mich., 1823. Ingham Port., 761.

—— John, b. 1770; set. Vt., 1777, Mich., 1833. Shiawassee, 442.

—— Lucius L., b. Hawley, 1816; set. Mich., 1839. St. Clair, 122.

—— Lydia, b. Hampshire Co., 1803? m. Alvah Whitmarsh of Mass., N. Y., and Ill. Lenawee Port., 1136.

—— Mary, m. 1815? Nathaniel Macumber of N. Y. and Mich. Newaygo, 267.

—— Mary A., of Northampton; m. 1835 Watson Loud of Mass. and Mich. Macomb Hist., 663.

—— Miles D., set. O., 1838. Washtenaw Hist., 1261.

—— Nancy, b. Somerset, 1773; m. 1796 Henry Weatherwax of N. Y. and Mich. Lenawee Hist. II, 234.

—— Orange, b. Berkshire Co., set. N. Y., O., 1831. Mich., 1854. Berrien Twent., 579.

—— Polly, b. Colerain, 1792; m. 1811 Daniel Jennings of N. Y. Hillsdale Port, 222; Lenawee Hist. I, 272; Lenawee Port., 395.

—— Rhoda, b. Sharon; m. 1820? Fisher Bullard of N. H. Kent, 1392.

—— Robert W., from near Pelham; set. N. Y.; d. 1839. Ingham Port., 750.

CLARK, Sophronia, b. Southwick, 1803; m. Henry W. Clapp of O. and Mich. Jackson Hist., 1010.

—— William A., b. Pittsfield; set. N. Y., 1820? Saginaw Port., 455.

—— William H., b. Hopkinton, 1805; set. Mich., 1845. Macomb Hist., 693.

CLARKE, Archibald S., set. N. Y., 1810? Jackson Hist., 968.

—— Franklin S., b. Berkshire Co., 1812; set. N. Y., Mich., 1843. Jackson Hist., 611.

—— John, Jr.,.b. Brewster, 1824; set. N.Y. Cal., Mich., 1860. Hillsdale Port., 263.

—— Linus, set. N. Y., 1825. Jackson Hist., 611.

—— Robert M., b. Brewster, 1825; set. Cal. Hillsdale Port., 263.

—— William B., set. N. Y., 1820? Saginaw Hist., 744.

CLEAVES, William S., b. Lowell, 1851; set. Mich., 1860. Upper P., 277.

CLEGG, Alice, b. Taunton, 1852; m. Asa L. Crane of Mich. Hillsdale Port., 842.

CLEMANS, Asa, b. Worcester, 1804? set. Mich., 1837. Hillsdale Port., 372.

CLEMENS, Jonathan, Revolutionary soldier; set. N. Y. Jackson Port., 341.

CLOUGH, Elijah, set. Mich., 1839. Oakland Port., 765.

COBB, John, set. Mich., 1834; d. 1875. Jackson Hist., 880.

COBURN, Jeptha, set. Mich., 1830. Oakland Port., 488.

—— Sallie, m. 1820? Daniel Stearns of N. Y. Newaygo, 274.

CODDING, Abiah, set. Vt., 1812 soldier. Berrien Port., 481.

CODY, Rufus, set. N. Y., 1800. Hillsdale Port., 715.

COFFIN, Lydia, b. Nantucket, 1780; m. 1797 Obed Macy of Mass., N. Y. and Mich. Lenawee Hist. II, 326.

COGSWELL, Asahel, set. N. Y., 1800? Saginaw Hist., 755.

COLE, Dyer, b. 1799; set. Mich. Lansing, 182.

—— Luther, set. N. Y., 1785. Monroe, 152.

—— Nathaniel, b. Rehoboth, 1794; set. N. Y., Mich., 1837. Macomb Hist., 650

COLEMAN, Almeda, m. 1820? John Russell of N. Y. and Mich. Jackson Hist., 955.

COLES, Columbus, b. Williamsburg, 1828; set. O., Mich., 1854. Isabella, 353.

—— Horace, set. O., 1839; d. 1882. Isabella, 353.

—— Oliver, b. Belchertown, 1790? set. N. Y. and Mich. Osceola, 255.

COLLIER, Charles S., b. Charlestown, 1803; set. N. Y., 1840, Mich, 1853. Oakland Biog., 76.

—— Susan, m. 1830? Samuel Andrews of Mich. Bay Gansser, 486.

COLLINS, Angeline, b. 1811; m. Alanson Flower of Mich. Oakland Port., 421.

—— Benjamin, from Cape Cod; set. N. Y., 1802. Berrien Hist., 326.

—— George, b. Wilbraham; set. Mich., 1830? Washtenaw Past, 165.

—— John, b. Hampshire Co., 1816; set. Mich. Genesee Port., 500.

—— Jonah S., b. Cape Cod, 1769; set. Mich. Genesee Port., 500.

—— Nathaniel, set. N. Y., 1825? Newaygo, 278.

COLT, Clara or Clarissa, m. 1825 Elnathan Phelps of Mass. and Mich. Oakland Biog., 607; Oakland Port., 640.

—— George, b. Pittsfield, 1807; set. Fla., 1828, Cuba, 1836, Mich., 1853. Clinton Port., 385.

—— Sylvia E., b. Pittsfield, 1796; m. 1813 Charles Larned of Mich. Wayne Chron., 325.

COLTON, John B., b. Conway, 1827; set. Mich., 1844. Kent, 264.

COLVER, Calvin, b. 1788; set. Mich. Washtenaw Hist., 590.

COMAN, Samuel, set. N. Y., 1800; Mich., 1835. Hillsdale Port., 700.

COMINGS, Chester, from Worcester County, set. Mich., 1837. Allegan Hist., 219, 253

COMSTOCK, John, b. 1774; set. N. Y., 1788, Mich., 1830. Lenawee Hist. I, 497. Lenawee Port., 648.

—— Nathan, set. N. Y., 1788. Lenawee Hist. I, 497.

—— William, set. Mich., 1850? Muskegon Port., 434.

CONANT, Charles R., b. Franklin Co., 1814; set. Vt., 1823, Mich., 1851. Jackson Port., 594.

CONE, Obed, b. 1792; set. N. Y., 1825? Mich., 1853. Lenawee Hist. II, 130.

CONGDON, William T., b. near Boston; set. N. Y., 1830? Ingham Port., 246.

CONKLIN, Ebenezer H., b. Lenox 1790; set. N. Y., 1806, Mich., 1831. Washtenaw Hist., 1336.

CONN, George, set. N. H., 1795? N. Y Clinton Port., 719.

CONNABLE, Abbie, b. Bernardston; m. 1830? James C. Bontecou of R. I., Mass. and O. Northern M., 474.

CONVERSE, Benjamin, b. Belchertown, 1813; set. Mich., 1834. Lenawee Port., 1207.

—— Ephraim, b. Brookfield, 1779; res. Belchertown; set. Mich., 1851. Lenawee Port., 1207.

—— James, of Northampton; set. Mich., 1840. Lenawee Hist. I, 513.

—— Maria L., b. Northampton, 1832, m. 1854 George T. McKenzie of Mich. Lenawee Hist. I, 513.

COOK, Amelia, m. 1825 Justin Cook of Mich. Washtenaw Hist., 1307.

—— Edwin, b. Hadley, 1812; set. N. Y., 1834, Mich. Lenawee Port., 353.

—— George, b. Hampshire Co., 1828; set. Mich., 1845. Washtenaw Hist., 1307.

—— Justin, b. Hampshire Co., 1802; set. Mich., 1845. Washtenaw Hist., 1307.

—— Levi, b. Bellingham, 1792; set. Mich., 1815. Detroit, 1033.

—— Martin E., b. Shelburne Falls; set. N. Y., 1820? Jackson Hist., 791.

—— Randolph, b. 1831; set. Mich., 1845. Washtenaw Hist., 1307.

—— Samuel, set. Vt., N. Y., 1800? Calhoun, 75

—— Vienna, b. Bellingham, 1795; m. 1820 Benjamin Taft of Mass. Oakland Port., 225.

COOLEY, Chester, b. Berkshire, 1790? set. N. Y., O., Mich., 1850. Kalamazoo Port., 888.

—— Dennis, b. Deerfield, 1789; set. Ga., Mich., 1827. Macomb Hist., 817.

—— Geogre, b. Deerfield, 1819; set. Mich., 1830. Ionia Hist., 290.

—— George N., b. Conn. Valley, 1810; set. N. Y., Mich. Kent, 653.

Cook, Jerusha M., b. S. Deerfield, 1810; m. 1840 Philip Reeve of Mich. Washtenaw Past, 219.

Cooley, Joanna, b. Lowell, 1825; m. Solon T. Hutchins of Mich. Midland, 288.

—— Leonard, set. N.Y., 1800? Mich., 1842. Lenawee Port., 594.

—— Orsimus, set. Mich., 1830; Genesee Hist., 410.

—— Reuben, set. N. Y., 1811. Kalamazoo Hist., 433.

—— Russell, b. Deerfield; set. Mich., 1830. Ionia Hist., 290; Washtenaw Hist., 689.

—— Sally, m 1800? Lemon Copley of O. and Mich. Genesee Port., 620.

—— Smith, set. N. Y.. 1840? Huron, 287.

—— Sophronia, b. 1811; m. Sylvester Scott of Mich. Clinton Port., 666. 912.

—— Thomas, set. N. Y., 1804. Washtenaw Port., 235.

—— Zadoc. b. 1793; set. O. 1825, Mich., 1833. Oakland Biog., 367.

Coolidge, Henry H., b. Leominster, 1805 or 11; set. Mich., 1836. Berrien Hist., 146; Berrien Port., 213; Berrien Twent., 154, 286; Cass Hist., 90.

Coon, Huldah. m. 1800? Elijah Knox of Mass. and N. Y. Kalamazoo Port., 983.

Cooper, Jeremiah, set. N. Y , 1810. Lenawee Illus., 90.

—— John, b. Plymouth; set. Me., 1820? Mich., 1865. Ionia Port., 746.

—— Sarah, b. Cheshire, 1803; m. 1821 Edmund B. Dewey of N. Y. Lenawee Illus., 90

Copeland, Emeline, m. 1835? David Burton of Me. and Mich. Midland, 240.

Cossett, Isabinda, m. 1810? Asaph Robinson of O. Branch Port., 556.

Cotrell, Lucy, b. Worthington, 1817; m. 183 7 James Rogers of Mass., Mich. and O. Lenawee Port., 915.

Cotton, Otis W., set. N. Y , 1808; La., 1818, Mich., 1828. Macomb Past., 168.

Coulson, Lovina, m. 1815?William Pratt. of Mass. and O. Hillsdale Port., 827.

Courtis, William M., b. Boston, 1842; set. Mich., 1883. Wayne Land. Appendix 28.

Covey, Hiram, b. Mt. Washington, 1802; set. N. Y., 1814, Mich., 1837. Oakland Hist., facing 218.

Cowan, N. B., b. 1810; set. Mich., 1840. Clinton Port., 456.

Cowan, Sally, m. 1805? Elkanah Ring. Saginaw Hist., 757.

Cowles, Horace, see Coles.

—— Israel T., b. Belchertown, 1854; set. Mich., 1878. Wayne Land. Appendix, 119.

—— Proctor P., b. Amherst, 1818; set. Mich., 1858. Upper P., 277.

—— Shepard B., b. Amherst, 1826; set. N. Y., 1830? Mich., 1836. Grand Rapids City, 622; Kent, 1354.

—— Sylvester, b. Amherst, 1795; set. N. Y., 1830? O., 1836. Grand Rapids City, 622.

Cowls, Samuel, b. Hatfield, 1766; set. O. Lenawee Hist. II, 116.

—— Sophia, b. Williamsburg, 1796; m. 1821 John Wilson of N. Y. and Mich. Lenawee Hist. II, 116.

—— Sophia, m. 1825? George H. Smith of Mass. and Mich. Jackson Port., 451.

Cox, James N., b. Fairhaven, 1844; set. Mich. 1869. Houghton, 213; Northern P., 400; Upper P., 303.

Crafts, Frances, m. 1832 Warren Pease of Mich. Washtenaw Hist., 1348.

—— Solomon C., set. Mich., 1842. Jackson Hist., 881.

Crandell, Edgar B., b. Cheshire; set. N.Y., Mich., 1878. Grand Rapids City, 119.

—— Stephen R., b. W. Stockbridge, 1836; set. N. Y., Mich., 1878. Grand Rapids City, 119; Mecosta, 491.

Crandle, Betsey, b. 1787; m. 1802 Jacob Hoadley of Mass., N. Y. and Mich. Lenawee Hist. II, 94.

Crane, Abraham, 1812 soldier, set. N. Y., 1825? Allegan Twent., 170.

Crane, Albert, b. Taunton, 1815; set. Mich. 1832. Hillsdale Port., 842, 845.

—— George, b. Norton, 1783; set. N. Y., 1804, Mich., 1833. Lenawee Hist. I, 252, 509; II, 466; Lenawee Port., 371.

—— Hannah, m. 1835 Sylvanus Kennedy of Mich. Lenawee Port., 223.

—— John, set. Ct. Hillsdale Port., 223.

—— Samuel, set. Ct., N. Y., 1810. Hillsdale Port., 223.

—— Turner, b. Norton, 1789; set. N. H., N. Y., 1816, Mich., 1833. Hillsdale Port 845; Lenawee Hist. II, 102 483; Lenawee Illus., 87; Lenawee Port., 569.

CRANSON, Elisha, b. near Boston, 1782; set. N. Y., 1815? Mich., 1830. Washtenaw Port., 419.

—— John, set. N. Y., 1825? Mich., 1832. Clinton Port., 987.

CRAPO, David, b. Dartmouth; set. O., Mich., 1854. Ionia Port., 736.

—— Henry H., b. Dartmouth, 1804; set. Mich., 1856. Branch Port., 149; Genesee Hist., 179.

CRAW, Farley, b. Cheshire, 1824; set. N.Y., 1827, Mich., 1845. Genesee Port., 303.

CRESSY, Erastus, of Rowe; set. Mich., 1842. Allegan Hist., 472.

CRISSEY, William S., b. 1806; set. N. Y., 1811, Mich., 1855. Kent. 533.

CRITTENDEN, Chauncy, set. N. Y., 1830? Kalamazoo Port., 825.

—— John, b. Conway, 1796; set. R. I., N. Y., 1816, Mich., 1831. Macomb Hist., 577, 906; Macomb Past, 146.

—— Levi, set. Mich., 1835. Macomb Hist., 794.

—— Orris, set. Mich., 1834. Hillsdale Port., 375.

CROCKER, Joseph, b. Cape Cod, 1801; set. N. Y., 1830? Osceola, 249.

CROFOOT, Joseph, b. 1811? set. N. Y. Berrien Hist., 405.

CROSBY, Hale E., b. Ashburnham, 1816; set. Mich., 1844. Berrien Port., 900.

—— Warren, set. N. Y., 1840? Mich. Muskegon Port., 276.

CROSS, Darius, b. Rowe or Buckland, 1814; set. Mich., 1837. Lenawee Hist. II, 309; Lenawee Illus., 383; Lenawee Port., 1025.

—— Eunice, m. 1785? David Peabody of N. H. Calhoun, facing 112.

—— Prudence, b. Rowe, 1807; m. 1828 Aaron S. Baker of Mich. Lenawee Hist. II, 109.

CROSSMAN, Nathaniel, b. Taunton; set. N. Y., 1805? Calhoun, 133.

CROVER, Amanda, of Worcester, m. 1853? Dennis Wakefield of Mich. Lenawee Illus., 284.

CUDWORTH, Mrs. A. L., set. Mich., 1828. Wayne Chron., 74.

CULVER, Martin, b. Chester; set. N. Y., 1826, Mich., 1837. Jackson Port., 296.

—— Marvin, b. Chester, 1807; set., N. Y. 1828, Mich., 1837. Jackson Port., 296.

CUMMINGS, Elvira, m. 1840? John Bonner of Pa. and Mich. Newaygo, 445.

—— Mary A., b. Royalston, 1805? m. Samuel S. Burpee of Mich. Calhoun, 76.

CURRIER, Hannah, m. 1820? Hugh Tolford of N. H. and Mich. Lenawee Port., 683.

—— Jacob, set. Mich., 1836. Berrien Hist., 402.

CURTIS, Hannah, m. 1805? Jonathan E. Davis of N. Y. Washtenaw Hist., 979.

—— Jeremiah, set. N. Y., 1800? Saginaw Hist., 729.

—— Moses, of Dudley, set. N. Y., 1800? Kalamazoo Hist., facing 476.

CURTISS, Waterman F., b. 1806; set. N.Y., Mich., 1859. Gratiot, 266.

CUSHING, James H., set. N. Y., 1825? Mich., 1851. Cass Twent., 687.

CUTLER, Dexter, b. 1811; (name changed from Shepherd) set. Mich., 1838. Northern M., 343.

—— Dwight, b. Amherst, 1830; set. Mich., 1848. Muskegon Port., 142; Ottawa Hist., 49.

CUTTER, Catharine, m. 1830? Peter Bradt of N. Y. Saginaw Hist., 908.

—— E. B., set. Ill., 1852, Mich., 1880. Saginaw Hist., 551.

DALRYMPLE, James, of Colerain, set. N. Y., 1018. Oakland Biog., 113.

—— Polly, b Colerain, m. 1815? Joseph Bancroft of N. Y. and Mich. Oakland Biog., 113.

DAMON, I. B. T., b. Hampshire Co., 1826; set. Mich., 1850? Saginaw Hist., 821.

DANA, Edmund, b. Cambridge, 1739; set. England. Bay Gansser, 374.

—— Mary, m. 1850? James H. Clapp of N. Y. and O. Grand Rapids City, 438.

DANIELS, David H., of Brimfield; set. Mich., 1832. Kalamazoo Hist., 383.

—— Elijah, b. 1793; set. N. Y.; d. 1839. Ingham Port., 733.

—— Elizabeth, m. 1805? Zenus Roberts of Mass. and Pa. Lenawee Port., 601.

—— Tamer, b. Hingham; m. 1810? Thaddeus Hopper of N. Y. and Mich. Berrien Twent., 338.

DARLING, Ephraim, b. 1791; set. Mich. Washtenaw Hist., 593.

—— Joseph, set. N. Y., 1804, Mich., 1844. Jackson Port., 324, 824.

DARLING, Lewis, b. 1812; set. N. Y., Mich. 1836. Jackson Port., 545.

—— Matilda A., b. Mendon, 1820; m. 1840 Stephen T. Hardy of Mich. Monroe, 587.

—— Pascal, set. N. Y., 1804, Mich., 1834. Jackson Port., 824.

—— Reed, b. Springfield, 1785; set. N. Y., Mich., 1834. Kalamazoo Hist., 309.

—— Simon, set. Mich., 1829. Ingham Hist., 463.

DARWIN, S. A., b. Pittsfield, 1813; set. Mich., 1836. Ingham Port., 221.

—— Seth C., set. N. Y., 1817, Mich., 1835. Ingham Port., 221.

DAUBY, Alexander J., b. near Springfield; set. N. Y., 1820. Jackson Port., 243.

DAVIS, Asa, set. N. Y., 1802. Lenawee Port., 232.

—— Bela, set. Vt., 1795? Macomb Past, 167.

—— Calvin, b. Hubbardston, 1793; set. N. Y., 1804, Mich., 1824. Macomb Hist., 726, 773; Macomb Past, 355.

—— Dolly, m. 1790? Lemuel Foster of Mass. and Mich. Jackson Port., 745.

—— Ebenezer, b. Conway, 1800; set. N. Y., 1827, Mich., 1831. Lenawee Hist. II, 130.

—— Jehiel, b. Wilbraham, 1787; set. Mich. 1831. Oakland Port., 612.

——, Jonathan E., b. Hubbardston, 1788; set. Vt., N. Y., 1805? Mich., 1843. Macomb Hist., 866; Macomb Past, 167; Washtenaw Hist., 979.

—— Joseph, b. 1800; set. N. Y. Branch Twent., 830.

—— Joshua, b. Barre, 1750; set. N. H., 1758, Vt., 1763. Detroit, 1186.

—— Levi, b. Vt., set. New Salem, 1805, N. Y.. 1816. Branch Port., 459.

—— Lucy, m. 1800? Isaac Rogers of N. Y. and O. Jackson Hist., 925.

—— Nathaniel, b. Petersham, 1715; set. N. H., 1758, Vt., 1763. Detroit, 1186.

—— Olive, m. 1820? James S. Merchant of Me. and Mich. St. Clair, 752.

—— Parnal, b. Monson, 1789; m. 1812 Joseph Belknap Jr. of Mass., N Y. and Mich. Lenawee Hist. II, 473.

DAVIS, Paul, b. near Boston; Revolutionary soldier; set. Vt., N. Y. Branch Port., 459.

—— Sally, b. Hubbardston, 1791; m. Abijah Owen of N. Y. and Mich. Macomb Hist., 755.

—— Samuel C., b. Lee, 1779; set. Mich., 1839. Jackson Port., 286.

—— Solomon, set. N. Y., 1810? Hillsdale Port., 959.

—— Willard, b. Princeton; set. Mich., 1837. Ingham Hist., 520.

—— William, b. 1799? set. N. Y. Washtenaw Hist., 1427.

DAWES, George W., b. Goshen, 1847; set. Mich., 1865. Gratiot, 457.

DAY, Erastus, b. Dalton, 1780; set. Canada, 1812? N. Y., Mich., 1826. Macomb Hist., 695, 791.

—— Esther H., m. 1873 Reuben Hatch Jr. of Mich. Traverse, 77.

—— Harry, of Dalton, set. N. Y., 1805? Macomb Hist., 695.

—— Pelatiah, b. Salem, 1776? set. N. Y., 1800? Clinton Port., 536.

—— Sarah, m. 1800? Charles Foote of Mass. and N. Y. Hillsdale Port., 461.

DEAN, Ailes, of Adams, b. 1818; m. 1838 Erastus S. Jenks of Mass. and Mich. Ionia Hist., 291.

—— Alexander, b. 1793; set. Mich. Kent, 1333.

—— Benjamin, b. New Ashford, 1806. set. Mich., 1858. Midland, 187.

—— Benjamin F.,b. Peru,1839; set. Mich., 1862. Midland, 363.

——, Ellen, m. 1860? Stephen R. Crandell of N. Y. and Mich. Grand Rapids City, 119.

——, Emily, m. 1835? J. D. White of N. Y. and Mich. Washtenaw Hist., 1055.

—— Harry, b. Westfield, 1799; set. Mich., 1837. Grand Rapids Hist., 180; Grand Rapids Lowell, 108.

—— Jessie F., b. Berkshire Co., 1856; m. George O. Rockwell of Mich. Midland, 265.

—— Mary A., b. Lee, 1854; m. William C. Plumer of Mich. Midland, 195.

—— Nelson K., b. Lee, 1852; set. Mich., 1854. Midland, 191.

DEAN, Rhoda K., of Taunton; m. 1815?
Rufus Read of Vt., N. H. and Mich.
Kalamazoo Hist., 477; Kalamazoo Port.,
630.

—— Stoel E., b. Pittsfield, 1847; set.
Mich., 1877. Midland, 196.

DEFOREST, Luther, b. 1796; set. N. Y.,
1820? Saginaw Hist., 745.

DE FORREST, Heman P., b. N. Bridgewater, 1839; set. Mich., 1889. Wayne
Land, appendix, 29.

DE LAND, Charles V., b. N. Brookfield,
18-6; set. Mich., 1830. Jackson Port.,
219; Saginaw Hist., 465.

—— Samantha, b. 1824; m. Benjamin W.
Rockwell of Mich. Jackson Hist., 701.

—— William R., b. Brookfield, 1792 or 5;
set. N. Y., Mich., 1830. Jackson Hist.,
142; Jackson Port., 219; Saginaw Hist.,
465.

DELANO, Israel, of Pembroke, b. 1765;
set. N. Y. Allegan Hist., 233.

—— M. A., b. Fairhaven, 1848; set. Mich.,
1868. Upper P., 344.

—— Stephen B., b. Providence? 1795;
set. N. Y. Kalamazoo Port., 640.

DELL, William H., b. 1820; set. Mich.,
1845. Washtenaw Hist., 497.

DEMING, Almond, set. O. 1834. Allegan
Twent., 188.

—— Emerson, b. Northampton, 1832;
set. O., 1834, Mich., 1863. Allegan
Twent., 188.

—— Eunice, m. 1800 David Southwick of
Mass. and N. Y. Kalamazoo Port , 738.

DENFIELD, William F., b. Natick, 1857;
set. Mich., 1884. Saginaw Port., 780.

DENHAM, Cornelius, b. Franklin Co.; set.
N. Y., 1820; d. 1828. Branch Port.,
236.

—— Cornelius, b. Conway, 1817 or 8; set.
Ill., N. Y., Mich., 1865. Branch Port.,
236; Branch Twent., 438.

DENISON, Asa W., set. Mich., 1845. Kent,
695.

DENNIS, Mary E., b. Concord; m. 1848
John D. Williams of Mich. Clinton
Port., 506.

DENNISON, Lovisa A., b. N. Lee, 1849; m.
Stoel E. Dean of Mass. and Mich. Midland, 197.

DENSMORE, Julina, of Conway, m. 1830?
Artemas Chase of N. Y. and Mich. Lenawee Hist. II, 3z9.

—— Rufus, set. Mich.; d. 1847. Gratiot,
491.

DERAINVILLE, Patience, m. 1815? Ephraim
Braley of N. Y. Midland, 194.

DEWEY, Amy, m. 1825? James H. Cushing
of N. Y. and Mich. Cass Twent.. 688.

—— Elizabeth, m. 1810? Ira Barnes of
N. Y., O. and Mich. Hillsdale Port.,
498.

—— Jonathan, set. N. Y., 1820? Oakland Port., 716.

—— Rowland, b. Westfield, 1803; set. O.
Branch Port., 495.

—— Stephen E., set. O., 1823. Branch
Port., 495.

DE WITT, Sarah, b. Belchertown, 1803;
m. 1827 Samuel Hinkley of N. Y. and
Mich. Lenawee Hist. I, 267; Lenawee
Port., 488.

DEXTER, Maria, m. 1845? Ransom D.
Tucker of Mich. Mecosta, 492.

—— Meribah, b. New Bedford, 1770 or 7;
m. 1797? Henry Jennings of N. Y. Lenawee Hist. II, 154; Lenawee Port., 534.

—— Samuel, set. N. Y., 1810? Saginaw
Hist., 728.

—— Samuel W., b. Boston, 1792; set.
N. Y., Mich., 1824. Washtenaw Hist.,
267; Washtenaw Past, 680; Wayne
Chron., 273.

DIBBLE, Philo, set. N. Y., 1800? Calhoun,
73.

DICKENS, Phebe, b. 1796; m. John Oliver
of N. Y. Jackson Hist., 1108.

DICKINSON, Abigail, set. Mich., 1835; m.
1836 George Salisbury of Mich. Bean
Creek, 49.

—— Asa C., b. Great Barrington; set.
N. Y., Mich., 1848. Wayne Chron.,
358; Wayne Land., 686.

—— George W., b. Granby, 1809; set.
N. Y., 1831, Mich., 1835. Grand River,
appendix 20; Kent, 201, 260.

—— Nathan, b. Amherst, 1799; set. Mich.,
1836. Macomb Past, 337.

—— Obed, of Amherst, set. Mich., 1836.
Branch Hist., 255.

DICKMAN, Sarah A., of Hopkinton, b. 1818;
m. 1848 Wellington Chapman of Mich.
Saginaw Port., 856.

DINSMORE, William, set N. Y., 1830?
Mich., 1836. Ionia Port., 559.

DIXON, George H., b. Nantucket, 1800;
set. N. Y., 1840? O., Mich. Detroit,
1401.

DOAN, Mrs. Emily, b. 1803; set. Mich.,
1835. Washtenaw Hist., 498.

DOANE, Elisha, b. Worcester, 1796; set.
Vt., N. Y., O., Mich., 1824. Kalamazoo
Hist., 304, 310.

—— Isaiah, b. Earlham? set. N. Y., 1820?
O. 1835? Berrien Twent., 951.

DODGE, Charles D., b. Ipswich, 1849; set.
Mich. Ingham Port., 322.

—— George H., b. 1834; set. Mich., 1856.
Clinton Past, 366.

—— Harvey, of Charlton, b. 1800; set.
Mich., 1856. Clinton Past, 366.

—— Hervey, b. Beverly, 1806; set. N. Y.,
O. Ingham Port., 322.

—— Lucretia, m. 1820? Thomas Kinney
of Mass. and N. Y. Lenawee Port.,
386.

—— Mary A., of Dudley, m. 1856 George
H. Dodge of Mich. Clinton Past, 366.

DOLBEAR, Avery, b. Templeton, 1789;
set. N. Y., 1810? Mich, 1842. Lenawee
Hist II, 469.

DOLE, Cordelia, m. 1840? William K.
Farnsworth of Ohio. Saginaw Port.,
620.

—— Linus, set. N. Y., 1820? Isabella,
256.

—— Nancy, b. Shelburne, 1832; m. 1852
Hart L. Upton of Mass. and Mich. Clinton Port., 870.

DONALDSON, Irene, m. 1820? Clark Worden
of Mich. St. Clair, 725.

DONELSON, Abel, of Colerain, set. Mich.,
1827. Genesee Hist., 186.

—— Ira, b. Colerain, 1790; set. Mich.,
1837. Oakland Biog., 174; Oakland
Hist., 307.

DORR, Solomon F., b. Brookfield, 1785;
set. N. H., 1820? Mich., 1834. Washtenaw Hist., 1341.

—— Susan, of Boston, m. 1800? Cyrus
Baldwin of N. Y. Washtenaw Hist.
962.

DORRANCE, William H., set. N. Y., 1840?
Washtenaw Past, 437.

DOTY, Samuel, b. Plymouth, 1681; set.
Conn. Washtenaw Past, 43.

DOUGLAS, Clinton, b. Sandisfield, 1788;
set. N. Y., 1805. Clinton Past, 193.

—— Sarah, m. 1816 John Buttolph of N.Y.
and Mich. Ionia Port., 558.

DOUGLASS, Caleb S., b. Amherst, 1809;
name changed to Solomon Gilbert.

DOWNER, Charlotte, m. 1835? James Harris
of Vt., N. Y. and Mich. Clinton Past,
66.

DOWNING, O. E., b. Charlestown, 1824;
set. Mich., 1876. Upper P., 446.

DOWSE, Sarah J., b. Littleton? 1827; m.
Samuel P. Youngman of Mich. Ionia
Port., 678.

DRAKE, Larnard, b. 1783; set. Mich. Clinton Port., 363.

—— Melvin, b. Easton, 1805; set. Vt.,
1811, Mich., 1830. Oakland Hist., 333;
Oakland Port., 733.

—— Walter, b. 1808; set. Mich., 1830.
Clinton Port., 362.

DRAPER, Charles, b. Marlborough, 1811;
set. Mich., 1833. Oakland Port., 265.

—— William, b. Dedham, 1780; set. Mich.,
1833. Oakland Port., 265.

DRURY, Samuel F., b. Spencer, 1816; set.
Mich., 1838. St. Clair, 125.

DRYER, Allen, of Stockbridge, b. 1772;
set. N. Y., 1800? Clinton Port., 516,
617; Ingham Hist., 203; Ingham Port.,
345.

—— Harriet L., b. Stockbridge, 1823;
m. 1844 Anthony McKey of Mich. Lenawee Hist. II, 384.

—— John, set. N. Y., 1808. Macomb
Hist., 882.

—— Thomas F., b. Richmond, 1801; set.
N. Y., 1808. Macomb Hist., 882.

DUMBLETON, Caroline, m. 1840? George
W. Grosvenor of Mich. Grand Rapids
City, 724.

DUNBAR, William, b. W. Stockbridge
1807; set. Mich., 1832. Monroe, 355.

DUNHAM, ——, set. N. Y.; d. 1830. Allegan Hist., 463.

—— Aaron, set. N. Y., 1820? Lenaeew
Port., 992.

—— Betsey, b. Attleboro; m. 1800? Otis
Hicks of N. Y. Macomb Hist., 797

—— John, 1812 soldier, set. N. Y., 1814?
Clinton Port., 743.

DUNN, Joel, b. 1775; set. Mich., 1831.
Washtenaw Hist., 1251.

DUNN John, b. 1765? set. Vt. Hillsdale Port., 584.

DURAND (or Durant), Almira, b. 1806; m. 1827 Silas Wheelock of Mich. Washtenaw Hist., 1091; Washtenaw Port., 620.

DURKEE, Charles M., b. 1829; set. O., Mich., 1854. Ionia Port., 702.

—— Martin, set. O. 1835? Ionia Port., 702.

DURPHY, H. C., b. 1816; set. Mich., 1849. Ottawa Hist., 120.

DWIGHT, C. G., set. Mich., 1865. Kalamazoo Port., 976.

—— Emma, m. 1871 Sylvester P. Hicks of Mich. Kent, 1219.

—— Martha A., b. Belchertown; m. 1853 Edward W. Barber of Mich. Jackson Port., 258.

—— Norman, b. 1815; set. Mich., 1838. Washtenaw Hist., 851.

—— Peregrine, b. 1795; set. N. Y.; d. 1842. Jackson Port., 258.

DYER, Jotham, set. Vt., Mich., 1828. Jackson Hist., 621.

EAGER, Benjamin, b. Lancaster, 1812; set. Vt., N. Y., Mich., 1836. Allegan Twent., 571; Kalamazoo Port., 586.

EAMES, Daniel, b. Dedham? 1780? set. N. Y. Kalamazoo Port., 370.

—— Persis, of Worcester, b. 1813; m. 1835 Charles A. Carpenter of Mich. Oakland Hist., 260; Oakland Port., 628.

EASTMAN, Elizabeth, m. 1785? Nathaniel Morrill of N. H. Jackson Hist., 771.

—— Jonathan, set. Vt. Berrien Port., 155.

—— Timothy, b. 1798; set. Me., 1822? Mich., 1835. Ottawa Hist., 117.

EATON, D. L., b. Ashburnham, 1822; set. Mich. Kent, 1214.

—— James, set. N. Y., 1800? Mich., 1828. Lenawee Port., 472.

—— Lucy, m. 1835? Elihu Sabin of N. H. and Ind. Berrien Twent., 477.

—— Ward, b. Boston; set. Pa., 1840? Branch Twent., 345.

EDDY, John, set. N. Y., 1800? Mich., 1832. Lenawee Port., 659.

EDDY, Jonathan, b. 1726; set. Me. Saginaw Port., 205.

—— William, b. Mansfield, 1752; set. Me. Saginaw Port., 205.

EDGERLY, James C., b. 1791; set. N. Y., 1814; Mich., 1822. Macomb Hist., 582.

EDGERTON, Ruth, m. 1820? William Rice of O. and Thomas Rowan. Genesee Port., 1049.

EDMONDS, Isabel, b. 1808; m. Laomi Robinson of Mich. Clinton Port., 899.

EDMUNDS, Hannah, m. 1815? Martin Luther of Vt. Clinton Port., 755.

EDSON, Miss C. P., of Yarmouthport, m. 1854 John C. Clarke of Mich. St. Clair,73.

EDWARDS, John M. b. Northampton, 1820; set. Mich., 1848. St. Clair, 121.

EGGLESTON, Spencer, b. Sheffield; set. N. Y., 1810? Jackson Hist., 622.

ELDREDGE, Daniel,b. 1745; set.Conn. Lenawee Hist. I, 135; Lenawee Port., 937.

ELDRIDGE, Caleb, b. Berkshire Co.; set. N. Y., 1835? Kent, 1259.

—— Mary, b. 1800; m. Willit G. Green of N. Y. Clinton Port, 214.

ELDRIDGEN, Elisha, b. 1789; set. Mich. Washtenaw Hist., 592.

ELLIS, Horace, b. 1795; set. N. Y., 1820? Mich., 1855. Clinton Port., 696.

—— John, b. Ashfield, 1815; set. Mich., 1843. Grand Rapids Lowell, 722.

—— William, b. Springfield; set. Vt., N. Y. Mich., 1854. Lenawee Port., 590.

—— William L., set. N. Y.; d. 1862. Hillsdale Port., 666.

ELLISON, Eliab, set. N. Y., 1810? Ionia Port., 266.

ELLSWORTH, Melinda L., m. 1830? Warren J. Ashley of Mich. Isabella, 495.

EMERSON, B. F., b. Middleton, 1838; set. Mich., 1868. Upper P., 342.

—— George W., set. O., 1810, Mich., 1830; d. 1837. Hillsdale Port., 878.

—— Jesse, of Wendell, set. O., 1810. Hillsdale Port., 878.

EMMONS, James, set. O., 1810? Cass Twent., 438.

ENSIGN, Horace, set. O., 1830? Kalamazoo Port., 736.

ENSIGN, Lavina, m. Jonathan Hayden of N. Y. Branch Port., 598.

ESTABROOK, Seth, b. 1795; set. N. Y., 1820? Saginaw Port., 939.

ESTES, Benjamin, set. Me., 1800? N. Y.; d. 1850. Lenawee Hist. I, 177; Lenawee Port., 1216.

——C. H., b. 1836; set. Mich., 1838. Traverse, 92.

——Deborah, b. 1804; m. 1822, Libni Kelley of N. Y. and Mich. Lenawee Hist. I, 177.

——Edy, b. Marshfield, 1810; m. John Fraser of N. Y. and Mich. Kalamazoo Hist., facing 506.

——Jerome, Co. D. 61st. Mass. Infantry; d. 1889. Grand Rapids Lowell, 369.

——Lucy B., m. 1842 Enos Canniff of Mich. Lenawee Port., 1200.

——Sylvanus, b. Plymouth Co., 1794; set· N. Y., Mich., 1832. Hillsdale Port., 740·

ESTEY, Israel B., b. Royalston? 1811; set. N. H., Vt. Clinton Port., 227.

ETHERIDGE, Samuel, b. Adams, 1788; set· Mich., 1836. Branch Twent., 622.

EVELETH, Charles, b., 1807? set N. Y., 1830? Mich., 1853. Clinton Port., 958.

EVERETT, Franklin, b. Worthington, 1812; set. N. Y., 1840, Mich. 1846. Grand Rapids Lowell, 241; Grand River, appendix 21; Kent, 261, 999.

——Tyler, set. N. Y., 1820? Jackson Hist., 1085.

EWELL, Consider, set. Mich., 1835? Macomb Hist., 787.

——Samuel, b. Hampshire Co. 1799; set. N. Y., 802, Mich., 1836. Macomb Hist., 655; Macomb Past, 27.

EWERS, Henry M., b. Wendell, 1800. set. N. Y. Branch Port, 610.

FAIRBANKS, Abigail, m. 1800? Charles Crosby of Conn. and Mich. Lenawee Port., 737.

FALES, Fanny, m. 1810? Joel Brown of Vt. Muskegon Port., 122

——Mary, b. Hampshire Co., 1783; m. Levi L. Lawrence. Berrien Port., 617.

FALL, John, set. O. Mich., 1825. Ingham Port., 702.

FALLEY, John W., b. Westfield, 1814; set. N. Y. and O. Hillsdale Port., 249.

FARMER, John, b. Boston; set. N. Y., 1770. Detroit, 1085.

FARNHAM, Melinda, of Conway; m. 1815? William Holloway of Mass. and N. Y. Lenawee Hist. II, 475.

FARNSWORTH, Charles, b. Hawley, 1802; set. N. Y., O., Mich., 1837. Lenawee Port., 647.

——William K., set. N. Y., 1840? Saginaw Port, 620.

FARNUM, Fanny, b. Pamsa? m. Joseph Chapin of N. Y. and Pa. Kalamazoo Port., 824.

FARRAR, Asa, b. Northfield, 1760; Revolutionary soldier; set. N. Y., 1800? Detroit, 1141.

——Daniel, Revolutionary soldier; set. N. H. Genesee Port., 898.

——John, b. Rutland, 1793; set. N. Y., 1808? Mich., 1817, Detroit, 1141.

——Sullivan, set. N. Y., 1800? Mich. 1834. Macomb Hist., 883.

FARRINGTON, Erastus C., b. Norfolk Co., 1824. Gratiot, 300.

FAULKNER, Almira or Elmira, b. Colerain, 1790; m. 1809 John Gragg of Mass. and Mich. Hillsdale Port., 658; Lenawee Hist. I, 180.

FAUNCE, Alden, set. O.; d. 1863. Isabella, 276, 396.

—— William H., b. New Bedford, 1819; set. Mich. Ingham Port., 531.

FAXON, Caroline, b. Conway, 1801; m. George Russell of N. Y. and Mich. Branch Port., 605.

FAY, Francis, set. Mich. 1850? Monroe, 360.

—— James, set. N.Y., 1810? Jackson Hist., 995.

—— Louise, of Southboro; m. 1828, Luther H. Trask of Mich. Kalamazoo Port., 239.

—— William, b. Hampden Co., 1821; set. O., Va., Mich., 1884. Muskegon Port., 173.

—— William H., set. O., 1825? d. 1882, Muskegon Port., 173.

FEGLES, Sally, b. 1804; m. 1820? Addiniram Bradley of N. Y. and Mich. Branch Twent., 768.

FENNER, James L., b. 1777; set. N. Y. Allegan Hist., 238.

FENSON, ames, set. Canada, Mich., 1863, Lake Huron, 229.

FENTON, John, set. Vt., 1781. Lenawee Hist., I, 477.

—— Mary A., b. Cambridge, 1817; m. 1842, Levi Gustin of N. Y. Lenawee Illus., 166.

—— Seth, b. 1781; set. Vt., 1781, Pa. Lenawee Hist. I, 477.

—— Stephen, b. Middlesex Co. 1791; set. N. Y., 1820? Lenawee Illus., 166.

FERRY, —— (grandfather Dexter M. Ferry of Detroit), set. N. Y., 1800? Wayne Chron. 442.

—— Chester, set. N. Y., 1820; Kent, 535,

—— William M., b. Granby, 1796; set. N. Y., Mich., 1823. Grand River, appendix, 22; Ottawa Hist., 38.

FERSON, William G., set Mich. 1836. Berrien Hist., 158; Berrien Twent., 150.

FESSENDEN, Eben, b. Worcester Co., 1800? set. Vt., Canada. Macomb Past, 186.

FIELD, Abigail, b. 1789; m. Ira Humphrey of N. Y. and Mich. Jackson Hist., 832.

—— Charles E., b. Greenfield, 1850? set. Ill. Branch Port, 616.

—— Thomas, b. 1782; set. N. Y., 1820? Mich. 1833. Jackson Port, 681.

FIELDING, William, set. N. Y., Mich., 1831. Jackson Port, 231.

FIELDS, Jonathan E , set. Mich. 1833. Washtenaw Hist., 229.

FIFIELD, Enoch, b. Salisbury, set. N. H., Mich., 1830. Jackson Port., 747.

—— Henry, of Essex Co., set. Mich. 1834. Ingham Hist., 313.

FINNEGAN, John B., Taunton, 1831; set. Mich., 1832. Washtenaw Port., 426.

FISH, Betsey, b. Barnstable Co., 1783; m. 1800? Orrin F. Sessions of Vt. and Mich., Kent, 752; Oakland Port., 714.

—— David, set. N. Y., 1800. Jackson Hist., 855,

—— Sarah B., b. Barnstable; m. 1825, Joseph Goodspeed of Mass., O., and Mich. Cass Rogers, 337.

FISHER, Erastus, b. Northfield, 1814; set. Vt., N. Y., Mich., 1840. Kent, 1003; Mecosta, 462.

—— Fanny., m. 1825? Lorenzo Aldrich of Canada and Mich. Mecosta, 402, 419, 527.

—— Joel, b. near Boston, 1780; set. N. Y., 1800. Lenawee Hist. I, 155.

—— John, b. 1784; res. Franklin Co. set. Mich., 1836. Lenawee Port., 504.

—— John, b. Charlemont, 1829; set. Mich. 1836. Lenawee Port., 505.

—— Joseph P., b. Dedham, 1800; set. N. H., Mich., 1834. Oakland Port, 767.

—— Olive D., b. 1820; m. 1845, Solomon F. Sears of Mich. Washtenaw Hist., 666; Washtenaw Port., 340.

—— Pliny, set. N. Y.,1830? Mich., Lenawee Port., 253.

—— Timothy, set. N. H., 1810? Oakland Port, 767.

FISK, Abigail, b. Worcester, 1808; m. 1831, Joseph I. Talmadge of Mich. Lenawee Hist. I, 251.

—— Abigail, m. Joseph Richardson of N. Y. (1812 soldier). Branch Port, 311.

—— Adaline, m. Asa Kingsbury of Mich. (b. 1806). Cass Hist., opposite 160.

—— Daniel, b. Worcester, 1772; set. N. Y., 1802. Lenawee Illus., 228.

—— Ebenezer, b. Franklin Co., 1815; set Mich., 1839. Lenawee Port, 335.

—— Frank, b. Ashfield, 1836; set. Mich 1838. Ionia Port., 410.

—— Jabez, b. Wendell, 1794; set. N. Y. 1802; Mich., 1833. Lenawee Illus., 228; Lenawee Port., 1042.

—— James, set. Vt., 1820? Kent, 1300.

—— Joseph, set. Mich., 1838, d. 1877. Ionia Port, 410.

—— Joseph, b. Charlemont or Windsor 1810; set. N. Y., Mich., 1834. Allegan Hist., 156; Allegan Twent., 571; Kalamazoo Port., 934; St. Clair, 119.

—— Roswell of Berkshire County, bought land 1837. Allegan Hist., 219.

FISKE, Ebenezer, b. Wenham, 1762; set. N. H. Branch Port., 341.

FITCH, John M., b. Bedford, 1811; set. N. H., 1833; Mich., 1836; Clinton Port., 263.

FITTEN, James, of Lawrence, set. Mich., 1835. Hillsdale Hist., 220.

FITTS, Harrison, b. Oxford, 1815; set. N. Y., 1840? Mich., 1851. Lenawee Port., 867, 953.

FLAGG, Fidelia, m. 1832, Josiah Bond of N. Y. Lenawee Illus., 104

FLAGG, Nancy, of Stowe, b. 1814; m. 1837, Richard H. Whitney of Mass., and Mich. Lenawee Hist. II, 393; Lenawee Illus., 468.

—— Tabitha, m. 1841 Josiah Bond of N.Y., and Mich. Lenawee Illus., 104. ᵗ

FLANDERS, Zebulon, b. Newburyport, 1760; set. N. H. Genesee Port., 868.

FLETCHER, Addison, set. N. Y., 1840? Washtenaw Hist., 1082.

—— Jemima, m. 1800? Samuel Underwood of N. Y. and Mich. Jackson Hist., 933.

—— Joel, b. Westford, 1786; set. Maine, Mich. Kalamazoo Port., 236.

—— Lorenzo C., b. Lowell, 1815; set. Mich., 1839. Genesee Hist., 310.

—— William, set. Mich., 1820. Berrien Hist., 132.

FLINT, Sarah A., m. 1830? Lewis M. Edson of N. Y. Detroit, 1139.

FLOOD, Martin, set. Wisconsin, d. 1873. Ionia Port., 694.

FLOWER, Andrew, set. Vt., 1810? N. Y., Mich. Oakland Biog., 380; Oakland Hist., 114.

—— William, b. Ashfield; set. N. Y., 1800? Macomb Hist., 697.

FLOWERS, Clarissa, m 1810? William Brown of N. Y.; d. 1821. Gratiot, 324.

FOBES, Mehitable, of Bridgewater; m. 1784, Benjamin Packard of Mass., and Vt., Stˑ Joseph, 84.

FOLLETT, J. I., b. Dalton, 1818; set. O.. Ind. 1842, Mich., 1852. Traverse, 91.

—— Nathan, b. 1793; set. Mich. Washtenaw Hist., 592.

—— Sabra, b. 1775; m. Reuben Wilson of N. Y. and Mich. Branch Port., 188.ⱼ

FOOTE, Charles, b. 1740; set. N. Y. Hillsdale Port., 461.

—— Freeman, set. Vt., 1785? Jackson Hist., 1121.

FORBES, H. N., set. Mich., 1836. Ingham Hist., 299.

—— Jortin, b. Buckland? 1812; set. N. Y.ᵗ Mich. Washtenaw Hist., 1395.

—— Levi, set. Canada 1830? Isabella, 503.

FORD, Ansel, b. Cummington, 1788; setˑ O., 1838. Lenawee Port., 1137, 1810.

—— Charles, b. Cummington, 1809; setˑ O., 1850. Lenawee Port., 810, 871 1137.

FORD, Eugene E., b. Cummington, 1841; set. O., 1850, Mich., 1869. Lenawee Past, 316.

—— Gardner, set. Mich., 1846. Macomb Past., 316.

—— George F., b. Cummington, 1838; set. O., 1850. Lenawee Port., 810.

—— Hezekiah, 4th, b. Abington, 1759; res. Cummington, set. O., 1842. Lenawee Port., 1137.

—— Levi B., b. Cummington, 1836. set. Vt., 1849, O., 1850, Mich., 1863. Lenawee Port., 1136.

—— Philena, b. Plainfield, 1807; m. 1828 Horace Simmons of O. and Mich. Branch Twent., 807.

—— Tamezin, b. 1810; m. Walter Foote of N. Y. and O. Hillsdale Port., 838.

—— William, b. Berkshire Co; set. N. Y., Mich., 1833. Washtenaw Port., 418.

FOSDICK, George, b. Nantucket; set. Va., Ind., 1822., Mich.,ˌ 1830., Ind., 1838; d. 1865. Cass Rogers, 348.

—— James H., b. 1827; set. Mich., 1866. Allegan Twent., 167.

FOSTER, Abel, b. Dudley, 1767; set. R. I. Lenawee Hist. I, 92.

—— Abiel, Sr., b. Andover, 1735; set. N. H. Berrien Port., 886.

—— Betsey, m. 1870? Dr R. H. Henderson of N. Y. and Mich. Lenawee Port., 506.

—— Daniel, b. Cape Cod; set. N. Y., Mich., 1842. Kalamazoo Port., 969.

—— John R., set. N. Y., Mich., 1833. Lenawee Port., 1040.

—— Laura, b. Sutton or Dudley, 1795; m. 1811, David Bixby of Mass., N. Y., and Mich. Lenawee Hist. I, 91; Lenawee Port., 1021.

—— Lemuel, b. Dudley, 1762; set. N. Y., 1807. Jackson Port., 745.

—— Lemuel, Jr., b. Leyden, 1793; set. N. Y., 1807, Mich., 1836. Jackson Port., 745; Washtenaw Hist., 993.

—— Moses, b. near Boston; set. Vt., 1810? N. Y. 1820. Jackson Port., 476.

—— Nancy, b. Franklin Co., 1808; m. Charles A. Hebard of N. Y. and Mich Kent, 1396.

—— Theron, set. N. Y., Mich., 1836, Cal. Kent, 1005.

FOWLER, Elizabeth, m. 1810? Samuel Averill of Mich. Oakland Port., 935.

—— Frederick, b. 1791; set. O., 1814; Mich., 1834. Hillsdale Hist., 328.

—— Mary A. of Westfield; m. 1844, L. S. Noble of Mich. St. Clair, 589.

—— Richard, set. O., 1816; Mich.. 1834. Hillsdale Port., 530.

FOX, Anna O., b. Lowell; m. 1875, Charles S. Hazeltine of Mich. Grand Rapids City, 197.

—— Aruna, set. O., 1835? Clinton Port., 864.

—— Emeline, b. 1832; m. 1847, Noah Long of Mich. Clinton Port., 864.

—— Frederick, set. N. Y., 1840? Ind., 1857; Mich., 1866. Newaygo, 232.

—— Lewman, set. N. Y., 1830? Kalamazoo Port., 513.

FRANCIS, Lois, b. 1808; m. 1830, George W. Williams of Mich. Oakland Port., 194.

——, Roxy, m. 1840? Henry Huyck of O. and Mich. Gratiot, 324.

FRANCISCO, Dwight, b. 1798; set. N. Y 1815? Kent, 1299.

FRANKLIN, Mary, m. 1820? Eli Lacy of N. Y. and Mich. Clinton Past., 124.

FRARY, David, set. O., 1804; Mich., 1817. Lenawee Hist. II, 134.

FRASER, Adkins, b. 1782, set. N. Y. Isabella, 451.

—— James G., set. N. Y., 1820? Ill.,1853. Clinton Port., 786.

FREEMAN, Juliana B , b. Attleboro, 1822; m. 1863, Benjamin L. Hicks of Mich., Lenawee Hist. I, 160; Lenawee Illus. 321.

—— Ruel A., b. Attleboro, 1838; set. Mich., 1843. Lenawee Port., 668.

—— William, b. Attleboro, 1796; set. Mich , 1842 or 3. Lenawee Hist. I, 160, 245; Lenawee Port., 668.

—— William B., b. Attleboro, 1820; set. Mich., 1842. Lenawee Hist. I, 245.

—— William H., b. Sutton, 1831; set. Mich. Grand River, appendix, 26.

FRENCH, Abel, set. N. Y., 1820? Mich., 1844. Ionia Port., 350.

—— Apollos, b. Taunton; set. Vt., 1800? Genesee Hist., 266, 276.

FRENCH, Cyrus V., b. Berkley, 1833; set. Mich., 1838. Jackson Port, 465.

—— Harvey, b. 1789; set. Mich. Washtenaw Hist., 592.

—— John B., set. N. Y. Genesee Port., 261.

—— Lydia A., m. 1810? John Beebe cf N. Y. Kalamazoo Port., 525.

—— Matilda, b. Northampton, 1790? m David Fox of. N. Y. and Penn. Genesee Port., 668.

—— Nathaniel of Berkshire Co.; set. N.Y., 1810? Calhoun, opposite 124.

—— Samuel, set. N. Y., 1820? Wis. Northern M., 456.

—— Vernon, b. Berkley, 1810; set. Mich., 1838 or 9. Jackson Hist., 795, Jackson Port., 298, 465.

FREY, Ellen of Athol, m. 1854, C. R., Pattison of Mich. Washtenaw Hist., 575.

FRIEZE, Henry S., b. Boston, 1817; set. R. I., Mich., 1853, or 4, Washtenaw Hist., 995; Washtenaw Past, 668.

FRINK, James, of Williamstown; set. Mich., 1838? Shiawassee, 397.

FROST, Allen L., b. Williamsburg, 1804; set. N. Y., Mich., 1835. Macomb Hist., 698.

—— Bezaleel, set. N. Y., 1815? Macomb Hist., 698.

—— Frederick, set. Vt. 1800? Jackson Port, 581.

—— Josiah, b. Williamsburg, 1763; set. N. Y., 1803. Detroit, 1217; Jackson Port., 856.

—— Josiah, b. Williamsburg, 1791; set. N. Y., 1803. Detroit, 1217.

—— Mary, b. Springfield; m. 1810? Timothy Rockwell of Canada. Washtenaw Hist., 792.

—— Samuel, b. 1786; set. Vt., 1810? N. Y., 1824; Mich., 1841. Oakland Port, 346; Mabomb Hist., 822.

FROTHINGHAM, George E., b. Boston, 1836; set. Mich. Washtenaw Hist., 996.

FRY, Jeduthan, b. 1815; set. Pa., Mich., 1834. Ingham Hist., 292.

FRYE, Hiram of Andover; set. Mich., 1838. Ingham Hist., 119; Lansing, 48.

FULLER, Bethany, m, 1800? Levi Wood of N. Y. Hillsdale Port., 404.

——Betsey, b. 1802. m. I. W. Munger of N. Y. Genesee Port., 1014.

——Electa, d. 1883; m. James Morrill of O. and Mich. (1812 soldier). Branch Port., 535.

——Elizabeth, m. James Phelps of Mass. and N. Y. Clinton Port, 984.

——James, b. Ipswich, 1770; set. N. H. N. Y., 1815. Ingham Hist. opposite 308.

——Jason, set. N. Y., 1816. Genesee Port., 1015.

——John, b. 1788; set. N. Y., Mich., 1837, Jackson Hist., 795.

——Joshua, b. Rehoboth, 1701; 'set. Conn. 1722. Grand Rapids City, 177.

——Lucy, b. 1789; m. 1808, Peter Sears of Mass. and Mich. Washtenaw Hist., 665; Washtenaw Port , 340.

——Mary, b. Warwick, 1786; m. Pearl Cannon of N. H., Vt., N. Y., and Mich. Macomb. Hist., 724-5.

——Philo C., b. Berkshire Co.; set. N. Y., 1815? Grand Rapids City. 178; Kent, 1009.

——Sophia, b, 1801; m. 1825? Philip Wells of Mich. Oakland Port, 639.

GAINES, Emeline E., b. Leyden, 1818; m. Charles A. Shattuck of N. Y. Hillsdale Port., 923.

GALE, Brooks, set. Vt, 1788? Detroit, 1189

——ELBRIDGE G., set. Mich. 1844. Genesee Hist., 57.

GALLAGHER, Louise, of Charlestown; m 1865? Wm. G. Burchfield of Colorado. Washtenaw Past, 177.

GALLUP, ——, b. 1800; set. N. Y., Mich., 1844. Jackson Hist., 1104.

GAYNARD, Stata, m. 1825? Daniel Burt of O. Muskegon Port, 347.

GARDNER, Daniel, b. Brimfield; set. N. Y. 1812? d. 1824. Allegan Hist., 362; Allegan Twent., 284; Kalamazoo Port., 701.

——Lebeus, b. Hingham, 1829; set. Mich., 1850. Jackson Hist., 796.

——Lydia, of Nantucket; m. 1796, Stephen Walker of R. I. and N. Y. Detroit, 1128A; Grand RapidsLowell, 982; Wayne Chron., 163.

—— W. A. H., b. Hancock, 1819; set. N. Y. 1825, Mich. 1855. Kent, 1261.

GARLAND, HORACE W., b. Boston, 1855; set. Ia. 1855, Mich. 1863, Tex., Kan., Mich., 1894. Berrien Twent., 706.

GARLIC, LUCY, b. Lanesboro; m. 1814 Benjamin Colegrove of Penn. and Mich. Lenawee Port., 204.

GARLICK, HORACE, b. Boston, 1809; set. Conn., N. Y., 1818, Mich. Macomb Hist., 699.

—— SAMUEL, b. Boston; set. Conn., ₁N. Y., 1818, Mich. d. 1830. Jackson Port., 317. Macomb Hist., 699.

GARVEY, SARAH E., set. Mich., 1848. Cass Twent., 360.

GASTON, ELIJAH, set. N. Y. and Mich. d. 1841. Ingham Port., 687.

GATES, AARON of Conway, set. N. Y., 1810? Jackson Port., 461.

—— CYNTHIA, m. 1795? Samuel P. Noyes of N. Y., Branch Port., 496.

—— ELIZABETH, m. 1800? Issac Amaden of N. Y. Washtenaw Past., 182.

—— INCREASE S., b. Conway, 1800?; set. N. Y., Mich., 1839. Jackson Port., 461.

—— PERSIS of Worcester; m. 1740? Adonijah Rice of Mass. and Vt. Jackson Port., 726.

——SARAH, m..1790? Nicholas Chamberlain, of N. Y. Kalamazoo Port., 381.

GAY, ABNER, b. Dedham; set. N. H. Muskegon Port., 153.

—— EDWARD A., b. Boston, 1829; set. N. Y. Mich., 1833. Lansing, 506; Washtenaw Hist., 779.

—— TIMOTHY, b. Boston, 1801; set. Mich., 1833. Lansing, 506.

—— WILLIAM, set. Penn. 1825? Canada and O. Clinton Past, 101.

GIBBENS, JOHN E., b. Berkshire Co., 1822; set. Mich. Jackson Hist., 1141.

GIBBS, DAVID, b. 1800; set. N. Y., 1820? Vt, 1825? Ionia Port., 316; Macomb Hist., 657.

—— DEBORAH, of Barnstable Co., m. Elisha Lewis of N. Y., O. and Mich. Hillsdale Port., 799.

—— JOHN M., set. O., 1836? Mich., 1854. Ionia Port., 451.

—— LOVILLA C., b. Berkshire Co., 1836; m. 1858, John J.Maynard of Mich. Ionia Port., 451.

—— SAMUEL A., b. 1833; set. O., 1838., Mich. 1854. Ionia Port., 629.

GIBSON, SALLY, m. 1816? Stephen Parkhurst of N. Y. Branch Twent., 340.

GIDLEY, EDWIN, set. Mich., 1850? Clinton Port., 580.

—— MARY, m. 1803, Reuben Buck of N. Y. Lenawee Hist. II., 287.

GIFFORD, ANNA, m. 1810? Benjamin Rounsville of N. Y. Ingham Port., 833.

—— PHEBE, m. 1820? Stephen M. Mosher of N. Y. Hillsdale Port., 894.

GILBERT, CHARLES, b. 1760? set. Wis. Hillsdale Port., 284.

—— DANIEL, b. Sheffield, 1786; set. N. Y.; Mich., 1844. Branch Port., 292.

—— FRANCIS B., b. Greenfield, 1818; set. Mich., 1837 or 40. Grand Rapids Lowell, 680; Kent, 1014.

—— HIRAM R., b. Worthington, 1834; set. Mich., 1854. Genesee Port., 612.

—— ISAAC, b. 1810; set. Mich., 1840? Ma comb Hist., 795.

—— LYDIA, m. 1820? Alvah Gannett of N. Y. Hillsdale Port., 284.

—— SOLOMON, b. Amherst, 1809; set. Mich. 1845. St. Clair, 675.

—— STEPHEN, set. N. Y.. Mich., 1835. Cass Twent., 601.

—— THOMAS D., b. Greenfield, 1815; set Mich. 1835. Grand Rapids Lowell, 679; Kent, 261, 1014; St. Clair, 124.

GILES, EBENEZER, b. Townsend, 1759; set. Vt. Jackson Port., 548.

—— EPHRAIM, set. Vt., 1800? Mich., 1845. Jackson Port., 548.

GILL, SAMUEL, set. N. Y., 1810? Muskegon Port., 378.

GILMAN, JOHN T., 1812 soldier; d. 1884; set. N. Y., Mich. Genesee Port., 816.

GILMORE, ARETUS, b. 1792; set. O. 1815? Clinton Port., 584.

—— REUBEN, set. O. 1840? Jackson Port., 700.

GILSON, FRANK R., b. Charlestown, 1848; set. Mich., 1885. Berrien Port., 285.

GLEASON, ARCHIBALD, set. O., 1830? Newaygo, 440.

—— NATHANIEL, b. 1774; set. N. Y. 1800, Mich., 1830. Lenawee Hist. I, 302.

GLOVER, CHARLES W., b. 1791; set. N. Y., 1797, Mich., 1833. Washtenaw Port., 630.

—— ORVILLE B., b. Upton, 1804; set. N. Y. Mich., 1839. Cass Twent., 65, 781.

GODDARD, EZRA G., b. Worcester, 1823; set Mich., 1862. Saginaw Port., 774.

—— REBECCA S., b. Plymouth; m. 1830? George Perkins. Macomb Hist., 801.

—— RUFUS, set. N. Y., 1825? Mich., 1838. Ionia Hist., 354.

GOFF, ELECTA, m. 1820? Anson Crawford of N. Y. and Mich. Ionia Port., 671.

—— SEWALL S., b. Royalston, 1811; set. N. Y Mich., 1829. Lenawee Illus., 99; Lenawee Port., 935.

—— TIMOTHY B., b. 1790; set. N. Y., 1820 Mich., 1827. Lenawee Hist. I, 181.

GOODALE, ISAAC, b. 1755; set. Vt. 1790? Oakland Port., 758.

—— LYDIA C., b. Amherst, 1822; m. Silas Kimberly of Mich. Ionia Port., 569.

—— NORMAN C., b. Amherst, 1813; set. Mich. 1835. Washtenaw Hist., 853.

GOODELL, ELECTA, m. 1825? Chas. Cooley of N. Y. and Mich. Washtenaw Hist., 1359.

—— JACOB, Revolutionary soldier; set. Vt., 1810? d. 1828. Clinton Port., 374.

—— RACHEL A., m. 1835? Isaac Thornton of O. Midland, 299

GOODING, CHRISTOPHER, set. N. Y., Mich., 1854. Kent, 573.

—— ELNATHAN, b. 1771; set. N. Y. Washtenaw Hist., 1429.

GOODMAN, ENOS, set. N. Y., 1810? Branch Port., 549.

—— THOMAS, b. South Hadley, 1790; set. N. Y. and Mich. Branch Hist. facing 341; Branch Port., 549.

GOODRICH, ACHSAH, b. 1791; set. Mich. Washtenaw Hist. 591.

—— LEVI H., b. Hadley, 1774; set. N. Y., 1800? Mich. Northern M., 352.

—— M. H., b. Conway, 1826; set. Mich., 1827. St. Clair, 122

—— MORELL, b. Conway, 1812; set. Mich., 1827. Washtenaw Hist., 500.

—— SARAH, b. Boston; m. 1830? Alonzo D Atherton of N. H. Clinton Port., 269.

GOODSPEED, JOSEPH, b. Sandwich, 1797; set. N. Y., 1828, Mich., 1836. Cass Rogers, 337; Cass Twent., 65.

GOODWIN, BETSY, of Hopkinton, m. 1800? Nathan Gould of Mass. and N. Y. Oakland Biog., 534.

—— JUSTUS, b. Lenox; set. N. Y. and Mich. graduate of Hamilton College, 1821. Branch Hist., 205.

GORHAM, J. M., b. Boston, 1825; set. Mich., 1849. Kent, 265.

GOULD, JAMES H., b. in Shaker Village, 1798; set. N. Y. and Mich. Berrien Port., 679.

—— NATHAN, of Hopkinton; b. 1767; set. N. Y. Oakland Biog., 534.

GRACE, JOHN C., set. Mich., 1830? Gratiot 295.

GRAGG, JOHN, b. Colerain, 1785; set. N. Y. 1825, Mich., 1826. Hillsdale Port., 658 Lenawee Hist. I, 180.

—— ROBERT, b. Colerain, 1811; set. Mich., 1825. Lenawee Hist. I, 180.

—— ROENA, b. Colerain, 1821; m. Robert Cox of Mich. Hillsdale Port., 658.

GRAHAM, HIRAM, b. 1816; set. N. Y. and Mich. Hillsdale Port., 521.

—— WANTON, b. Cheshire, 1790; set. N. Y., 1815? Mich., 1830? Lenawee Hist. I, 433.

GRANGER, DAVID, b. Sandisfield; set. N. Y., 1830? Kalamazoo Port., 917.

—— FRANCIS, Sr., b. Hampshire Co., 1806; set. N. Y., O., 1830, Mich., 1852. Branch Port., 597,

—— MRS. HARRIET, b. W. Springfield, 1797; set. Mich., 1834. Washtenaw Hist., 493.

—— ITHAMAR, b. Sheffield, 1796; set. N. Y. and Mich. Calhoun, 141.

—— THADDEUS, b. Sandisfield, 1765; set. O., 1810. Macomb Hist., 699, 796.

GRANT, CHARLES, b. Colerain, 1794; set. Mich. 1836? Saginaw Port., 547.

GRAVES, ESTHER P., b. Hampshire Co.; m. 1855, James W. Ransom of Mich. Kent, 1107.

—— ISRAEL, b. Whately, 1785; set. N. Y. Jackson Hist., 1101.

—— JEREMIAH, set. Ct. and Ill. Berrien Port., 345.

—— JOB, b. Greenfield, 1799; set. Mich., 1831. Lenawee Hist. II, 245.

—— LEBBEUS, set., N. Y. 1810? Kent, 743.

—— LYMAN, set. Mich., 1825? Washtenaw Port., 333, 516.

—— WATERS, of Colerain, set. N. Y., 1810? Lenawee Illus., 159.

GRAY, ——, b. Ashfield; set. Mich., 1827. Branch Hist., 244.

—— AMOS, set. Vt. 1800? Washtenaw Hist., 853.

—— Darwin L., b. Ashfield, 1824; set. Mich. 1836. Branch Twent., 247, 521.

—— Eli, of Ashfield, set. Mich. 1836. Branc Twent., 522.

—— Philip, of New Bedford; set.Mich. 1830? Kalamazoo Hist., 381.

—— Sarah A., of Worcester; m. 1838, Wellington Chapman of Mich. Saginaw Port, 856.

—— Thomas, Revolutionary soldier; set. N. Y., 1800? Wayne Chron., 216.

GREEN, Henry; b. Williamstown, 1820; set. N. Y., 1830 or 34, Mich., 1833 or 40. Kent, 770, Grand Rapids City, 559, 717.

—— Keziah, m. 1820? Samuel Wilson of Vt. and N. Y. Genesee Port., 537, 655.

—— Nathaniel, b. 1787? set., O. Newaygo, 369.

—— Noah K., b. Windsor, 1808; set. Mich., 1835. Lenawee Illus., 412; Lenawee Port., 914.

—— Sarah, m. 1820? Appollos Long of N. Y. Lenawee Port., 312.

—— William W., b. 1839; set. N. Y., 1840 Ill., Mich., 1902. Berrien Twent., 408.

—— Willit G., b. 1800; set. N. Y., 1825? Mich., 1840. Clinton Port, 214.

GREENLEAF, John G., b. Haverhill, set. Mich., 1820? Berrien Twent., 651.

GREGORY, Noah, b. 1803; set. Canada, Mich., 1836. Jackson Port, 864.

GREY, Patience, b. 1777; m. 1800? Billions Stocking of N. Y. Grand Rapids Lowell, 390, Kent, 1137.

GROSS, Johab, b. Eufield, 1790; set. Mich., 1832. Oakland Hist., 283.

GROSVENOR, Ebenezer O., b. Grafton or Paxton, 1783; set. N. Y., 1825, Mich. Hillsdale Port., 391, Monroe, 448.

—— George W., set. Mich,, 1840? Grand Rapids City, 724.

—— Ira R., b. Paxton, 1815; set. Mich. 1835. Monroe, 448.

—— Lemuel D., b. Paxton, 1830; set. N. Y, 1852, Ill., Mich. Jackson Port, 633.

GUILFORD, Erastus., b. Northampton; set. O., Mich., 1825. Kalamazoo Hist., 440.

GURNEY, Charles W., set. Mich., 1837 or 40., Clinton Past, 503; Shiawassee, 527.

GUYLFORD, Caroline, b. 1816; m. Joseph Harper of Mich. Cass Hist., 175.

36   PIONEERS FROM MASSACHUSETTS

HADSELL, Fred A., set. Mich., 1855. Cass Twent., 365.

HAGUE, Fannie I., m. 1867, Charles Smith of Mich. Northern P., 410.

HAIGHT, Mary J., m. 1840? Allen Kennedy of Mich. Jackson Hist., 944.

HALBERT, Seth, set. N. Y., 1825? Midland, 211.

HALE, C. D., b. Berkshire Co.; set. Mich., 1862. Lake Huron, 143.

—— Charles P., b. Bernardston, 1828; set. Mich., 1851. Kalamazoo Hist., 482; Kalamazoo Port., 446.

—— David B., set. Vt., 1780? Ingham Hist., 483.

—— Henry B., b. 1808; set. Mich. Jackson Hist., 856.

—— Israel, set. Mich., 1866, O. Lenawee Port., 422.

—— L. D., b. Franklin Co., 1806; set. N. Y., 1818; Mich., 1839. Washtenaw Hist., 1001.

—— Mary F., b. Norwich, 1848; m. 1867. Martin Odell of Mich., Lenawee Port., 422.

—— Stephen, set. N. Y., 1818. Washtenaw Hist., 1001.

—— Susan, m. 1810? Ebenezer Stuart of N. Y. Macomb Hist., 805.

—— Zedock, set. Vt., Wis., Mich.; d. 1866 Kalamazoo Port., 407.

HALL, Abner, b. Dedham, 1755; set. Vt. 1800? Lenawee Hist. I, 418; Lenawee Port 253.

—— Alfred, b. Berkshire Co., 1796; set N. Y., Mich., 1836. Jackson Hist., 903.

—— Catherine, m. 1815? Newland Sampson of N. Y. and Mich., Hillsdale Port. 369.

—— E., set. N. Y., 1800? Washtenaw, Hist., 1398.

—— Eunice of Lanesboro; m. 1800? Abner Bagg of Mass. and N. Y. Wayne Chron., 357.

—— George C., b. 1820; set. N. Y. Sanilac, 248.

—— Julia, m. 1835? James Westover of Mass., Ct. and Ind. Genesee Port., 579.

—— Prince B., set. Vt., 1790? Harvard graduate. Lenawee Port., 1201.

—— Rowena, m. 1830? Storm Arnold of Mich. Oakland Biog., 623.

—— Rufus, set. Mich., 1825? Oakland Biog., 310.

—— Seth, b. Franklin Co., 1815; set. N. Y. and Mich. Hillsdale Port., 692.

—— Susan, b. Berlin; m. 1830? Stephen Peckham of N. Y. Kent, 1318.

HALVERSON, Joseph, b. 1630; set. N. Y.; Mich., 1841. Traverse, 318.

HAMILTON, Abigail, b. 1792; set., Mich., Washtenaw Hist., 590.

—— Increase S., b. Cummington, 1810; set. N. Y. 1818; Mich., 1835. Lenawee Port., 1076; Lenawee Hist. II, 237.

—— John L. b. Cheshire? 1797; set. N. Y., O., 1834; Mich., 1837; Ind. Lenawee Port., 398.

—— Lucy, m. 1820? Peregrine Dwight of Mass. and N. Y., d. 1880. Jackson Port., 258.

—— Mila A., m. 1824, Frederick P. Hatch of Mass. and Mich. Homer, 46.

—— Milo D., b. Blandford, 1828; set. Mich., 1835. Homer, 45.

—— Obadiah, b. Pelham or Salem; set. N. Y., 1818. Lenawnee Hist. II 237; Lenawee Port., 399; 1076.

—— Patrick, b. Stockbridge, 1794; set. Mich., 1825. Cass Hist., facing 188.

—— Samuel W., b. Granville, 1801; set. Mich., 1835; d. 1851. Homer, 45; Mecosta, 322.

——Thomas J., b. 1820? set. N. Y., Mich., Ia. Clinton Past., 215.

—— Walter, b. Brookfield, 1790? set. Vt., 1820? N. Y. Saginaw Port., 765.

—— Warren, b. Madison Co.? 1816; set. Mich., 1833. Washtenaw Hist., 621.

HAMLIN, Hannah, m. 1825? Orrin Wilcox of N. Y. and Mich. Genesee Port., 457.

HAMMATT, Abigail D. of Nantucket; m. 1832? Gilbert Hatheway of Mass. and

Mich. Grand Rapids Lowell, 648; Macomb Hist., 908.

HAMMOND, George H., b. Fitchburg, 1838; set. Mich., 1854. Detroit, 1153; Wayne Land., Appendix, 126.

HAND, Edward, set. Mich., 1845? Lenawee Port., 1025.

—— James H., set. N. Y., O., 1835? Mich., 1844. Branch Port , 398.

HANDY, Caleb, set. N. Y., 1815? d. 1824. Washtenaw Port., 334.

HARDING, George D., b. Boston, 1848; set. N. Y., Mich., 1870. Hillsdale Port., 322.

HARKNESS, Hannah, m. 1812? Richard B. Sergeant of N. Y. Clinton Port., 752.

HARLOW, Amos R., b. Shrewsbury, 1815; set Mich., 1849; Houghton, 162. Northern P., 5.

HARMON, Henry, set. N. Y., Mich., 1866. Kalamazoo Port., 943.

—— Polly, b. 1800, m. Almon Hart of Mich. Hillsdale Port., 572.

—— Sarah, m. 1860? Martin T. Ryan of Mass. and Mich. Grand Rapids City, 372.

HARPER, Caroline Guilford, b. Northampton, 1816; set. Mich., 1835. Cass Twent., 66.

HARRIMAN, Lucinda, of Lawrence; m. Wm. E. Syms. Berrien Port., 661.

HARRINGTON, Ebenezer, set. N. Y., 1825? Kalamazoo Port., 426.

—— Eli F., b. E. Bradfield? 1839; set. Mich., 1858. Grand Rapids Lowell, 267; Kent, 421.

—— Jeremiah, b. Greenfield, 1774; set. Mich., 1820. St. Clair, 631.

—— Mary E., b. Worcester, 1845; m. Morris Holcomb of Mich. Kent, 1033.

HARRIS, Betsey, b. 1798; m. Oliver C. Roberts of Penn. Mecosta, 416.

—— Celestia L., b. Heath; m. 1858, Wm. F. Coles of N. Y. and Mich. Osceola, 255.

—— Joseph, set. Mich., 1850? Washtenaw Port., 355.

HARRISON, A., b. Williamstown, 1802; set. Mich., 1825. St. Clair, 121.

—— Chloe, b. Williamstown, 1786; m. 1814, Benj. Barrett of Mass. and Vt. Lenawee Hist. I, 176.

—— John, of Berkshire Co.; set. Mich., 1840? Gratiot, 327.

—— Lois, b. N. Adams; m. 1812, Herrick Willey of N. Y. Lenawee Illus., 444.

—— Maria L., b. Westfield, 1835? m. Henry R. Lovell of N. Y. and Mich. Genesee Port., 694.

HART, Almon, b. 1797; set. Mich. Hillsdale Port., 572.

—— George, b. Lynnfield; set. Vt., O., 1834; d. 1857. Hillsdale Port., 533.

—— Stephen, set. O. 1835? Newaygo, 279.

HARTSELL, Mary A., m. 1825? Henry Gilmore of Canada. Mecosta, 238.

HARTWELL, Betsey, m. 1800? Joseph Luce of Mass. and N. Y. Lenawee Hist. II, 233.

HARVEY, Charlotte, m. 1850? Elezer C. Knapp of Mich. Allegan Twent., 413.

HARWOOD, Ahaz, b. 1791; set. Vt., 1815? Mich., 1839. Macomb Hist., 855.

—— Alanson, set. N. Y., Mich., 1838. Ingham Hist., 478.

—— Harriet, b. Enfield, 1796; m. 1816, Jonah Gross of Mass. and Mich. Oakland Hist., 83.

—— William W., b. Berkshire Co., 1785; set. N. Y., 1789; Mich., 1824. Washtenaw Hist., 1264.

HASKINS, Hiram, b. Taunton, 1818; set. Mich. Jackson Hist., 641.

—— John, b. Taunton? 1785; set. Mich., 1834. Lenawee Hist. II, 217.

—— Lydia, b. Taunton, 1793; m. 1811, Sylvester Boodry of Mass. and Mich. Lenawee Hist. II, 336.

—— Samuel, Sr., set. Vt.; d. 1776? Jackson Port., 836.

—— William, of Taunton; set. Mich., 1834. Lenawee Hist. II 217.

HASTINGS, Henry, b. 1818; set. Wis., 1850? Mich. Upper P., 504.

HATCH, Frederick R., b. Blandford, 1803; set. Mich., 1832. Homer, 36, 46.

—— William, b. 1759; set. Nova Scotia. Lenawee Hist. I, 104.

HATHAWAY, Adeline M., b. 1806; m. 1836, Kelly S. Beals of Mich. Lenawee Port., 214.

—— Bathsheba, b. New Bedford, m. 1830? Vernon French of Mass. and Mich., Jackson Hist., 795; Jackson Port., 299.

—— Daniel, b. 1792? set. O. Gratiot, 278.

—— Elizabeth, m. 1835? Thomas J. Hoxie of N. Y. and O. Gratiot, 658.

—— Elizabeth, m. 1842, Richard De Greene of Mich. Lenawee Port., 657.

—— Hiron, b. 1799; set. N. Y., 1820? Macomb Hist., 588.

—— James, of Berkshire Co., set. Mich., 1834. Lenawee Hist. II, 242; Lenawee Port., 657.

—— Jeptha, set. Mich., 1806. Lenawee Port., 214.

—— Prudence, m. 1800? Jeremiah Cooper of Mass. and N. Y. Lenawee Illus., 90.

—— Tryphena, b. Heath; m. 1810? Elias Upton of Mass. and Mich. Clinton Past., 421; Clinton Port., 869.

—— Z., b. 1802; set. O., 1825. Berrien Hist., 253.

HATHEWAY, Gilbert, b. Plymouth Co., 1812; set. Mich., 1846. Grand Rapids Lowell, 648; Macomb Hist., 908.

—— James, S. P., b. Marion, 1834; set., Mich., 1853. Macomb Hist., 908.

—— Rufus C., b. Rochester; set. Mich., 1850? Grand Rapids Lowell, 648.

HAWES, Jason A., set. Wis., 1850? Northern P., 208.

HAWKINS, Abiel, b. Williamstown, 1797; set. Vt., N. Y., Mich., 1818. Washtenaw Hist., 1208.

HAWKS, Aaron, set. Mich., 1837. Lenawee Port. 255.

—— Anna, of Shelburne, b. 1774 or 1775? m. 1795? Rufus Smead of N. Y., and Mich. Lenawee Hist. I, 337; Lenawee Illus., 124.

—— Emeline, of Franklin; m. 1839, Henry B. Childs of Mass. and Mich. Grand Rapids City, 604.

—— John A., b. Franklin Co., 1809; set. Mich., 1833. Lenawee Port., 255.

HAYDEN, Jonathan, set. N. Y. Branch Port., 598.

—— Lavina, b. near Boston, 1790; m. Arnold Spencer of N. Y. Macomb Hist., 661.

—— Polly, b. Northampton; m. John Brown of N. Y. and O., an 1812 soldier. Branch Port., 598.

HAYNES, George A., b. Princeton 1858; set. Mich., 1881. Homer, 128.

—— Josiah, b. Franklin Co., 1808; set. Mich., 1834. Hillsdale Port., 793.

—— Mary, of Newbury, m. 1706, John Preston of Ct. Macomb Hist., 709.

HAYS, Willard, set. Mich., 1836. Allegan Hist., 367.

HAYWARD, David, 1812 soldier, set. N. Y., Northern P., 409.

—— Henry, b. Cummington, 1787; set. N. Y., 1810? Mich., 1833. Lenawee Hist. II, 149; Lenawee Port., 913, 998.

—— Ormand, b. near Boston, 1799? set. Vt., N. Y., Mich. Muskegon Port., 335, 395.

—— Stephen, b. near Boston, 1752; Revolutionary soldier; set. N. Y., 1785? Muskegon Port., 335.

—— Theodore, set. N. Y., 1810? Mich., 1834. Lenawee Hist. I, 428.

HAZARD, James, b. Russell, 1796; set. Mich., 1820? Macomb Hist., 824.

HAZLETON, Charlotte, m. 1830? Levi Forbes of Canada. Isabella, 503.

HAZZARD, James, b. 1769; set. N. Y., 1800? St. Joseph, 107.

—— William, b. Berkshire, 1798; set. N. Y., Vt., 1811, N. Y., Mich., 1817. St. Joseph, 107.

HEAD, Smith, set. O., Mich., 1855. Cinton Port., 632.

HEALY, Joshua, set. Vt., 1790? and N.Y. Kalamazoo Port., 863.

—— Nelson K., set., Mich., 1838. Allegan Hist., 186.

HEATH, James, b. Berkshire Co., 1793; set. N. Y., O., 1835 and Mich. Clinton Port., 905.

HEBARD, Charles A., b. Franklin Co., 1805; set. N. Y., Mich., 1839. Kent, 1396.

—— Ezra A., b. Leyden, 1830; set. N. Y. and Mich., 1839. Kent, 1396; Grand Rapids Hist., 224; Grand Rapids Lowell, 706.

HEMENWAY, Thomas, b. near Boston; set. N. Y., 1785. Lenawee Port., 438.

HEMINGWAY, Harriet N., of Prescott; m. 1854, Wm. P. Watterman of Mich. Jackson Hist., 818.

HENIMAN, Polly, m. 1850? Edwin Gidley of Mich. Clinton Port., 580.

HERBERT, William H., b. Northfield, 1844; set. Ind., 1855; Mich. Northern M., 507.

HERRICK, Eliza A., b. Hampshire, 1829; m. Justice C. Perry of Mich. Midland, 178.

—— Eunice, b. Pittsfield, 1821; m. Darius Rockwell of Penn. Midland, 197, 264.

—— Priscilla, m. 1810? Nahum Ward of Mass. and 1830? Israel Bissel of O. Hillsdale Port., 357.

HERSEY, Daniel T., b. Northampton, set. O., 1835? Kalamazoo Port., 626.

—— John, b. Cummington; set. N. Y., Mich., 1818. Oakland Hist., 139.

—— Susannah, b. 1783, m. Achish Pool of Mass. and N. Y. Macomb Hist., 758.

HEWES, George W., b. Lynnfield, 1822; set. Mich., 1865. Kent, 1029.

HEWITT, Mary, m. 1828, Henry Arnold of O. and Mich. Cass Twent., 614.

HIBBARD, Charles A., set. Mich., 1836. Grand Rapids City, 36.

—— John, b. N. Hadley, 1827; set. Wis., 1887; Mich., 1850. St. Clair, 317

HICKOX, Erastus, set. N. Y., 1820? Jackson Port., 401.

HICKS, Amos, b. 1776; set. N. Y., Mich., 1825. Ingham Port., 611; Washtenaw Hist., 876.

—— Benjamin, b. 1771? set. N.Y., Mich., 1835. Oakland Port., 362.

—— Betsey, m. 1800? James Case of N. Y. Oakland Port., 347.

—— Celia, of Taunton; m. 1819, David Willard of N. Y. Ionia Port., 695.

—— Ephraim, b. Dighton, 1793; set. N. Y, 1795, 1812 soldier; Mich., 1835. Lenawee Hist. I, 158; Lenawee Illus., 321.

—— Jabez, set. N. Y., 1795. Lenawee Hist. I, 158.

—— Otis, b. Attleboro, 1770? set. N. Y., 1800? Macomb Hist., 797.

—— Peleg, set. N. Y., 1812? Lenawee Port., 527.

HICOK, Arnold, of Berkshire Co., set. N.Y., 1820? Genesee Port., 744.

—— William T., b. 1814; set. N. Y. Genesee Port., 744.

HIGBEE, Loring, set. N. Y., 1796; d. 1862. Mecosta, 267.

HILBORN, Henry E., b. 1829; set. Mich., 1866. Detroit, 1436.

HILL, Asa, b. Adams, 1794; set. N. Y., 1815? Mich., 1841. Lenawee Hist. II, 317, 375.

—— Calvin R., set. N. Y. and Mich., 1835. Kent, 658.

—— Comstock F., b. 1835; set. Mich., 1837. Washtenaw Hist., 1285.

—— Darius G., set. N. Y., 1805? Mich., 1838. Genesee Port., 251; Oakland Port., 931.

—— Elijah, b. 1775; set. N. Y., 1804. Oakland Port., 429.

—— Elizabeth, of Franklin Co., m. 1810? John Fisher of Mass. and Mich. Lenawee Port., 505.

—— Etta A., b. 1859; m. Charles E. Warner of Mich. Mecosta, 356.

—— Fitch, set. Mich. 1837. Washtenaw Hist., 1285.

—— Hannah B., of Shutesbury; m. 1831, N. H. Hemingway of Mass. and Mich. Jackson Hist., 818.

—— John F., b. Worcester Co., 1838; set. N. Y., 1852; Mich., 1861. Saginaw Hist., 899.

HILTON, Emma of Boston; m. 1869, Rowland Connor of Mich. Saginaw Port., 619.

—— Sallie, daughter of Gov. Hilton of Mass. m. Samuel G. Langley. Berrien Port., 837.

HIMES, Joshua V., of Boston, set. Mich., 1864? Berrien Hist., 140.

HINKLEY, Ann, m. 1825? Zimri Sanderson of Mich. Washtenaw Port., 608.

—— Henry, b. Lee, 1808; set. N. Y. Berrien Port., 909.

—— Samuel, b near Barre, 1803; set. N. Y., 1830, Mich., 1834. Lenawee Hist. I, 266; Lenawee Port., 487.

—— Sarah S., b. Barre, 1828; m. Moses Carpenter of Mich. Lenawee Hist. I, 266.

—— Sophia J., b. Barre, 1830; m. Harmon G. Munger of Mich. Lenawee Hist. I, 266.

HINMAN, Henry, b. Stockbridge; set. N. Y., 1810? Kent, 1262.

HISCOCK, James, b. 1788; set. Penn., 1815? Mich., 1829. Washtenaw Hist., 1004; Washtenaw Past., 481; Washtenaw Port., 265.

HITCHCOCK, Mamie; m. 1816? Daniel Perry of N. Y. and Mich. Jackson Hist., 835.

—— Manley, 1812 soldier, set. N. Y., 1815? Jackson Port., 757.

—— Otis, b. 1795; set. N. Y., 1815? Ionia Port., 360.

HOADLEY, Jacob, b. 1779; set. N. Y., 1820? Mich., 1836. Lenawee Hist. II, 94.

HOBART, Israel, set. Mich., 1837; d. 1840. Jackson Hist., 627.

—— John, b. Townsend, 1782; set. N. Y., 1800? Jackson Hist., 859; Jackson Port., 604.

—— William, b. Groton, 1751; set. N. Y. Jackson Port., 604.

HODGE, Emily, m. 1810? Sebina Tryon of N. Y. Clinton Port., 700.

—— Milton H., b. Adams, 1825; set. Mich. 1836 or 1837. Jackson Hist., 1027; Jackson Port., 697.

—— Warner I., b. Adams, 1794; set. Mich., 1836; d. 1851. Jackson Hist., 831, 1027; Jackson Port., 696.

HOLBROOK, Bevajah, of Berkshire Co., set. N. Y., 1820? Detroit, 1121.

—— Thestor T., b. 1792; set. N. Y. and Mich. Hillsdale Port., 634.

HOLCOMB, Horace, b. 1790; set. Mich. Washtenaw Hist., 591.

HOLDEN, Amasa or Amadon, b. Northfied, 1795; set. Mich., 1844. Ingham Hist., 307; Lansing, 454.

—— M., b. Somerset, 183–; set. Mo., 1859, Mich. 1864. Muskegon Hist., 103.

HOLLOWAY, Butler, b. Conway, 1814; set. N. Y., 1816, Mich., 1833. Lenawee Hist. I, 291; Lenawee Port., 509.

—— Sarah, b. 1823; m. Garrett Rockwood of N. Y. and O. Genesee Port., 625.

—— Silas, b. Ashfield, 1812; set. N. Y., 1817, Mich., 1832. Lenawee Hist. II, 475.

—— William, b. 1781; set. N. Y., 1816 or 1817, Mich., 1833. Lenawee Hist. I, 291; Lenawee Hist. II, 475; Lenawee Port., 509.

HOLMAN, ——, b. Boston; set. Roxbury, N. H., 1790. Macomb Hist., 701.

HOLMES, ——, b. Boston, 1776; set. Canada; d. Buffalo, N. Y., 1836. Wayne Chron., 375.

—— Benjamin T., b. 1760; set. N. Y. Lenawee Port., 204.

—— Charles, D., b. W. Boylston, 1814; set. Mich., 1831 or 1833. Calhoun, 110; Kent, 1040; St. Clair, 123.

—— D. C., b. Berkshire Co., 1836; set. Mich., 1848. Jackson Hist., 1027.

—— Evelyn, b. Adams, 1830? m. 1st.—— Rathbun, m. 2d. 1878, M. H. Hodge of Mich. Jackson Port., 698.

—— Jeremiah, b. 1806; set. Vt., 1816? Mich., 1835. Lenawee Hist. II, 360.

—— John C., b. Salem, 1809 or 1819; set. Mich., 1835. St. Clair, 119; Wayne Chron., 304.

—— Milton, set, N. Y., 1830? Jackson Port., 698.

—— Thomas, b. W. Boylston, 1815? set. Mich. Calhoun, 110.

HOLT, Clara M., m. 1886, Dwight C. Clapp of Mich. Clinton Port., 617.

—— Nicholas M., b. Berkshire Co., 1801? set. Vt., 1820, N. Y., 1839, O., 1854. Saginaw Port., 750.

HOMES, William, b. Berkshire Co., set. N. Y., 1830? Mich., 1853. Newaygo, 458.

HOOLEY, Ann, m. 1840? Averill Burnett of Mich. Jackson Port., 300.

HOPKINS, Levi, b. Gt. Barrington, 1750; set. Va., 1795. Lenawee Port., 912.

—— Mark, set. N. Y., 1806, Mich., 1824. St. Clair, 676.

—— Pitt, set. N. Y., 1790? Oakland Hist., 150.

—— Samuel, Presbyterian clergyman, of Great Barrington, grandfather of Darius Hopkins of Pa. Kalamazoo Port., 589.

—— Samuel F., b. Berkshire Co., 1803; set. N. Y., 1806; Mich., 1824. St. Clair, 676.

HOPPIN, Thaddeus C., set. N. Y., 1820; Mich., 1844; d. 1859. Berrien Port., 783; Berrien Twent., 338.

HORTON, Edward S., b. Warwick,' 1844; set. Mich., 1856. Wayne Land., appendix, 224.

HOSFORD, Franklin H., set. O. 1840? Kent, 1220.¹

HOSMER, Artemus, b. Concord, 1788; set. Mich., 1818. Wayne Chron., 118.

—— Rufus, b. Stowe, 1819; set. Mich., 1838. Ingham Hist., 112; Oakland Hist., 46.

HOUGH, Samuel, set. Conn.; N. Y., 1800? Branch Port., 455.

HOVEY, Horace, set. O., 1815? Mich., 1842. Clinton Port., 480.

—— William, b. Concord, 1812; set. Mich., 1856. Kent, 1045.

HOWARD, Alfonzo, set. N. Y., 1840? Saginaw Hist., 652.

—— Daniel, b. Bridgewater; set. Vt., 1810? Wayne Chron., 346.

—— Edgar, b. Bristol Co., 1822; set. Mich., 1836 or 1838. Detroit, 1393; Kent, 1045; Wayne Chron., 66.

—— Hepzibah P., b. Easton, 1817; m. 1838, Joseph H. Manning of Mich. Washtenaw Port., 483.

HOWE, Aaron, b. N. Y., 1820? set. Mich. Lenawee Hist. II, 440.

—— Daniel, set. N. Y., 1810? Genesee Port., 758.

—— Frederick A., set. N. Y.; Mich., 1834 or 1835. Berrien Hist., 228; Berrien Twent., 431. 483,

—— Hollis, b. Marlboro, 1801; set. N. Y., 1820? Mich., 1837. Lenawee Hist. II, 440.

—— Irena, m. 1825? Solomon Gage of N. Y. Washtenaw Hist., 852.

—— Priscilla of Andover; m. Thomas Bliss of N. Y. and Mich. Kalamazoo Port., 509.

HOWES, Ezra, b. E. Dennis, 1787; set. N. Y., Mich., 1830. Lenawee Hist. II, 151.

—— John, b. E. Dennis, 1797; set. N. Y., Mich., 1847. Lenawee Hist. II, 152.

HOWLAND, Amy of Westport; m. 1856 Chas. H. Richmond of Mich. Washtenaw Hist., 1035

—— Gilbert, set. N. Y., 1800. Hillsdale Port., 343.

—— John, b. Greenfield, 1797 or 1798, set. N. Y., 1822, Mich., 1843. Washtenaw Hist., 593, 1211.

—— Jonathan, b. Adams, 1789; set. N. Y., 1800 or 1810, Mich., 1846, d. 1871. Hillsdale Hist., 294; Hillsdale Port., 513; Lenawee Hist. I, 426; Lenawee Hist. II, 214; Lenawee Port., 958.

—— Mary E. m. 1860? Addison P. Halladay of Mich. Lenawee Port., 456.

—— Samuel, b. Middlebury, 1811; set. Mich., 1836. Kent, 261.

HOXSIE, Content, b. 1771; m. John W. Kelley of Mass., Me., and Mich. Lenawee Port., 1216.

—— John, set. N. Y., 1780? Lenawee Port., 1217.

—— Lydia, b. N. Adams, 1790; m. Jason B. Wolcott of N. Y., O. and Mich. Hillsdale Port., 942.

HOYT, Calvin, set. N. Y., and Mich., 1841. Gratiot, 397.

—— Frances M., m. 1825? Samuel Stevens of N. Y. Muskegon Port., 316.

—— Nancy, b. New Braintree, 1780; m. 1810? Samuel Ewell of N. Y. and Mich. Macomb Hist., 655; Macomb Past., 27.

HUBBARD, Edwin F., b. 1812; set. Mich., 1850. Lenawee Illus., 337.

—— Electa, b. Goshen; m. 1840? Daniel W. Reed of Mass. and N. Y. Allegan Twent., 116.

—— Elizabeth W., of Northampton; m. 1840, Wm. L. Greenly of Mich. Lenawee Hist. I, 101.

—— Francis E., b. S. Hadley, 1815; set. N. Y. Genesee Port., 758.

—— Henry, set. O., 1835. Ionia Port., 705.

—— Miss J. E., b. 1834; m. 1852, Chas. M. Durkee of O. and Mich. Ionia Port., 705.

—— James, b. Brimfield; set. N. Y., 1820? Mich., 1835. Kalamazoo Port., 856; Midland, 282.

—— John, Revolutionary soldier; set. N. Y., 1785? Clinton Port., 450.

—— Jonathan, b. 1732; set. N. Y., 1800. Kalamazoo Port., 856.

—— Samuel, of Boston; bought land 1836. Allegan Hist., 270, 293.

—— Thomas, of Hampden Co.; bought land 1836–37. Allegan Hist., 269, 353.

HUDSON, Polodore, b. Williamstown, 1797; set. Mich. Kalamazoo Port., 413.

—— William P., set. O., 1820? Muskegon Port., 347.

HULL, Daniel E., set. O., Mich., 1867. Lenawee Port., 487.

—— Harry D., b. Westfield, 1854; set. O., Mich., 1867. Lenawee Port., 487.

HUME, Moses, b. Berkshire Co.; set. N. Y., 1810? Mich., 1854. Clinton Port., 881; Lenawee Port., 924.

HUMPHREY, Minerva S., b. Lanesboro, 1829; m. 1848, Stephen M. Mead of Mass., O. and Mich. Lenawee Port., 942.

HUNT, Alfred H., set. N. Y., 1835? Kent, 1048.

—— Lorano, b. New Salem, 1795; m. Levi Davis of N. Y. Branch Port., 459.

—— Lucy A., of Braintree; m. 1851, Lebeus Gardner of Mich. Jackson Hist., 796.

—— Nathan, set. N. Y., 1800? Ionia Port., 844.

—— Ruth S., b. Salem, 1829; m. 1851, John Kirby of Mich. Lenawee Illus., 82.

—— Theophilus C., b. Holliston, 1809; set. Canada, Mich., 1859. Mecosta, 379.

HUNTER, Silas O., set., N. Y., 1830? Muskegon Port., 267.

HUTCHENS, —— of Berkshire Co.; set. N. Y., 1790? Lenawee Hist. I, 257.

HUTCHINSON, Noah, set. N. Y., 1800? Calhoun, 184.

HUTCHISSON, Ephraim, set. N. Y., 1790? Jackson Hist., 832.

HYDE, Caleb, of Berkshire Co., set. Broone Co., N. Y., 1800? Calhoun, 75.

—— Ebby, b. Berkshire Co., set. N. Y., 1800. Calhoun, 75,

—— Eliza M., b 1820; m. 1840? Ebenezer Nethaway of Mich. Clinton Port., 610.

IDE, Miss B., b. 1831; set. Mich., 1832. Washtenaw Hist., 501.

INGALLS, Stephen, b. 1755; set. N. Y. Lenawee Hist. II, 79.

INGERSOLL, Rev. E. P., of Lee, set. Mich., 1837. Clinton Past, 503; Clinton Port., 503. Shiawassee, 527.

—— Erastus, of Lee, set. N. Y., Mich., 1825. Shiawassee, 529.

—— Stephen, b. Lynn, 1782; set. N. Y., Mich., 1843. Lenawee Hist. II, 357; Lenawee Port., 742.

INGHAM, Anthony, of Lawrence, set. Mich., 1835. Hillsdale Hist., 220.

JACKSON, Abigail M., b. Newton Falls, 1814; m. 1834, Luther Haskins of Mich. Lenawee Hist. II, 217.

—— Eliza, b. Salem, 1813; m. 1832, John B. Griswold of Mich. Saginaw Hist., 824.

—— Hannah, b. Hampshire Co., m. 1840? Luther Clapp of Mich. Gratiot, 362.

—— Mary, b. Newton,1755; m. 1775, Abner Hall of Mass., Vt. and Mich. Lenawee Hist. I, 418; Lenawee Port., 253.

—— Mary B., m. 1802, Thomas Manley of Vt. Macomb Hist., 734.

—— William, set. N.Y., 1830? Conn. Gratiot, 373.

JAMES, Luther, b. Goshen, 1803; set. Mich., 1835. Washtenaw Hist., 501, 814.

—— Sophia, b. Goshen, 1792; m. 1815, Thomas Sears of Mass., N. Y. and Mich. Washtenaw Hist., 818; Washtenaw Port., 228.

JANES, Isabella of Northfield; m. 1822, John Howland of N. Y. and Mich. Washtenaw Hist., 1211.

JENISON, Charles O., b. Boston, 1843; set. Wis. 1877, Mich. 1882. Ionia Port., 735.

JENKINS, Ella, b. Berkshire Co.; m. 1860. Stephen R. Crandall of N. Y. and Mich. Mecosta, 491.

JENKS, Ellen M., b. Belchertown, 1825; m. 1853, Henry P. Howe of Mich. Lenawee Hist. II, 441.

—— Erastus S., b. Cheshire, 1814; set. Mich. 1844. Ionia Hist., 291.

—— Laban, set. N. Y., Mich., 1821, d. 1829. Oakland Hist., 319.

JENNEY, Benjamin, set. O., 1835? Ionia Port., 377.

—— Ebenezer, b. New Bedford; set. Vt., 1790? Macomb Hist., 731.

—— James, set. N. Y., 1840? Washtenaw Hist., 856.

—— William, b. Middlesex Co., 1812; set. Mich., 1843. Macomb Hist., 591.

JENNINGS, Henry, b. New Bedford, or near Boston, 1777; set. N. Y., 1799. Lenawee Hist. II, 154; Lenawee Port., 534.

—— Isaac, set. Mich., 1837. Clinton Past. 503; Shiawassee, 527.

—— Stephen, set. N. Y., Mich., 1843. Genesee Hist., 311.

—— Zera, set. N. Y., 1815? Lenawee Port., 330.

JENNISON, Polly, m. 1800? Daniel Brown of Vt. and N. Y. Washtenaw Hist., 969; Washtenaw Port., 255.

—— William, b. Boston, 1800? set. N. Y., Pa., La. Saginaw Port., 1036.

—— William, b. Boston 1826; set. Mich., 1853. Wayne Chron., 399.

JEWELL, Silas T., set. O., d. 1869. Gratiot, 225.

JEWETT, Betsey, b. Littleton, 1804; m. Daniel Chatterton of Mich. Isabella, 204.

—— Eleazer, b. 1799; set. Mich., 1826. Saginaw Hist., 209.

—— Joseph, b. Dudley, 1803; set. N. Y., 1828, Mich., 1836. St. Joseph, facing 134.

JIPSON, Webster, set. N. Y., 1800? Kent, 788.

JOHNSON, Azubah, b. Bridgewater, 1797; m. Chester Cooley of N. Y. and Mich. Kalamazoo Port., 888.

—— Daniel, set. N. Y., 1800? Calhoun 109.

—— Elbridge N. set. Mich., 1834. Genesee Hist., 241.

—— Electa, m. Amasa Preston of O. and Mich. and d. 1863. Berrien Hist., 301.

—— Lucy, b. Worcester Co., 1797; m. Samuel Stevens of Mass. and Mich. Hillsdale Hist., 229.

—— Lutheria, b. 1815? m. Z. M. Marsh of N. Y. and Mich. Ingham Port., 602.

—— Mary, b. Worcester Co., 1803; m. Samuel Stevens of Mass. and Mich. Hillsdale Hist., 229.

—— Norman, set. N. Y., 1840? Kent, 1339.

—— Obadiah, b. 1735; set. Conn. Ingham Port., 312.

—— Stephen O., b. Westfield, 1847; set. N. Y., Mich., 1884. Wayne Land., 737.

—— Rev. W. W., b. Winstown? 1817; set. Mich., 1835. Kent, 263.

—— William A., b. Ashby, 1859; set. Mich., 1880? Grand Rapids City, 252.

—— William W., b. Williamstown, 1786; set. N. Y. Isabella, 401.

JONES, Benaiah, Jr., b. Berkshire Co ; set. O., 1810? Mich., 1828. Jackson Port., 429.

—— David S., b. Wisdom, Franklin Co., 1844; set. Mich., 1863. Jackson Port. 208.

—— Elisha of Berkshire Co., set. O., 1825. St. Clair, 579.

—— Jonathan of Leverett, set. N. Y., 1790. Allegan Hist., 390.

—— Joseph P., b. 1834; set. O., 1837. Mich., 1857. Hillsdale Hist., 218.

—— Mrs. Lois (wife of Benaiah), b. Peru, 1790. Hillsdale Hist., 125.

—— Polly, m. 1825? Alexander Barrett of Mich. Ionia Port., 461.

—— S. A., b. Berkshire Co., 1817; set. O., 1835, Mich., 1837. St. Clair, 579.

—— Sullivan, set. N. Y., 1830? d. 1880. Newaygo, 193.

JOSLIN, Frederick W., b. Hubbardon, 1845; s et. Ind., Mich., 1872. Mecsts, 273.

—— John. set. N. Y., 1810? Mich., 1835. Washtenaw Hist., 745.

JOY, David, b. Rehoboth, 1724; set. Vt., N. Y. Jackson Hist., 1091.

JOYCE, Angie C., b. Duxbury, 1857; m. 1879, George E. Wilde of Mich. Northern P., 206.

JUDD, Elliott E., b. S. Hadley, 1841; set. Mich., 1852. Kent, 272, 1054.

—— George E., b. S. Hadley, 1838; set. Mich., 1852. Kent, 1054.

—— John E., b. 1838; set. Mich. Kent, 272.

—— Levi, b. S. Hadley, 1795; set. N. Y., 1820? Saginaw Port., 283.

—— Rhoda, b. Berkshire Co., m. 1810? Samuel Scott of N. Y. Newaygo, 277.

—— Samuel, b. S. Hadley, 1806; set. Mich., 1852. Kent, 264, 1053.

KAPLE, John H., b. Tyringham, 1817; set. Mich., 1838. Wayne Land., appendix 55.

KAUFFER, Hale P., b. Methuen 1840; set. Mich. Kalamazoo Port., 867.

KEENEY Jonathan B., b. 1815; set. Mich., 1837. Clinton Past, 346.

KEITH, Mary G., m. 1820? William R. DeLand of Mass. and Mich. Saginaw Hist., 465.

—— Olivia M., b. Worcester Co., 1815; m. 1839, Edwin Adams. Jackson Hist., 848.

KELLEY, Abigail, m. 1820? Abiel Densmore of Me. and Mich. Jackson Hist., 885.

—— John W., b. Cape Cod 1768; set. Me., 1800? Mich., 1839. Lenawee Port , 1216.

—— Libni, b. Dennis, 1799; set. Me., N. Y., 1824, Mich., 1836. Lenawee Hist. I, 177.

—— Ruth, b. 1768; m. Nathan Harkness of N. Y. Lenawee Hist. II, 461; Lenawee Port., 612.

KELLOGG, Anna, b. Berkshire Co., m. 1810? Ephraim Towner of N. Y. Washtenaw Port., 625.

—— Catharine M., b. Sheffield, 1808; m. Job Whitney of Mich. Kent, 634.

—— Ebenezer W., b. Hadley, 1815; set. Mich., 1839. Gratiot, 450.

KELLOGG, Hosmer, of Sheffield, b. 1815? set. Mich., Monroe, 147.

—— Joseph, b. 1778; set. N.Y. Kalamazoo Port., 574.

—— Nathaniel, set. N. Y., 1820? Jackson Hist., 657.

KELSEY, Elisha, b. Sheffield; set. Conn., Wis. Hillsdale Port., 660.

KEMP, Joseph, b. Shelburne, 1813; set. N. Y., 1828, Mich., 1845. Northern P., 473.

KENDALL, Adelaide, m. 1850, Cornelius Selfridge of N. Y. and Mich. Oakland Port., 784.

—— Eleanor, b. Worcester Co., m. 1808? Jonas Bennett of N. Y. Branch Port., 310.

—— George, b. Greenfield, 1813, set. N.Y., 1831, O. 1833, Mich. 1840. Grand Rapids Lowell, 682; Kent, 1054.

—— Henry D., b. Greenfield; 1815; set. O. 1839, N. Y. 1844, Mich. 1879. Grand Rapids Lowell, 709.

—— JOHN, b. Greenfield, 1825; set. N. Y. 1831, O. 1833, Mich. 1847. Grand Rapids Lowell, 653; Kent, 261.

—— Mary, b. Westminster, 1768; m. David McGee of N.Y. and Mich. Jackson Port., 812.

KENFIELD, Erastus of Belchertown, b. 1801; set. O. 1834. Allegan Hist., 252; Kalamazoo Port., 513.

—— William S., b. Belchertown, 1831; set. O., 1834?, Mich., 1855. Allegan Hist., 252; Allegan Twent., 328; Kalamazoo Port, 513.

KENNEDY, Chauncy, b. 1818; set. Mich. 1840. Cass Hist., 144; Cass Twent. 353.

KENNY, Munnis, set., Mich. Washtenaw Hist., 671.

KENT, Ann, m. Luther Hanchett of N. Y., O. and Mich. Hillsdale Port, 319.

—— Lydia, m. 1800? William Wright of N. H. and N. Y. Genesee Port., 897.

—— Mariner, of Newburyport: b. 1757; set. N. H., 1798. Lenawee Hist. I, 213; Lenawee Port., 298.

—— Richard, b. Newburyport, 1786; set. N. H., 1798, Mich. 1835. Lenawee Hist. I., 213; Lenawee Port., 298, 655.

—— Rufus, b. Hampshire Co., 1820; set. Penn., 1841, Mich., 1856. Mecosta, 381.

KERR, William W., b. Cambridge, 1843; set. Canada, 1844, Mich. Sanilac, 191.

KERWIN, James, set. Mich., 1866. Lake Huron, 173.

KETCHAM, Betsey, b. Clarksburg, 1798; m. 1815, William W. McLouth of N. Y. and Mich. Lenawee Hist. I, 193.

KEYES, Eli, b. 1808; set. O., Mich., 1837. Branch Port, 501.

—— George, b. Springfield, 1830; set. Mich 1837 Branch Port, 501.

—— James, b. Newburyport, 1789; set. N. Y.. 1817. Lenawee Port., 1205.

—— Sarah B., b. Townsend, 1813; m. 1831, Edwin D. Crane of N. Y. and Mich. Lenawee Port., 1205.

KEYS, Pardon, set. N. Y., 1825? Washtenaw Hist., 815.

KIDDER, Alfred, b. Boston, 1840; set. Mich., 1860? Upper P., 431.

KILBOURN, David, set. N. Y., Mich., 1836. Branch Twent., 449.

KILBURN, Elijah, b. Great Barrington, 1813; set. Penn. Lenawee Port., 642.

KIMBALL Daniel, b. Haverhill, 1779; set· N. H., 1800; Mich., 1851. Lenawee Hist· I, 348.

—— Darius, set. N. H., Penn., N. Y., Mich., 1846. Lenawee Port., 779

KIMBERLY, Silas, b. Ashfield, 1814; set. Mich., 1828. Ionia Port., 569.

KINDLE, Dolly, m. 1780? James Stuart of N. Y. Genesee Port., 622.

KING, Amos, b. near Boston; Revolutionary soldier, set. N. Y. Hillsdale Port., 467.

—— Asabel, b. 1781; set. N. Y., Mich., 1837. Jackson Hist., 199.

—— Augusta A., of Taunton; m. 1860? U. W. Lawton of Mich. Jackson Hist., 663.

—— David, set. N. Y., 1820? Clinton Port., 538.

—— David, b. 1786; set. N. Y. Allegan Hist., 454.

—— Eunice, m. 1810? Smith Bailey of N. Y. Kent, 1373.

—— George, b. Hampshire Co., 1800; set· N. Y., 1802, Mich., 1831. Washtenaw Hist., 1401.

—— Henry, d. Ohio, 1862. Berrien Port., 672.

—— James, set. N. Y., 1815? Mich., 1845. Kent, 1221.

—— Polly, m. 1800? Martin Culver of Mass., N. Y. snd Mich. Jackson Port., 296.

—— Simon, set. N. Y., 1800? Jackson Port., 309.

KINGMAN, Malaney, m. 1820? Dexter Mitchell of N. Y. and Mich. Northern M., 321.

KINGSBURY, Asa, set. Mich., 1860? Jackson Port., 406.

—— Asa, b. Newton, 1806; set. O., 1830 ' Mich., 1833 or 6. Cass Hist., 144, facing 160; Cass Rogers, 328; Cass Twent., 70,552,644.

—— Charles, b. Norfolk Co., 1812; set. Me., Mich., 1835 or 7. Cass Hist., 179; Cass Twent., 71.

—— Elijah, b. Franklin Co. 1796; set. Mich., 1839. Cass Twent., 71.

KINGSLEY, Charles R., b. Bernardston, 1831; set. Mich., 1839. Berrien Port, 426; Cass Twent., 71.

—— Elijah, b. Franklin Co., 1796; set. Mich., 1838. Berrien Port., 426; Cass Hist., 266.

—— Esther, b. Becket; m. 1803, David Frary of O. and Mich. Lenawee Hist. II, 135.

—— George W., set. Mich., 1833. Berrien Twent., 715.

—— Lydia C., b. Swansea, 1822; m. 1841, Simeon C. Wilson of Mich. Berrien Twent., 468.

—— Moses, b. Brighton, 1810; set. Mich., 1830. St. Clair, 121.

KINNEY, Amos L., set. Canada, Mich., 1855. Genesee Port., 443.

—— Hutchins, b. 1789; set. Penn., O. Branch Port., 610.

—— John S., b. Alford, 1827; set. N. Y., O., Mich. Lenawee Port., 386.

—— Thomas, set. N. Y., 1835? Lenawee Port. 386.

KIRBY, George, b. Berkshire Co., 1806; set. Mich., 1838. Wayne Chron., 379.

—— Lydia, m. 1830? Simon Jones of N. Y., O. and Mich. Gratiot, 423.

—— Sarah, m. 1790? Benjamin Estes of Maine and N. Y. Lenawee Port, 1216.

—— Thankful, m. 1830? Abraham T. Huff of N. Y. and O. Gratiot, 521.

KITTREDGE, Albina S., m. 1840? Charles W. Rich of Me. and O. Osceola, 196.

KNAPP, Brundage, set. O., 1830? Mecosta, 513.

—— Chauncey, b. 1798; set. Mich., 1830. Washtenaw Hist., 1085.

—— Ebenezer, set. N. Y., 1810? Mich. Kalamazoo Port., 541.

—— Rachel, m. 1820? Edmund W. Mead of N. Y. and O. Newaygo, 476.

KNEELAND, Clara, m. at Sandisfield, 1811, Sparrow Snow of Mass. and. O. Detroit 1269; Wayne Land., 820.

KNIGHT, Stephen H., b. Salem, 1862; set. Mich., 1889. Wayne Land., 748.

—— William, b. Northampton, 1806 or 7; set. N. J., 1827, Mich., 1834. Lenawee Hist. I, 336; Lenawee Illus., 123, 439; Lenawee Port., 433.

KNOWLTON. Ephraim A., b. Cape Ann, 1813; set. Vt., O., Mich., 1846. Branch Port., 470; Branch Twent., 249.

—— William, b. Wenham; set. Vt., 1815, O. Branch Port., 470.

KNOX, Elijah, b. Blandford, 1773; set N. Y. Kalamazoo Port., 983.

KRIGER, Michael, set. Ind., 1835? Newaygo, 257.

LADD, John, b. 1774; set. N. Y., 1800? Lenawee Port., 519.

—— John, b. Cheshire, 1786; set. N. Y., 1816. Lenawee Hist. I, 413.

—— John, set. N. Y., 1820? Lenawee Port., 1038.

LAIRD, Jonas, b. 1792; set. N. Y. Hillsdale Port., 935.

LAMB, Nahum, b. Charlton, 1794; set. N.Y., 1815? Mich. 1834. Lenawee Hist. I, 108.

—— Otis, b. Greenville, 1790; set. Canada 1810, N. Y. 1816, Mich. 1823. Macomb Hist., 831; Macomb Past, 280.

LANDMAN, William J., b. Boston, 1873; set. Mich. Grand Rapids Lowell, 789.

LANDON, George, b. Sheffield, 1795; set. Mich. 1831. Monroe, 431.

LANE, Bereah H., b. Enfield, 1800; set. Mich. 1834. Bean Creek, 35; Lenawee Port., 1098.

—— Irene, b. Chesterfield, 1774; m. David Foote of N.Y. and Ill. Genesee Port.,907.

—— Nathaniel, of Enfield; set. Mich. 1834. Bean Creek, 36; Lenawee Port., 1098.

—— Nathaniel, b. Enfield, 1830; set. Mich. 1834. Lenawee Port., 1098.

LANG, Henry, b. 1829; set, Mich. 1844. Cass Hist., 145.

—— Oscar, b. 1816; set. Mich. 1844. Cass Hist., 145.

LANGDON, Reuben, b. Tyringham, 1777; set. N. Y. 1795? Lenawee Hist. II, 339.

LANGLEY, S. G., set. Mich. 1832. Berrien Twent., 178.

LAPHAM, Elizabeth, m. 1780? Gilbert Howland of Mass. and N. Y. Hillsdale Port., 343.

—— Elizabeth M., b. Hancock 1822; m. Samuel Jones of Mich. Oakland Port., 789.

—— Joshua, b. 1778; set. Mich. 1830? Oakland Biog., 183; Oakland Port., 789.

LARNED, Charles, b. Pittsfield; graduated at Williams College 1806, set. Mich. 1815? Wayne Chron., 323.

—— Cynthia, b. Springfield; m. 1830? James Grant of N.Y. and Mich. Macomb Hist., 729,

LATHROP, Charles A., b. W. Springfield, 1816; set. Mich. Macomb Hist., 703.

—— Edward, b. W. Springfield; set. Mich.; d. 1863. Macomb Hist., 703.

—— Freeman, b. Hawley, 1837; set. Mich. 1868. Kent, 1064.

—— Joseph, b. W. Springfield, 1834; set. Mich. 1836. Wayne Land., 749.

—— Seth, b. W.Springfield,1818; set. Mich. 1837. Macomb Hist., 799.

—— Solomon, set. Mich. 1836. Wayne Land., 749.

LAW, Levi J., b. Salem 1854; set. Mich. 1881. Northern M., 123.

LAWRENCE, Calvin, b. 1814; set. N. Y. 1840, Mich. 1848. Lenawee Port., 764.

—— Levi L., b. Hampshire Co., 1783; set. N. Y., O., Mich. Berrien Port., 617.

—— Wolcott, b. near Pittsfield, 1786; set. Mich. 1816. Monroe, 244.

LAZELL, George, b. 1799; set. Mich. 1825. Washtenaw Hist., 502, 1365.

LEACH, Reliance, b. Bridgewater; m. 1795? Noah Turrell of Mass. and N. Y. Hillsdale Port., 612.

LEARNED, Edward, b. Roxbury; set. N. Y. 1810? Huron, 257.

LEE, Asa, set. O., 1820? Saginaw Port., 617.

—— Elias, set. O. 1811. Macomb Hist., 831,

—— Lucy, b. Amherst; m. 1815? George W. Emerson of Mass. and Mich. Hillsdale Port., 878.

—— Lucy, m. 1835? Henry Morris of Vt. Gratiot, 401.

—— Mary, b. Concord, 1777; m. 1796, Oliver Williams of Mass. and Mich. Shiawassee, 158.

—— Mason, b. Taunton, 1779; set. N. Y., Mich. 1833. Berrien Port., 462; Cass Twent., 72.

—— Permelia, b. 1804; m. Joel Clark. Kalamazoo Port., 466.

—— Rebecca, b. Barre, 1780, m. 1800, Benjamin Wing of N. Y. and Mich. Washtenaw Hist., 870.

—— Rowland H., b. Roxbury, 1805; set. O. 1811. Macomb Hist., 831.

—— Sarah, of Westfield; m. 1721, Daniel Hayes of Conn. Lenawee Port., facing 187.

LEET, Mary, m. 1820? Joseph Moon of O. and Mich. Genesee Hist., 471.

LEGG, Polly, m. 1810? Ebenezer Knapp of N. Y. and Mich. Kalamazoo Port., 541.

—— Sophronia, b. Orange, 1777; m. 1801, Abram Aldrich of N. Y. and Mich Branch Port., 360; Branch Twent., 674.

LELAND, Mary A., m. 1830? Israel E. Phelps of N. Y. and Mich. Ionia Port., 583.

LENOX, Rosanna, m. 1830? Chauncey D. Fox of Mich. Isabella, 186.

LEONARD, Edwin S., b. North Adams, 1835; set. Mich. Clinton Past, 428.

—— H. F., b. Plymouth County, 1848; set. Mich. 1867. St. Clair, 758.

—— Isaac R., soldier of 1812; set. N. Y. Genesee Port., 405.

—— Levi, set. O. 1814. Branch Port., 610.

—— Rone, m. Hutchins Kinney (b. 1789) of Penn. and O. Branch Port., 610.

—— Sallie M. of Middleborough, b. 1846; m. Fred J. Brown of Mich. Ingham Port., 365.

—— Susan, of Wrentham, m. 1810? Ephraim Wilbur of N. Y. Hillsdale Port., 189.

LEWIS, Anna, b. Springfield; m. 1878, Alexander W. Morrison of Mich. Clinton Past, 203.

—— Benjamin, set. N. Y. 1820? O., Mich., Wis. Hillsdale Port., 799.

—— Cyrus A., b. Grafton, 1832; set. R. I., Mich. 1851. Washtenaw Hist., 1016.

—— Elisha, b. Barnstable County, 1800? set. N. Y., O., Mich. Hillsdale Port., 799.

—— George F., b. Harvard 1828; set. Mich. 1835. Bay Hist., 96; Lake Huron, 96; Saginaw Hist., 469; St. Clair, 415.

—— Isaac, b. Boston; set. N. Y. 1820? Berrien Port., 136.

—— John, b. Walpole, 1750? set. N. Y. 1785? Lenawee Port., 1125.

—— William, Sr., set., N. Y. 1810? Branch Twent., 842.

—— William, b. 1799; set. Mich. 1832, Cal. 1849. Macomb Past, 611.

LILLEY, Zenas, set. N. Y. 1810? O. Lenawee Port., 822.

—— Zenas Jr., set. N. Y. 1820? O. 1834. Lenawee Hist. I, 117.

LILLY, Alanson, b. Franklin Co., 1817; set. O. 1832. Kalamazoo Port., 327.

—— Austin, of Ashfield; set. O. 1832. Kalamazoo Port., 327.

LINCOLN, Abiathar, set. Vt., N. Y., Mich., 1835. Jackson Port., 748.

—— Abiathar, Jr., set. Vt., N. Y., 1829, Mich. 1837. Jackson Port., 748.

—— Benjamin F., b. Wareham, 1831; set. Oregon, 1853, Vt. 1862. Traverse, 311.

—— Charity, b. Taunton, 1782; m. 1803, George Crane of N. Y. and Mich. Lenawee Hist. I, 253, 510; Lenawee Port., 371, 636.

—— Ephraim, b. Berkshire Co., 1786; set. N. Y. 1805. Jackson Port., 671.

—— Mercy, b. Taunton, 1785; m. 1st Tisdale Walker of Mass. and N. Y.; m. 2d 1816, Ephraim Hicks of Mich. Lenawee Hist. I, 159; II, 336; Lenawee Illus., 320.

—— Otis, set. N. Y., 1805. Jackson Port., 671.

LINDSAY, Isaac, set. N. Y., 1790. Branch Hist., 306.

LINDSEY, Lucius L., b. 1804; set. N. Y., Mich. 1841. Kalamazoo Port., 286.

LINDSLEY, Joseph A., b. Salem 1842? set. Mich. Washtenaw Hist., 502.

LINES, Mary, m. 1845? Charles Donwall of N. Y. Jackson Hist., 620.

LINNELL, Elijah, b. Barnstable, 1799; set. N. Y., Mich. Lenawee Illus., 106.

LINSEY, Robert, b. Colerain, 1797; set. N. Y. Hillsdale Port., 705.

LITCHFIELD, Jemima, b. Chesterfield, 1813; m. A. C. Clarke. Jackson Hist., 969.

LITTLE, Mrs. Ruth (wife of Henry), b. Monson, 1800; set. Mich. 1831. St. Clair, 119

LITTLEJOHN, John, of Martha's Vineyard; set. Mich. 1840. Allegan Hist., 154.

LIVERMORE, James, b. 1789; set. Me., Mich., 1835. Ingham Port., 198.

—— Mary Ann, m. 1812? Ebenezer O. Grosvenor_of Mass. and N. Y. Monroe, 448.

—— Samuel, set. Penn. 1820? Saginaw Port., 481.

LOCKE, Reuben, set. N. Y. 1825? Ionia Port., 510.

—— Russell, set. N.Y., Mich. 1835. Ionia Port., 510.

LOMBARD, Annie A., of Acushnet; m. 1860? Benjamin F. Lincoln of Ore. and Vt. Traverse, 311.

—— Frank W., b. Springfield, 1843; set. Ind. 1846; Mich. 1864. Traverse, 264.

LOMIS, Jacob L., set. N. Y. 1800? Oakland Biog., 526.

—— Thomas N., set. N. Y. 1800? Oakland Hist., 157.

LONG, A. H., set Mich. 1844. Cass Twent., 354.

—— Appolos, b. 1790; set, N. Y. 1820? Lenawee Port., 312.

—-- Henry,set.Mich.1844. Cass Twent,354.

—— O. N., b. Franklin Co., 1813; set. N.Y., Mich., 1837. Cass Hist., 304.

—— Oscar,set Mich.1844. Cass Twent ,354.

LONGLEY, Angie R. of Franklin Co. m. 1860, Andrew F. Ashley of Mo. and Mich. Upper P., 444.

LOOK, Henry M., set. Mich. 1830? Oakland Hist., 48.

—— Thankful, b. Martha's Vineyard, 1800; m. Walter Harris of Vt. and Mich. Lenawee Port., 196.

LOOMIS, Anjenette, b. 1811; m. Fowler J. Preston of Mich. Berrien Port., 117; Berrien Twent., 949.

—— Daniel, b. Pittsfield, 1782; set. N. Y. 1820. Lenawee Hist. I, 123.

—— Daniel A., b. Lanesboro, 1811; set. N. Y. 1820. Lenawee Hist. I, 123.

—— John, b. Hampden Co., 1827; set. Mich. 1836. Saginaw Hist., 899.

—— Josiah, 1812 soldier; set. Mich. 1836. Saginaw Hist., 899.

—— Lucinda, b. Hinsdale, 1785; m. 1802 Jesse Millard of N. Y. and Mich. Lenawee Hist. I, 296.

—— Mary, b. Hampden Co.; m. 1815? William H. Fay of O. Muskegon Port., 173.

LORING, Julia, m. 1835? Harley C. Clark of N. Y. Macomb Hist., 790.

LOTHROP, George V. N., b. Easton, 1817; set. Mich. 1839 or 1843. Detroit, 1124; Wayne Chron., 341; Wayne Land., 761.

—— Martha, b. Enfield, 1798; m. 1825, Elijah Linnell Lenawee Illus., 107.

LOUD, Watson, b. Westhampton, 1806; set. Mich. 1846. Macomb Hist., 663.

LOVEJOY, James, b. Boston, 1849; set. Minn. 1867, Mich. 1875. Traverse, 282.

—— William, b. Greenfield, 1762; set. N.Y. 1810? Hillsdale Port., 201.

LOVELAND, Samuel H., b. Washington, 1832; set. N. Y., Mich. 1855. Gratiot, 369.

LOVERIDGE, Caleb, b. Deerfield, 1792; 1812 soldier; set. Conn., N. Y. 1820? Allegan Twent., 168; Kalamazoo Port., 335,

LOWE, Susanna, b. Ipswich, 1773; m. Benjamin Procter of Mass. and N. H. Macomb Hist., 835.

LOWELL, Josiah, b. 1791; set. N. Y. 1813?, Mich. 1840. Clinton Port., 64 or 641.

—— Nelson, b. Newbury; set. Mich. 1830? Jackson Hist., 665.

LUCAS, Isaac W., b. Salem; set. Mich. 1855? Berrien Twent., 381.

LUCE, Abijah, b. Martha's Vineyard 1781; set. R. I. 1835, Mich. 1845. Grand River, appendix 38.

—— Benjamin F., b. Pittsfield, 1816; set. Mich. 1837. Lake Huron, 226.

—— C. F. E., b. Danvers, 1808; set. N. Y., Mich. Genesee Port., 914.

—— Joseph, b. 1780; set.. N. Y. 1820? Lenawee Hist. II, 232.

—— Nancy, m. 1800? Bezaleel Frost of N. Y. Macomb Hist., 698.

LYMAN, Anna, of Westfield; m. 1802, Riley Williams of Vt. Lenawee Hist. I, 288.

—— Hannah, m. 1825? Joel Newman of Mich. Northern M., 381.

LYNCH, Almira, m. 1830? Armenius Owen of Mich. Branch Twent., 774.

—— Nancy, m. 1830? David Harrington of N. Y. and Mich. Jackson Port., 249.

LYON, Simeon of Dedham; set. Mich. 1843. Hillsdale Hist., 224.

—— Wakeman, set. N. Y. 1810? Genesee Port., 992.

LYONS, Diana, b. Colerain, 1809; m. Curtis Coman of Mich. Hillsdale Port., 701.

LYONS, Mellona, b. Colerain, 1814; m. Kellogg Haskins of Vt. and O. Jackson Port.,836.

MCARTHUR, ALEXANDER, b. Acton, 1786; set. Vt., Mich. Ingham Hist., 437.

MCBRIDE, MARY, b. Boston, 1804? m. John Newell of Mass. and Canada. Lenawee Hist. II, 393.

MCCARTY, JAMES, b. Roxbury, 1815; set. Mich., 1830. Saginaw Hist., 679.

MCCOLLUM, DANIEL, b. Berkshire Co., 1800; set. Mich. Monroe, 505.

MCCOMBER, ESTHER, m. 1805? Charles Campbell of Vt. and N. Y. Kalamazoo Port, 610.

MCCOY, JAMES, set. Mich., 1865. Lake Huron, 166.

MCELROY, NANCY M., b. Boston, 1771; m. Daniel Robinson of Vt. and N. H. Clinton Port., 613.

MCGEE, DAVID, b. Coleraine, 1760; set. N. Y., 1810? Mich.,1835. Jackson Port.,812.

—— THOMAS, b. Coleraine, 1790; set. N. Y., Mich., 1832. Jackson Port., 812; Jackson Hist., 670.

MCHENCH, WILLIAM, set. N. Y. d. 1867. Ingham Port., 681.

MCINTYRE, LUCINDA E., m. 1820? Shubal Baker of N. Y. Jackson Hist., 827.

MACK, ABNER, b. Montague, 1795; set. Vt., O., Mch., 1832. Kalamazoo Hist., facing 446.

MCKEE, ELECTA, m. 1815? David King of N. Y. Clinton Port., 538.

MACKINTOSH, MARY A., m. 1840? Wells Field of Mich. Kalamazoo Port., 737.

MCLOUTH, BENJAMIN, b. Cheshire; set. N. Y., Ind., Mich. d. 1868. Branch Port., 273.

—— DRAXA, b. 1789; m. Levi Fuller of N. Y. and Mich. Washtenaw Hist., 1428.

—— JANE, b. Worthington; m. 1884 Alfred Cheney of Mich. Branch Port., 272.

—— OLIVER C., b. 1784; set. Mich. Hillsdale Port., 259.

—— WILLIAM W., b. Cheshire, 1792; set. N. Y., 1815; Mich., 1835. Lenawee Hist., I, 193; Lenawee Illus., 190.

McNETT, SAMUEL; 1812 soldier; set. N. Y. Muskegon Port., 19'.

MACOMBER, HANNAH, b. 1807; m. Joshua Simmons of Mich. Oakland Port., 201, 602.

—— HARRIET, m. 1850? Nathaniel A. Armstrong of Mich. Cass Twent., 454.

MCOMBER, JAMES, b. Berkley, 1801; set. Vt., Mich., 1835. Cass Hist., 201; Cass Twent., 74.

MACOY, REBECCA, b. 1776; m. Elijah Smith of Vt., N. Y. and Mich. Kalamazoo Hist., 423.

MACUMBER, NATHANIEL, set. N. Y., 1815? Mich., 1827. Newaygo, 267.

MACY, ELIZA G., b. Nantucket, 1821; set. Mich., 1833; m. 1846, Dyer H. Mudge of Mich. Lenawee Hist. II, 325.

—— ELIZABETH, b. Nantucket, 1763; m. Uriah Barnard. Berrien Port, 217.

—— OBED, b. Nantucket, 1770; set. N. Y., 1827, Mich., 1833. Lenawee Hist. II, 326.

MAKEPEACE, MARTHA S., b. Brookfield; m. 1840, Edwin W. Giddings of Conn. Macomb Hist., 657.

MALCOLM, SAMUEL, b. 1815; set. Mich., 1837. Jackson Hist., 833.

MALLERY, AMANDA, b. Easthampton, 1822; m. 1839, Jonathan B. Keeney of Mich. Lenawee Hist. II, 434.

—— ZALMON, b. Montgomery, 1784; set. Mich., 1836. Lenawee Hist. II, 435.

MALLORY, AZRIAH, b. New Ashford, 1804; set. N. Y., 1820? Mich., 1837. Hillsdale Hist., 250; Kent, 1223.

—— OTIS, set. N. Y. 1819. Genesee Port., 441.

MANLEY, THOMAS, set. Vt., 1800. Macomb Hist., 734.

MANLY, JULIA E., b. Sandisfield; m. 1820? Thaddeus Granger of O. Macomb Hist., 797.

MANN, ESTHER, m. Thomas Richardson of Vt. and Canada. Genesee Port., 206.

—— ROBERT, b. Ipswich, 1831; set. Mich., 1849. Ingham Hist., 402.

MANNING, WILLIAM, b. Harvard, 1808; set. La., Mich. Washtenaw Port., 483.

MANSFIELD, JOSIAH, set. N. Y., 1815? Mecosta, 309.

MARBLE, CHARLES, set. N. Y., 1820, Mich., 1843. Lenawee Port., 1121.

—— EMMA, m. 1805? Peter Brewer of N. Y. Calhoun, 74.

—— JAMES, b. Salem; set. N. Y., Ind., 1844; d. 1848. Berrien Port., 707.

—— PHEBE, b. Taunton, 1794; set. N. Y., 1820; m. Samuel Brightman of N. Y. and Mich. Lenawee Port., 1121.

—— SARAH L., m. 1817, Augustus D. Dorrance of N. Y. Ingham Port., 853.

MARICK, POLLY, b. 1800? m. Daniel Hathaway of O. Gratiot, 278.

MARKHAM, SARAH H., b. Boston; m. 1870? William T. Lamoreaux of Mich. Kent, 1069.

MARRIS, ALVIRA, m. 1828, Humphrey Smith of N. Y. and Mich. St. Clair, 706.

MARSH, ELIZABETH, b. 1830; m. 1st, Homer A. Lewe; m. 2d, 1843, L. D. Halsted, Branch Twent., 590.

—— ELLEN M., m. 1st, 1850? Samuel Arnold of N. Y.; m. 2d, George W. Petty of Mich. Macomb Port., 147.

—— EMERSON, set. Mich., 1838. Branch Twent., 591.

—— HOLLISTER, F., b. 1808; set. N. Y., Mich., 1853. Kalamazoo Port., 284.

—— JUSTIN, b. Montague, 1796; set. N. Y., Mich., 1837. Monroe, 505.

—— LYDIA, b. 1786; m. Uriah Chappell of Ohio. Ingham Hist., 348.

—— Z. H., b. Montague, 1811; set. N. Y., Mich., 1845? Ingham Port., 602; Mecosta, ——.

MARTIN, AMOS, b. Franklin Co.; set. Mich. 1848. Wayne Chron., 73.

—— ELIZABETH, m. 1815? John Williams of Mass. and N. Y. Clinton Port., 504.

—— EXPERIENCE, m. 1770? Joseph Baker of Vt. and Mass. Lenawee Port., 303.

—— JULIA, b. Coleraine, 1817; m. 1840? Abram Hayner of N. Y. and Mich. Ingham Hist., 330; Lansing, 471.

MARTINDALE, ELISHA, b. Lenox; d. 1861. Hillsdale Port., 393.

—— T. D., set. O., 1820? Kent, 576.

MARVIN, NATHAN, b. Granville, 1786; set. Mich., 1832. Jackson Hist., 169.

MASON, BENJAMIN, b. 1738; set. N. Y. Ionia Port., 612.

—— BROOKS, set. N. Y. 1861. Muskegon Port., 467.

—— BROOKS, JR., b. Cheshire; set. N. Y. 1801. Branch Port., 465.

—— DAVID, b. 1791; set. N. Y., Pa. Lenawee Illus., 372.

—— H. L., b. Berkshire Co., 1841; set. Mich. 1852. Jackson Hist., 1028.

—— ICHABOD, set. N. Y. ?. 1864. Macomb Hist., 857.

—— ISAAC, b. 1798; set. N. Y. 1801. Muskegon Port., 467.

—— JOHN, b. Swansea, 1767; set. N. Y. 1801. Lenawee Hist. II, 480; Lenawee Port., 199.

—— JOHN L., b. 1800; set. N. Y. 1816. Kalamazoo Port., 914.

—— LUCY, b. Lanesboro, 1798; m. Seymour Mead of Mass., O. and Mich. Lenawee Port., 942.

—— LUCY D., of Berkshire Co.; m. 1830? Joseph N. Ferry of N. Y. Wayne Chron., 442.

—— LYMAN G., b. Belchertown, 1829; set. Mich. 1855. Muskegon Hist., 132.

—— MIAL, b. 1808; set. Mich., 1836. Washtenaw Hist., 1403.

—— OCTAVIUS, b. Cheshire 1795; set. N. Y., Mich., 1840. Branch Port., 465.

—— PHOEBE, m. 1800? Clark Chase of N. Y. Kalamazoo Hist., facing 423.

—— SALLY, b. Attleboro, 1798; m. Nathaniel Cole of N. Y. and Mich. Macomb Hist., 650.

MATHEWS, GIDEON, set. Mich. 1837. Kalamazoo Port., 855.

MATTHEWS, SALMON H., of Conway, set. Mich. 1827. Washtenaw, 629; Washtenaw Past, 805.

MAY, CELESTIA E., b. Sandisfield; m. 1820? Deacon Rockwell of Mich. Kalamazoo Port., 313.

—— CHARLES S., b. Sandisfield, 1830; set. Mich. 1834. St. Clair, 121.

—— DWIGHT, b. Sandisfield, 1822; set. Mich. 1834. Kalamazoo Hist., 119, 278; St. Clair, 119.

MAY, RUSSELL G., b. near Pittsfield, 1804; set. N. Y. 1826, Mich. 1837. Cass Twent., 440.

MAYHEW, GEORGE R., b. S. Abington, 1850; set. Mich. Kent, 1075.

MAYNARD, *Colonel,* 1812 soldier; set. N. Y. 1810. Jackson Port., 825.

—— EZRA, b. Conway; set. Mich. 1824. Washtenaw Hist., 1253.

—— JOHN W., set. Mich. 1824. Grand Rapids City, 321; Kent, 1075.

—— WILLIAM S., b. Berkshire Co., 1802; set. Mich. 1830. Washtenaw Hist., 270; Washtenaw Part, 684.

—— WILLIAM S., b. Sudbury, 1803; set. N. Y., Pa. Kalamazoo Port., 677.

MEACHAM, ALMON, set. O., d. 1852. Gratiot, 215.

—— POLLY A., b. Shelby, 1826; m. 1843, John Friend of N. Y. and Mich. Ionia Hist., 355.

—— SARAH, m. 1815, Asa Lee of O. Saginaw Port., 617.

MEAD, EDMUND W., set. N. Y. 1820? Ohio. Newaygo, 476.

—— GEORGE, Lanesboro, 1826; set. O. 1840, Mich. 1851. Lenawee Port., 942.

—— LUCY, b. Boston; m. 1805? Samuel Garlick of Ct., N. Y. and Mich. Macomb Hist., 699.

—— MINERVA L., b. Lanesboro, 1823; set. Mich. 1833; m. 1844, Joel Carpenter of Mich. Lenawee Hist. I, 299; Lenawee Illus., 151.

—— SEYMOUR, b. Lanesboro, 1789; set. O. 1847, Mich. 1851. Lenawee Port., 941.

—— STEPHEN M., b. Lanesboro, 1822; set. O. 1860, Mich. 1878. Lenawee Port., 941.

MEARS, ALBERT, b. Billerica, 1821; set. Mich. 1836 or 1837. Muskebon Hist., 132; Muskegon Port., 194.

—— CHARLES, b. N. Billerica, 1814; set. Mich. 1836. Muskegon Hist., 132.

MELLEN, MARTHA, of Hopkinton; m. 1755? Samuel Chamberlain. Berrien Port., 885.

MENTOR, EMILY, m. 1815? Ebenezer Harrington of N. Y. Kalamazoo Port., 426.

MERCHANT, JAMES S., set. Me., Mich. 1840. St. Clair, 752.

MERRIAM, ALMIRA, b. 1804; m. 1825? Obed Taylor of Mich. Washtenaw Hist., 697.

MERRICK, BENJAMIN P., b. Holyoke, 1877; set. Mich. Grand Rapids Hist., 793.

MERRILL, H. W., set. Mich. 1845. Wayne Chron., 81.

—— WELTHY, m. 1810? Seth C. Darwin of N. Y. and Mich. Ingham Port., 221.

—— WILLIAM G., b. Haverhill, 1800; set. Mich. 1847. Genesee Port., 845, 1036.

MERRILLS, ISAAC, b. Amesbury; set. N. H. 1770? Jackson Port., 783.

MERRITT, CHARLES A., set. O. 1851, Mich. 1855. Ingham Hist., 367.

MERRYFIELD, NANCY, m. 1830? E. F. Smith, Sr., of Mich. Ionia Hist., 303.

METCALF, PHINEAS, set. N. Y. 1820? Ionia Port., 282.

MILES, ELIJAH, b. Stockbridge; set. N. Y. 1810? St. Clair, 680.

—— EMILY, b. Ashfield, 1820? m. 1843 Alanson Lilly of Mich. Kalamazoo Port., 327.

—— JONATHAN EASTMAN, b. Hampden Co., 1782; set. N. Y. 1800. Bernier Hist., 462.

MILLARD, *Doctor,* set. N. Y. 1827, Mich. 1841. Ionia Port., 660, 670.

—— CHARLES, b. Berkshire Co., 1819; set. N. Y. 1827, Mich. 1840. Ionia Port., 660.

—— ELEAZER, b. Rehoboth; set. N. Y. 1760? Ionia Port., 674.

—— EUNICE, m. 1780? Enos Walker of Mass. and Vt. Jackson Port., 787.

—— LEANDER, b. 1824; set. N. Y. 1827, Mich. 1841. Ionia Port., 670.

MILLER, ASHUR, set. N. Y. 1840? Mich. 1853. Kent, 1079.

—— CHARLES, set. Mich. 1878. Lake Huron, 273.

—— CHARLOTTE, m. 1825? Absalom Traver of N. Y. and Mich. Lansing, 259.

MILLER, EVI, set. N. Y. 1810? Kent, 1400.

—— JOHN G., b. Northampton, 1822; set. Mich. Hillsdale Port., 909.

—— LAURA, m. 1820? Horace Coles or Cowles of Mass. and O. Isabella, 353, 388.

—— NORTON L., b. Berkshire Co., 1815; set. N. Y. 1818, Mich. 1832. Macomb Hist., 596; Macomb Past, 11.

—— RELIEF, b. Marlborough, 1775; m. 1797, William Weatherby of Vt., N. Y. and Mich. Lenawee Hist. I, 136; Lenawee Illus., 117; Lenawee Port., 1020.

—— SALLY, b. 1775; m. 1775, Stephen Ingalls of Mass. and N. Y. Lenawee Hist., II, 78.

MILLS, SARAH J., b. Great Barrington, 1818; m. 1846, Timothy Clark of Mich. Branch Port., 271; Branch Twent., 677.

—— STEPHEN, set .Vt., N. Y., Mich., 1837. Ingham Hist., 475.

MINER, JOSEPH P., set. O. 1840? Saginaw Hist., 879.

—— LINUS K., b. Springfield; set. N. Y., MITCHELL, ALONZO, b. Cummington, 1807; set. N. Y. 1820, Mich. 1831. Lenawee Port., 285.

—— CHARLES K., set. N. H., d. 1869. Isabella, 465.

—— DEXTER, set. N. Y. 1820? Mich. 1831. Northern M., 321.

—— JOSEPH, b. Nantucket; set. N. Y. 1820? Lenawee Port., 580.

—— MARTHA K., b. 1810; m. 1834. Charles M. Baldwin of Mich. Lenawee Illus., 343.

—— WILLIAM, b. Cummington, 1782; set. Mich. 1833. Lenawee Port., 285.

MOFFITT, GEORGE, b. Worcester Co., 1827; set. Mich. 1836. Washtenaw Hist., 1448.

—— HORACE, of Worcester, b. 1800; set. Mich. 1836, O. Washtenaw Hist., 1448.

MONROE, DAN, set. N. Y. 1816. Newaygo, 437.

—— DARIUS, b. Williamstown? 1796; set. N. Y. 1809, Mich. 1856. Branch Port., 544.

—— PHILETUS, b. Berkshire Co., 1815; set. N. Y. 1816, Mich. 1864. Newaygo, 437.

MONTAGUE, DANIEL M., b. 1825? set. N. Y., Mich. Genesee Port., 719.

—— DANIEL N., b. Hadley; set. N. Y. 1834, Mich. 1839. Genesee Hist., 368.

—— STILLMAN, set. N. Y. 1825? Branch Twent., 717.

MONTGOMERY, CHAUNCY, b. 1827; set. O. 1853, Ind. 1857, Mich. 1875. Upper P., 227.

—— HENRY, from near Boston; set. N. Y. 1800. Lenawee Hist. I, 395.

MOODY, WILLIAM, b. 1810; set. O. Gratiot, 361.

MOON, CLARISSA, b. Tyingham, 1790? m. Albert Stickney of O. Ingham Port., 486.

MOOR, ANNA, m. 1835? J. D. Doane of Mich. Washtenaw Hist., 708.

MOORE, AARON, b. Bolton? set. N. Y. 1810? Detroit, 1194.

—— DAYTON, set. O. 1840? Ind., Mich. 1854. Newaygo, 288.

—— ELIJAH, set. N. Y., d. 1840. Isabella, 477.

—— GEORGE F., b. Berkshire Co., 1832; set. N. Y. 1847, Mich. 1859. Detroit, 1161.

—— JOHN, of Berkshire Co.; set. N. Y. 1847, d. 1858. Detroit, 116.

—— JOHN, b. Berkshire Co., 1824; set. N. Y., Mich. 1868. Washtenaw Hist., 1021.

—— LILLIAN, of Berkshire Co., m. 1871, B. W. Wright of Mich. Upper P., 451.

—— LOREN, b. Coleraine, 1802; set. N. Y. 1803, Mich. 1831. Washtenaw Past, 182.

—— LOVELL, b. Shirley, 1797; set. Mich. 1831. Grand Rapids Lowell, 106; Grand Rapids Hist., 175; Kent, 263.

—— RHODA, b. Heath, 1790; m. Calvin Love of N. Y. and Mich. Lenawee Illus., 106.

—— WASHINGTON, of Coleraine; set. N. Y. 1803; 1812 soldier. Hillsdale Port., 997; Washtenaw Past, 182.

MORE, ZERUAH, m. 1820? Rowland Nimocks of N. Y. and Mich. Hillsdale Port., 452.

MORGAN, JOHN C., b. Chicopee, 1856; set. Mich. 1869. Berrien Hist., 235.

—— NANCY, b. 1780?; m. Daniel Nightingale of N. H. and Mich. Genesee Port., 589.

—— SAMUEL A., set. N. Y. 1830? Mich. 1840. Washtenaw Hist., 1269.

MORRILL, NATHANIEL, set. N. H. 1785? Jackson Hist., 771.

MORRIS, WILLIAM, set. Mich. 1820? Oakland Hist., 115.

MORRISON, Owen, b. Coleraine; set. N. Y. 1820? Lenawee Port.. 788.

—— Stephen A., b. Danvers, 1815; set. Mich. 1837. Allegan Hist., 334.

MORSE, Joseph B., set. N. Y., Mich. 1831. Genesee Port., 572.

—— Lemuel, b. 1779; set. N. Y. 1810? O. Lenawee Port., 898.

—— Lewis, b. Fitchburg, 1831; set. Mich. 1857. Lansing, 487.

—— Lewis L., b. 1800? set. Mich. 1857, d. 1871. Lansing, 487.

—— Lincoln, b. Fitchburg, 1833; set. Mich. 1857. Lansing, 487.

—— Lydia, m. 1815? John Canniff of N. Y.; m. 2d, John Bird of Mich. Lenawee Port., 1200.

—— Susanna, m. 1805? John Adams of N. H. Macomb Hist., 687.

MORTON, Ambrose, b. 1757; set. N. Y. Kalamazoo Hist., 543.

—— Ambrose, Jr., b. Stoughton, 1788; 1812 soldier; set. N. Y. Kalamazoo Hist., 543; Berrien Port., 246.

—— Eleazer, b. 1786; set. N. Y. 1806? Mich. 1834. Berrien Hist., 197.

—— Elijah, b. Hatfield, 1771; set. N. Y. 1815? Mich. 1834. Newaygo, 318.

—— John, set. N. Y., Mich. 1834. Hillsdale Port., 655; Lenawee Port., 580.

—— Maria, b. 1802; set. Mich. 1838; Washtenaw Hist., 504.

MOSELEY, Augustus C., b. Pittsfield, 1835; set. Mich. 1840. Branch Twent., 729.

—— Sarah, m. 1840? Maj. R. J. Barry of Mich. Jackson Port., 471.

—— Thomas, set. Mich. 1840. Branch Twent., 729.

—— Thomas, b. Pittsfield, 1794; set. Mo., N. Y., Mich., 1836 or 1841. Branch Port., 524; Branch Twent., 250.

MOSELY, William Augustus, b. Westfield, 1815; set. Mich. Branch Twent., 251.

—— William G., of Westfield; set. Mich. 1837. Grand Rapids Hist., 188; Grand Rapids Lowell, 115.

MOSES, Byron, set. Mich. 1850. Clinton Port., 590.

MOSHER, Stephen M., set. N. Y. 1820? Hillsdale Port., 894.

MOTT, Adam, b. near New Bedford; set. N. Y., Mich. 1829. Lenawee Port., 1080.

MOTTLES, Eunice, b. 1789; m. Jeremiah Van Wormer of N. Y. and Mich. Jackson Port., 863.

MOULTON, Nathaniel, set. N. Y. 1790? Lenawee Port., 1103.

MOWRY, Elisha, of Berkshire Co., set. N. Y. 1816. Washtenaw Hist., 1026.

—— J. B., b. Berkshire Co., 1809; set. N. Y., 1816, Mich. 1831. Washtenaw Hist., 1026.

MUNGER, Luke, b. Boston; set. O. Berrien Hist., 501.

MUNN, Horace, b. 1790? set. N. Y. Lenawee Port., 1020.

—— Israel, set. N. Y. 1800? Lenawee Port., 1057.

MURDOCK, Martha, b. Framingham, 1825; set. N. Y. 1828, Mich. 1839; m. 1st, 1845, John C. Ellis of Mich.; m. 2d, 1855, Dennis Warner. Washtenaw Hist., 868; Washtenaw Port., 524.

—— Samuel, b. Westminster; set. N. Y. 1828, Mich. 1839. Washtenaw Hist., 868.

—— Samuel W., set. Mich. 1850? Clinton Port, 527.

MURPHY, Daniel M., b. Erving, 1854; set. Mich. 1876. Clinton Port., 613.

MUSSEY, Dexter, b. Worcester, 1811; set. Mich. 1836. Macomb Hist., 225, 667.

MYERS, Mercy, b. Middlesex Co., 1787; m. 1810? Stephen Fenton of N. Y. Lenawee Illus., 166.

NASH, Andrew B., set. N. Y., Mo., 1870. Lenawee Hist. I, 403.

—— Augustus W., set. N. Y., 1840? Mich., 1854. Allegan Twent., 111; Kalamazoo Port., 563.

—— Ebenezer, of Longmeadow; set. Conn., 1785? St. Clair, 305.

—— Harrison, set. N. Y. before 1836. Branch Port., 311.

—— Joel, set. N. Y., 1830? Kent, 1341.

—— Jonathan E., b. Greenfield? 1820; set. Mich., 1846. Grand River, 246 and appendix, 47; Kent, 1341.

NEEDHAM, Johanna, b. Boston, 1817; m. 1839 James J. Newell of Mich. Lenawee Hist. II, 392.

NELSON, Eunice, m. 1810? Levi Hilton of N. Y. and Mich. Oakland Port., 582.

—— Ezra T., b. Milford, 1824; set. Mich., 1842 or 1845. Grand Rapids Lowell, 463; Kent, 1089.

—— George C., b. Milford, 1812; set. Mich., 1834. Grand Rapids Hist., 196.

—— Ichabod S., b. Deerfield; set. Mich., 1830. Cass Twent., 608.

—— James M., b. Milford, 1810; set. Mich., 1836. Grand Rapids Hist., 182; Grand Rapids Lowell, 109; Kent, 1090.

—— Josiah, b. 1773; set. N. Y. Gratiot, 695.

—— Josiah, set. N. Y., 1800? Ionia Port., 406.

NEWBURY, Edward C., b. Amherst, 1838; set Mich., 1840. Macomb Hist., 668.

NEWCOMB, Hezekiah, of Bernardston; set. N. Y., 1830? Detroit, 1163; Wayne Land., 783.

NEWELL, Hannah, b. 1798; m. Conrad House of N. Y. and Mich. Clinton Port., 934.

—— James J., b. Boston, 1816; set. Canada, 1818; N. Y., 1830; Mich., 1837. Lenawee Hist. II, 392.

—— John, b. Lynnfield, 1794; set. Canada, 1818. Lenawee Hist. II, 391.

—— Rhoda, b. Boston, 1772; m. Samuel Rogers of Mass. and N. Y. Lenawee Hist. II, 330.

NEWTON, Josiah, set. Vt., 1810?; 1812 soldier. Oakland Port., 935.

—— Lucy, m. 1825? Evert Hawley of N. Y. Mecosta, 443.

NICHOLS, Cynthia, m. Henry King of O. Berrien Port., 672.

—— Nathan, b. Berkshire Co.; 1812 soldier; set. N. Y., Mich., 1836. Clinton Port., 205.

—— Orna, b. 1800; m. 1818? Aretus Gilmore of O. Clinton Port., 584.

—— Soloma, m. 1835? Palmer Marsh of N. Y. and Pa. Midland, 313.

NICKERSON, Elkanah, of Harwich; b. 1806; set. Mich., 1867. Berrien Hist., 203.

—— Lewis, b. near Boston; set. N. Y., Mich., 1831. Hillsdale Port., 588.

—— Lewis, set. N. Y., 1810?; Mich., 1830. Lenawee Port., 1032.

NIGHTINGALE, Daniel, b. 1778; set. N. H., Mich., 1837. Genesee Port., 589.

NIMOCKS, Roland, set. N. Y., Mich., 1843 Hillsdale Port., 452.

NIMS, Dwight B., b. Conway, 1807 or 1808; set. N. Y., 1833, Mich., 1835 or 1865. Homer, 73; Jackson Hist. 156; Muskegon Port., 262.

—— Reuben, b. Berkshire Co., 1794; set. Vt., Mich., 1855. Macomb Hist. 485; Macomb Past, 219.

NOBLE, Abby, of Williamstown; m. 1825 George Landon of Mich. Monroe, 431.

—— Charles, b. Williamstown, 1797; set. O., Mich., 1818 or 1820. Detroit, 1224; Monroe, 151.

—— Daniel, b. Williamstown, 1807; set. Mich., 1830. Monroe, 166.

—— David A., b. Williamstown, 1802; set. Mich., 1831. Monroe, 250.

—— Deodatus, of Williamstown; set. Mich., 1832. Detroit, 1224.

—— Levi, b. Blandford, 1792; set. N. Y., 1810? Hillsdale Port., 335; Ionia Port., 577.

—— Nancy, m. 1800? Jacob L. Lomis of N. Y. Oakland Biog., 526.

—— William A., b. Williamstown, 1819; set. Mich., 1833. Monroe, 167.

NORRIS, John C., set. N. Y., Mich., 1837.
:Hillsdale (Port., 457.

NORTHAM, Frances E., b. 1816; m. Cyril
Adams of Mich. Jackson Hist., 1134.

——Samuel K., b. Williamstown, 1824;
set. Mich., 1839. Northern M., 397.

NORTHRUP, Lydia A., b. Cambridge,
1810; m. David Wright of Mich. Kent,
793.

NORTON, John, set. N. Y., 1805? Mich.,
1823; d. 1832. Oakland Biog., 163;
Oakland 'Hist., 151; Oakland Port.,
301.

——Trumbull, set. N. Y., Mich., 1830.
Branch Port., 385.

NOWLEN, Sophia, of New Marlboro; m.
1817? Philo C. Fuller of N. Y. and
Mich. Grand Rapids City, 178.

NUTTING, Abbie B., m. 1831, Dauphin
Brown of Mich. Kalamazoo Hist.,
482.

——Ransom, b. Leverett, 1818; set.
Mich., 1853. Kalamazoo Port., 786.

NYE, Nathan, b. Salem, 1770?; set. N.
Y., 1800? Macomb Hist., 834.

OAKS, Daniel, b. Worcester Co., 1835;
set. Mich., 1855. Osceola, 329.

OLDS, Amanda, m. 1840 Israel Hale of
Mass., Mich. and Ohio. Lenawee
Port., 422.

—— Daniel, Revolutionary soldier; set.
O., 1812? Mich. Jackson Port., 428.

—— Hanford, set. N. Y., 1810? Washtenaw Hist., 1269.

——James, set. O., 1810?Mich., 1830.
Lenawee Port., 1073.

——Lois, b. near Pittsfield; m. 1815?
Benaiah Jones, jr., of O. and Mich.
Jackson Port., 428.

—— Martin, b. Bolton; set. N. Y., O.,
Mich., 1834, Oregon. Branch Hist.,
268.

OLIVE, Susan, m. 1815? Adgate W. Collins of O. and Iowa. Bay Gansser,
421.

OLIVER, David, b. Lynn, 1787; set. O.,
1849, Mich. Gratiot, 600.

—— John, b. 1790; set. N. Y. Jackson
Hist.. 1108.

OMANS, Thomas G., 1812 soldier; set.
N. Y., Mich., 1830. Kent, 687.

ORMSBY, Lysander, b. Westhampton,
1815; set. Mich., 1837. Lenawee Port.,
306.

OSBORN, Asa, b. Berkshire Co., 1775;
set. N. Y., 1791 or 1807, Mich., 1836.
Lenawee Hist. I, 141; Lenawee Port.,
713.

—— James, b. Colerain, 1793; set. N. Y.,
1810? Mich. 1866. Lenawee Hist. I,
168; Lenawee Port., 261.

——Joel, of Berkshire Co., set. N. Y.,
1791. Lenawee Hist. I, 141

—— Richard, b. Lanesboro; set. N. Y.,
Mich., 1835. Ingham Port., 843.

—— Thomas, b. Loraine, 1784; set. N.
Y., Mich., 1848. Lenawee Hist. I, 96;
Lenawee Port., 421.

OSBORNE, David L., b. Salem, 1813; set.
Mich., 1836. St. Clair, 589.

PACKARD, Amasa, b. Bridgewater, 1788;
set. O., 1832. Berrien Hist., facing
434.

—— Bartimeus, b. 1769; set. N. Y., 1790?
Lenawee Illus., 292.

—— Benjamin, b. Bridgewater, 1760;
set. Vt., 1790?. St. Joseph,'83.

—— Elizabeth, m. 1840? Hiram Baldwin
of N. Y. Genesee Port., 889.

—— John F., set. N. Y., 1800? Washtenaw Hist., 624.

—— Laura A., b. Plainfield; m. 1859 Alfred S. Packard of Mich. Berrien
Hist., 439; Kalamazoo Port., 278.

——Vesta, m. 1770? Joseph Bailey of
Mass. and N. Y. Hillsdale Port., 299.

——William, b. Plainfield, 1808; set. N.
Y., O., Mich. Berrien Hist., facing
434.

PADDOCK, Ira, b. N. Y., 1788; set. Berkshire Co., Mass., N. Y., Mich. Branch
Port., 453.

PAGE, Hale 'W., b. Shirley, 1816; set.
Mich. Kalamazoo Port., 867.

PAINE, Edward W., b. S. Hadley, 1839;
set. Ill., 1860, Mich., 1866. Grand Rapids City, 924.

PAINE, Electa, of Williamsburg; m. 1790?
Josiah Frost of Mass. and N. Y.
Jackson Port., 856.

PALMER, Lydia, b. Leyden; m. 1800?
Samuel Coman of N. Y. and Mich.
Hillsdale Port., 700.

PARK, Eliza A., b. Southbridge; m. 1850?
Chancy R. Church of Mich. Jackson
Port., 197.

——— William, b. 1791; set. N. Y., 1815?
Saginaw Port., 636.

PARKER, Calvin, set. N. Y.; d. 1834.
Hillsdale Port., 800.

———Chloe, b. New Bedford; m. 1795?
Ebenezer Jenney of Vt. Macomb
Hist., 731.

———Ezra, b. Newton, 1731; set. N. H.
Northern P., 457.

——— Farrington, b. Weston, 1776; set.
N. Y., 1791. Lenawee Hist. II, 71.

——— Ira, b. S. Adams; set. N. Y., 1815?
Lenawee Hist. I, 176.

——— Isaac, of Boston; bought land in
Mich., 1836. Allegan Hist., 270, 293.

——— James, b. Hartford? 1788; set.
Mich., 1830. Macomb Hist., 757.

——— Jonathan D., set. Mich., 1837; d.
1888. Genesee Port., 995.

——— Joshua, set. N. Y., 1795? Lenawee
Port., 784.

———Timothy, set. N. Y., 1810? Washtenaw Port., 533.

———William M., b. N. Adams, 1779; set.
N. Y., 1793. Oakland Port., 291.

PARKMAN, Phebe, b. Enfield; m. 1825?
Bereah H. Lane of Mass and Mich.
Lenawee Port., 1098.

PARKS, Asa, set. N. Y., 1807. Washtenaw Hist., 1309.

— Ashley, b. Berkshire Co., 1802; set.
N. Y., 1807, Mich., 1835. Washtenaw
Hist., 504, 1309.

PARMANTER, Zeviah, of Northboro; b.
1805; m. 1826 David Blackmer of
Mass. and Mich. Monroe, appendix,
35.

PARMATUR, Charles, set. N. Y., 1810?
Northern M., 347.

PARMENTER, Lydia, b. Oakham, 1792; m.
Samuel D. Wells of N. Y. and Mich.
Macomb Hist., 740.

PARMETER, Luther L., b. Orange, 1815;
set. N. Y., 1822. Newaygo, 328.

———Nathaniel, set. N. Y., 1822. Newaygo, 328.

PARSONS, Andrew, b. Newburyport, 1782;
set. N. Y. Branch Port., 133.

———Caroline, of Sandisfield; m. Rev.
Water Warren who was b. 1800. Berrien Port., 820.

——— Chester, b. Sandisfield, 1799; set.
N. Y., 1802, Mich., 1826. Washtenaw
Hist., 504, 1405.

——— David, b. 1776; set. N. Y., 1800?
Mich., 1844. Oakland Port., 554.

——— E. W., b. Berkshire Co., 1830; set.
Mich., 1833. St. Clair, 590.

——— James M., b. W. Springfield, 1810;
set. Mich., 1864. St. Clair, 120.

——— John, set. N. Y., 1802; d. 1813.
Washtenaw Hist., 1405.

———John, set. N. Y., Mich., 1826. Washtenaw Hist., 1434.

——— Jonathan, b. W. Springfield, 1820;
set. Mich., 1835. St. Clair, 121.

——— Melissa, b. Belchertown, 1800; m.
Warren Isham of N. Y. and Mich.
Detroit, 1157.

———Orrin, b. Sandisfield, 1794; set. N.
Y., 1802, Mich., 1826. Washtenaw
Hist., 1371; Washtenaw Past, 576.

——— Philinda, b. Conway; m. Marvin
Gaston of N. Y. and Mich.; d. 1888.
Ingham Port., 687.

——— Sarah, of Granville; m. 1824 Samuel
W. Hamilton of Mass. and Mich. Homer, 45; Mecosta, 322.

PARTRIDGE, Levi W., b. Pittsfield, 1851;
set. Mich., 1880. Wayne Land., appendix, 142.

PATCH, Anson B., b. 1814; set. Mich.,
1840? Ionia Port., 400; Macomb Hist.,
745.

PATRICK, Asa. Jr., of Hampden Co.,
bought land in Mich., 1836. Allegan
Hist., 269.

PAYNE, Daniel, set. N. Y., 1830? Mich.,
1836. Clinton Port., 267.

PAYNE, Hiram, set. N. Y., 1825? Kent, 1266.

—— Stephen, set. N. Y., 1830. Lenawee Port., 924.

PEABODY, David, set. N. H., 1780? Calhoun, opposite 112.

PEARSON, William, Revolutionary soldier; set. Canada. Mecosta, 444.

PEASE, Orlo A., set. N. Y., 1840? Saginaw Port., 489.

—— Warren, set. Mich., 1832. Washtenaw Hist., 1348.

PEASHOT, Sarah; m. 1800? Benajah 'H. Granger of Mass., N. Y., and O. Branch Port., 597.

PECK, Sarepta, m. 1820? Daniel F. Bramble of N. Y. and Mich. Branch Port., 318.

—— W. H. b. Fair Haven, 1853; set. Mich. 1878. Midland, 279.

PECKENS, David, 1812 solider; set. N. Y. 'Washtenaw Port., 405.

PEEBLES, David, set. N. Y., 1810? Washtenaw Hist., 1032.

PEETS, Charles S., set. Canada, 1825? Newaygo, 352.

PEIRCE, Francis, b. Waltham; set. Pa., 1840? Mecosta, 522.

PEIRSON, Levi R., b. Richmond, 1827; set. Mich., 1849. Lenawee Port., 710.

PENNELL, John, b. 1796; set. N. Y., 1825. Kent, 1301.

PENOYER, Jacob, of Lee, b. 1774; set. N. Y. Genesee Hist., 364.

PEREN, Lucy, m. 1798 Ezra Carpenter, Jr. of N. Y. and Mich. Washtenaw Port, 403.

PERKINS, Cyrus E., b. Lawrence, 1847; set. Mich. 1854. Grand Rapids City, 336.

—— George, b. Plymouth; set. Mich., 1831. Macomb Hist., 801.

PERRIN, Friend, set. Mich., 1834. Wayne Chron., 76.

PERRY, Betsey, m. 1800? James L. Fenner of N. Y. Kalamazoo Port., 607.

—— Chester, b. 1801; set. N. Y., Mich., 1824. Genesee Port., 944.

—— Daniel, set. N. Y., 1820? Mich. 1832. Jackson Hist., 835.

PERRY, Elizabeth, b. 1760; m. Ezra Parker of Conn. and Mich. Oakland Port., 292.

—— Sallie, m. 1820? Martin Durkee of Mass. and O. Ionia Port., 702.

—— Sarah, b. Beverly, 1815; m. David Taggart. Branch Port., 316.

—— 'William, b. Concord, 1790? set. N. Y. Clinton Port., 716.

PERSONS, Festus, b. 'Chester; set. N. Y. 1815? Newaygo, 382.

PETERS, G. 'W., set. N. Y., 1820? Mich. 1826. Washtenaw 'Hist., 863.

PETERSON, Polly P., m. 1830? Lewis Snyder of Mich. Jackson Hist., 889.

—— Reuben, b. Boston, 1862; set. Mich., 1890. Grand Rapids Hist., 207; Grand Rapids Lowell, 711.

PETTIBONE, Rosewell, set. N. Y., Mich., 1827. 'Hillsdale Hist., 256.

PETTIS, Edward, b. Pittsfield, 1818; set. 'Mich., 1826. Kent, 512.

—— Eliza T., m. 1837, Thomas J. Hamilton of Mich. and Ia. Clinton Past. 215.

PHELPS, Alfred, of Pittsfield; set. Mich., 1828. Oakland Hist., 287.

—— Benjamin, of Pittsfield; set. Mich., 1825. Oakland 'Hist., 286.

—— Edwin, b. Pittsfield, 1828; set. Mich., 1833. Oakland Biog., 687; Oakland Port., 640.

—— Elijah, set. Mich., 1831. Macomb Past., 316.

—— Elnathan, b. Pittsfield, 1799; set. Mich., 1833. Oakland Hist., 116; Oakland Port., 639.

—— Huldah A., b. 1826; set. Mich., 1830. Washtenaw Port., 266.

—— Josiah L., b. 1814; set. Mich., 1831. Macomb Past, 316.

—— Mary E., of Springfield; m. 1867, George C. 'Wetherbee of Mich. Detroit, 1172.

—— Norman, set. Mich., 1830. Washtenaw Port., 266.

—— Paulina, m. 1818. John Everett of N. Y. and 'Mich. Washtenaw Port., 353.

PHELPS, Rhoda, b. Pittsfield, 1794; m. 1815 or 16, Johnson Niles of N. Y. and Mich. Oakland Hist., 285, 295; Oakland Port., 894.

PHILIPS, Malaney, m. 1820? James W. Wadsworth of Mich. Allegan Twent., 199.

PHILLIPS, Abiathar, b, 1774; set. N. Y. Hillsdale Port., 665.

—— Abiathar, b. Franklin Co., 1804; set. N. Y., Mich., 1868. Hillsdale Port., 665.

—— Alanson, b. 1804; set. Me., 1830? Mich., 1835. Levawee Hist. II, 336.

—— Jonathan, set. N. Y., 1800? Oakland Port., 882.

—— Zebedee, set. N. Y., 1825? Ingham Port., 495.

—— Zebulon, set. N. Y.; d. 1833. Isabella, 287.

PHIPPEN, Mary L., b. Lynn; m. 1826. Thaddeus Hampton of Mich. Berrien Port., 488.

PICKERING, Rebecca, b. 1793; m. Fisher A. Darling of Mass. and Mich. Monroe, 587.

PIERCE, Abbie, m. 1830? Joel Oaks of Mass. Osceola, 329.

—— Abner G., b. Cambridge; set. N. Y 1850, Mich. Lenawee Port., 646.

—— Asa, b. 1790; set. N. Y., 1814, Mich. 1835. Genesee Hist., 283.

—— Asa T., b. Rehoboth; set. Mich., 1835. Genesee Hist., 283.

—— Experience, m. 1810? David Peckens of N. Y. Washtenaw Port., 405.

—— Isaac, b. Berkshire Co., 1803; set. N. Y., 1811, Mich., 1835. Kalamazoo Hist., opposite 344; Kalamazoo Port., 782.

—— James H., b. Bristol Co., 1822; set. Ill., 1842, Mich., 1879. Allegan Twent., 255.

—— Joshua, set. N. Y.; d. 1849. Genesee Port., 816.

—— Mary, m. John T. Gilman of N. Y.; d. 1866. Genesee Port., 816.

—— Nathan, b. 1770; set. N. Y., 1800? Washtenaw Hist., 817.

PIERCE, Nathan, b. Cheshire, 1790; set. N. Y., 1795, Mich. 1831 or 32. Calhoun, 129; Kalamazoo Port., 315; Washtenaw Hist., 817.

—— Orrin R., b. Cambridge, 1849; set. N. Y., 1850, Mich., 1875. Lenawee Port., 646.

—— Orrison A., b. 1847; set. Mich., 1869. Jackson Hist., 691.

—— Peter, b. Boston; 1812 soldier; set. Penn., 1820? Saginaw Port., 987.

—— Sarah, m. 1810? Joseph Rogers of N. Y. Jackson Port., 394.

PIERSON, Edwin D., b. Richmond, 1819; set. Mich., 1847. Lenawee Port., 675.

—— Franklin D., set. N. Y., 1810. Saginaw Port., 649.

PILLSBURY, Emily E., b. 1815; m. William S. Robinson of N. Y. and Mich. Macomb Port., 216.

PIPER, Giles A., b. Boston, 1840; set. Ill., Mich. Kalamazoo Port., 380.

—— Moses, set. Vt., Mich., 1838. Ingham Hist., 474.

PITCHER, Bathsheba, m. 1810? Thomas Sloan of N. Y. Gratiot, 274.

PITTS, Frances, of Cambridgeport or Charlestown; m. 1836, Charles Merrill of Mich. Detroit, 1220; Wayne Chron., 144.

—— Polly, m. 1812? Peleg Hicks of N. Y. Lenawee Port., 527.

PIXLEY, Benona H., b. Great Barrington, 1808; set. Mich., 1833. Jackson Hist., 905.

—— Laney, b. Barrington, 1793; m. Asa Hewett of N. Y. and Mich. Hillsdale Port., 334, 464.

—— Richard B., b. Great Barrington, 1801; set. Mich., 1836 or 38. Jackson Hist., 162, 905.

PLACEWAY, Joseph, set. N. Y., Mich., 1834; d. 1859. Ingham Port., 847.

PLATT, George W., b. Pittsfield; set. Mich., 1837. Berrien Twent., 151, 364.

—— James M. b. Pittsfield; set. Mich 1850? Berrien Twent., 785.

PLUM, Sarah, m. 1815? Samuel Gill of N. Y. Muskegon Port., 378.

POMEROY, Fanny, b. Southampton; m. 1830? Phineas Strong of N. Y. Kent, 1140.

—— Henry, b. 1786; set. Mich. Washtenaw Hist., 592.

——Silas, b. 1792; set. N. Y. 1820, Mich 1837. Jackson Hist., 1125.

POMROY,Levi, b. 1792; set. N. Y., Mich. Hillsdale Port., 703.

POND, Darius, set. N. H., 1810? Kent, 1285.

POOL, Achish, b. Ashfield, 1776; set. N. Y., 1810. Macomb Hist., 758.

—— Lydia, b. Abington, 1791; m. 1815. Brackley Shaw of Mass., N. Y. and Mich. Lenawee Hist., I, 424; II, 438; Lenawee Port., 237.

—— Marilla, of Savoy; m. 1820? Obediah Bliss of Mass. and N. Y. Grand Rapids Lowell, 699.

—— Olive, m. 1830? Alden Nash of O. and Mich. Kent, 596.

—— William H., b. Ashfield, 1808; set. N. Y., Mich., 1848. Macomb Hist., 758.

POPE, Oliver C., b. Middlesex Co., 1793; set. N. Y., Mich., 1835. Hillsdale Hist., 151; Hillsdale Port., 880.

PORTER, Allen, b. Franklin Co., 1795; set. N. Y., 1806. Lenawee Port., 858.

——Caroline, b. 1808; m. 1832, Job Whitney of O. and Mich. Kent, 633.

—— Jane E., m. 1835? Joseph S. Snow of Mich. Saginaw Port., 668.

—— Seth J., b. Williamstown; set. N. Y., Mich.; d. 1834. Ingham Port., 420.

POTTER, J. M., b. Cheshire, 1839; set. Mich., 1856. Ingham Port., 828.

POWELL, John L., b. 1780; set. N. Y., 1804 or 06. Ionia Hist., 349; Ionia Port., 395.

—— Milo, b. 1808; set. Mich., 1836. Cass Hist., 305.

—— Robert, b. 1791; set. Mich. Washtenaw Hist., 591.

POWER, Arthur, b. Adams, 1771; set. N. Y., 1810? Mich., 1830? Lenawee Hist., I, 522.

PRATT, Aaron, set. N. Y., 1806. Berrien Port., 738.

——Alpheus, b. Sherburne, 1793; set. N. Y., 1819, Mich., 1833. Lenawee Hist., I, 407.

—— Alva, b. Deerfield or Whately, 1796; set. N. Y. 1806; d. 1873. Berrien Port., 738; Washtenaw Port., 523.

—— Charles, b. Cheshire; set. N. Y., 1810? Mich., 1833. Lenawee Hist., II, 435.

—— Daniel L., Plainfield, 1820; set. O., 1830, Mich., 1845. Hillsdale Hist., 115; Hillsdale Port., 872; St. Clair, 120.

—— Eldridge G., b. S. Boston, 1805; set. N. Y., Mich., 1832. Macomb Hist., 599.

—— Elizabeth, b. 1783; m. Joseph Johnson of N. Y. Hillsdale Hist., 294.

—— Henry M., b. S. Framingham, 1842; set. Mich., 1864. Hillsdale Hist., 215.

—— Ira, set. N. Y. Kalamazoo Port., 267.

—— Jacob, b. 1784; set. N. Y., O., 1836, Mich., 1839. Ionia Port., 547.

—— Josiah, Sr., Revolutionary soldier; set. Vt., 1790? Macomb Hist., 708; Macomb Past, 468.

—— Linas, set. N. Y., 1815? Mich. Jackson Port., 325.

—— Lucy, b. Belchertown, 1778; m. Ephraim Converse of Mass. and Mich. Lenawee Port., 1207.

—— Mercy, b. Taunton; m. 1800? Nathaniel Crossman. Calhoun, 133.

—— Naomi, b. 1810? m. Willard Felshaw of N. Y. and Mich. Jackson Port., 325

—— Noah, set. Me., 1835? Newaygo, 321.

—— Wellington H., b. S. Framingham, 1843; set. Mich., 1864. Hillsdale Hist., 215.

—— William, set. O., 1830. Hillsdale Port., 872.

PRAY, Ellen, m. 1810? Joseph Young of N. Y. Shiawassee, 530.

PRESTON, Fowler J., of Whately? set.
Mich., 1829; d. 1843. Berrien Port.,
117; Berrien Twent., 173, 949.

—— John, of Andover, set. Conn., 1810?
Macomb Hist., 709.

PRICHARD, Ephraim, b. Great Barrington, 1790; set. O., Mich. Gratiot, 482.

PRIEST, Laura, b. Nottingham? m. 1840?
Abner G. Pierce of Mass., N. Y. and
Mich. Lenawee Port., 646.

PRIOR, Elizabeth, m. 1845, John Bam-
ber of Mich. Oakland Port., 595.

—— Frederick, b. 1801; set. Mich., 1835.
Oakland Biog., 577.

—— Philo, b. Pittsfield, 1829; set. Mich.,
1835. Oakland Biog., 577.

PROCTER, Benjamin, b. Gloucester, 1767;
set. N. H. Macomb Hist., 835.

PROCTOR, John, b. Groton; set. Vt.,
1820? Kent, 665.

PROUTY, —— b. Worcester Co., 1775;
set. Washington Co., N. Y., 1810?
Macomb Hist., 723.

PULLEN, Lucy, b. 1792; set. Mich. Washtenaw Hist., 592.

PURINTON, Hulda, b. Franklin Co., 1791;
m. Zenas Atwood of N. Y. and Mich.
Ingham Port., 371.

PUTNAM, Albert T., b. Worcester, 1821;
set. Mich., 1841. Jackson Hist., 149.

—— Benjamin W., b. Orange, 1843; set.
Mich., 1865. Kent, 1106.

—— R. W., b. Lowell, 1837; set. Mich.,
1872. Washtenaw Hist., 1226.

PUTNEY, Aaron, b. 1769; set. N. Y. Kalamazoo Port., 264.

QUATERMASS, Richard, set. N. Y., 1810?
Oakland Biog., 141.

QUIMBY, Elizabeth, b. 1797; m. James
H. Gould of N. Y. and Mich. Berrien Port., 679.

RAMSDELL, Gideon, b. Cummington,
1783; set. N. Y., 1800. Lenawee Hist.,
I, 253.

—— Ruth, b. 1801; m. Sylvanus Estes
of Mich. Hillsdale Port., 740.

RAMSEY, Sarah S., of Granville; m. 1847,
J. Austin Scott of Mich. Washtenaw
Hist., 1039.

RAND, Louisa, m. 1825? Rufus Goddard
of N. Y. and Mich. Ionia Hist., 354.

—— Thomas J., b. Charlestown? 1806;
set. Mich., 1849. Muskegon Hist.,
facing 73.

RANDALL, Isaac, set. N. Y., 1810? Saginaw Port., 978.

—— Mehitabel, m. 1820? Seth Robinson
of Mass. and O. Gratiot, 542.

—— Snow, b. Hanover, 1754; set. Vt.
Branch Port., 637.

RANKIN, Otis, set. Mich., 1836. St.
Clair, 727.

RANNEY, Ebenezer, set. N. Y., 1800?
Kalamazoo Port., 609.

—— Edwin, set. N. Y., 1840? Mich., 1854.
Newaygo, 192.

—— George, set. N. Y., 1833; d. 1842.
Hillsdale Port., 871.

—— Hannah, b. 1782; m. Abiather Phillips of N. Y. Hillsdale Port., 665.

—— Joel, b. Ashfield; set. N. Y., Mich.,
1877. Ingham Hist., 182; Ingham
Port., 226.

—— Lucius, b. Ashfield, 1819; set. N.
Y., Mich., 1842. Hillsdale Port., 871.

—— Lucretia, b. Ashfield or Buckland,
1819; m. 1837, Darius Cross of Mich.
Lenawee Hist. II, 310; Lenawee Illns.,
383; Lenawee Port., 1025.

—— Mary, b. Ashfield; m. 1835? Augustus F. Daniels of Mich. Lenawee
Port., 362.

—— Sarah S., b. E. Granville, 1826; m.
J. Austin Scott of N. Y. and Mich.
Washtenaw Past, 121.

RANSOM, Epaphroditus, b. Hampshire
Co., 1799; set. Vt., Mich., 1833 or 37.
Governor. Berrien Hist., 132; Branch
Port., 125; Kalamazoo Hist., 117.

RASH, George, b. 1788; set. Mich., 1824.
Washtenaw Hist., 875.

RATHBUN, Hiram, set. N. Y., 1815?
Shiawassee, 209.

RAWSON, Elias, from near Boston; set.
Mich., 1830. Kalamazoo Hist., 508.

—— Theodore, set. Mich., 1840? Lenawee Port., 649, 684.

RAY, George, b. Great Barrington, 1819; set. O., 1832; Mich., 1855. Traverse, 246.

RAYMOND, Mary, m. Aaron Rood of Vt. and Mich. Genesee Port., 351.

READ, Ainsworth, set. Mich., 1840? Clinton Past, 152.

—— Titus R., b. Peru; set. N. Y., Mich. Berrien Port., 349; Cass Hist., 176.

REDDINGTON, Teresa, m. 1840 Addison Tracy of O. and Mich.; d. 1872. Grand Rapids City, 292.

REDINGTON, Nathaniel, set. O., 1825? Mich., 1844. Ionia Port., 221.

REED, Abigail, b. near Boston, 1784; m. 1807 Elisha Cranson of N. Y. and Mich. Washtenaw Port., 419.

—— Ainsworth, set. Mich., 1850? Clinton Past, 486.

—— Amasa, set. Ill., 1840? Washtenaw Port., 499.

—— Bethuel, set. N. Y., 1840, Ind. Clinton Past, 374.

—— Daniel W., b. Chesterfield; set. N. Y., 1845. Allegan Twent., 116.

—— Isaac, set. Canada, 1820? Mecosta, 192.

—— Joseph B., b. 1807; set. Mich. 1836. Jackson Hist., 889.

—— Lydia M., b. Wendell, 1794; m. 1814 Obadiah Rogers of Mass. and Mich. Lenawee Hist. I, 168; II, 247.

—— Martha A., of Yarmouth; m. 1835? James F. Joy of Mich. Detroit, 1062.

—— William, b. near Boston, 1805; set. Mich., 1830? Ionia Hist., 190.

REESE, Jacob, b. W. Stockbridge; set. N. Y. Berrien Port., 704.

REMMELE, Hannah, m. 1805? Linus Clarke of N. Y. Jackson Hist., 611.

RENIFF, Naomi, b. 1790; set. N. Y., 1811; m. William Minor of O. Lenawee Hist., I, 421.

REYNOLDS, Joshua, b. Berkshire Co., Revolutionary soldier; set. Vt., N. Y. Saginaw Port., 750.

RHEA, Thomas A., b. Dartmouth, 1823; set. N. Y., Mich., 1868. Monroe, appendix, 47.

RICE, Abel, b. Worcester; set. Vt., 1759. Jackson Port., 726.

—— Adonijah, b. Worcester; set. Vt.; d. 1802. Jackson Port., 726.

—— Clark, set. N. Y., Mich., 1840. Gratiot, 207.

—— Elizabeth, b. Boston; m. 1850 Henry C. Lacy of Mich. Clinton Past, 124.

—— Erastus, b. Franklin Co., 1811; set. O., Mich. Branch Port., 199.

—— Gershom, b. 1805; set. Mich., 1835. Mecosta, 322.

—— Joseph, Jr., b. Conway, 1780; set. N. Y., 1802, Mich., 1845. Lenawee Port., 598.

—— Lucy, m. 1800? Washington Moore of N. Y. Washtenaw Hist., 1432.

—— Lucy, of Conway, m. 1806 William Moore of N. Y. and Mich. Wayne Chron., 253.

—— M. H., b. Concord? set. Wis., Mich. 1849. Northern P., 479.

—— Nancy M., b. Brookfield, 1828; m. 1851 Stanley G. Wight of Mich. Wayne Chron., 170.

—— Paul, of Boston, set. Mich., 1840? Clinton Past, 124.

—— Sarah, b. E. Sudbury, 1801; m. Calvin P. Frost of N. Y. and Mich. Jackson Port., 856.

—— Serepta, m. J. L. Root of O. Hillsdale Port., 667.

RICE, Sophia, b. Conway, 1809; m. 1827 Chauncy M. Stebbins of Mich. Ionia Port., 312.

—William, set. O., 1820? Genesee Port., 1049.

RICH, Charles, b. 1771; set. Vt., 1785; member of Congress. Genesee Port., 1047.

—— Charles W., set. Me., 1840? O. 1864. Osceola, 196.

—— Estes, set. Mich., 1831. Calhoun, 176.

——Thomas, of Warwick, set. Vt., 1785. Genesee Port., 215, 927.

RICHARDS, Daniel W., b. Amherst, 1829; set. N. Y., Mich., 1844. Genesee Hist., 352; Genesee Port., 927.

—— James, set. O., 1850? Mich. Mecosta, 392.

—— Lena of Springfield, m. 1872 James W. Caldwell of Mich. Detroit, 1398.

—— Willard, set. N. Y., Mich., 1844. Genesee Port., 927.

—— Willard, b. Framingham, 1806; set. N. Y., Mich., 1854. Hillsdale Port., 333.

——William, set. N. Y., Mich., 1844. Genesee Hist., 312.

RICHARDSON, —— b. Attleboro, May 13, 1746; set. N. H. Kent, 713.

——Ebenezer, set. N. Y., 1820? O. 1836. Newaygo, 298.

—— Jared, set. N. Y., 1810? Jackson Hist., 1055.

—— Lusanah, of Cummington; m. 1790? Obadiah Hamilton of Mass. and N. Y. Lenawee Hist. II, 237; Lenawee Port., 399.

—— Thomas, set. Canada, 1840? Midland, 192.

RICHMOND, Betsey, b. Dalton, 1798; m. William C. Smith of N. Y. and Mich. Hillsdale Port., 877; Lenawee Hist. II, 289.

—— James, set. N. Y., 1815? Canada. Kent, 1382.

—— Jonathan, set. N. Y., 1810? member of Congress. Washtenaw Hist., 1035.

RICHMOND, Rebecca, b. Dighton; m. 1812? Daniel Foster of N. Y., O., and Mich. Hillsdale Port., 845.

—— William, of Westport, set. N. Y., 1907. Grand River, appendix, 57.

RIGGS, Susan, b. 1820? m. Manford Felton of Mich. Gratiot, 352.

RILEY, H. H., b. Great Barrington, 1813; set. Mich. 1842. St. Clair, 124.

RING, E. J., b. Hampden Co., 1824; set. O., 1857, Mich., 1865. Saginaw Hist., 691.

RIPLEY, Abner, b. Plymouth Co.; set N. Y. 1810? Saginaw Hist., 692.

—— William K., set. Me., 1850? Saginaw Port., 529.

RISING, Oliver, set. O., 1820? Kent. 713.

ROBBINS, John, set. N. Y., 1830? Mich. Gratiot, 181.

—— John A., b. Pittsfield; set. N. Y., 1825? Mich., 1855. Ionia Port., 198.

—— Lucy, b. 1802; m. Samuel D. Kenney of Canada. Kalamazoo Port., 341.

——Milton B., set. Mich., 1836. Cass Hist., 267.

—— Wendell Phillips, b. Barnstable Co., 1851; set. Mich., 1869. Berrien Port., 147.

ROBERTS, Polly A., b. Berkshire Co., 1821; m. 1845 Jesse B. Odell of Pa. and Mich. Lenawee Port., 601.

——Zenas, set. Pa., 1830? Lenawee Port., 601.

ROBIE, Mary G., of Salem; m. 1837 David L. Osborne of Mich. St. Clair, 589.

ROBINSON, Bartlett, b. 1776; set. N. Y., 1810? Lenawee Port., 432.

—— Eliza H., b. Falmouth, 1807; m. Thomas J. Tasker of Mass. Saginaw Port., 942.

——Fanny W. b. Plainfield, 1824; m. Levi G. White of Mich. Gratiot, 543.

—— Gain, b. Clark's Island or Hardwick, 1765 or 1771; set. N. Y., 1800? Lenawee Hist. I, 379, 524; Lenawee Port., 1103.

—— Hiram B., b. Springfield, 1823; set. Mich., 1852? Branch Twent., 659.

ROBINSON, Jeremiah A., b. Concord, 1812; set. O., 1852, Mich., 1858. Jackson Hist., 700; Jackson Port., 305.

—— John, b. 1805; set. N. Y., 1824, Mich., 1836; d. 1854. Kalamazoo Port., 429.

—— Joshua N., set. O., 1840? Gratiot, 378.

—— Nahum, 1812 soldier; set. Pa. Branch Port., 443.

—— Peleg, set. N. Y.., 1795? Jackson Hist., 1153.

—— Robert, b. Duxbury, 1762; set. N. Y., 1800? Lenawee Hist. II, 89.

—— Seth, of Plainfield; set. O., 1830? Gratiot, 543.

ROBY, E. A., b. Middlesex Co., 1811; set. Wis., Mich. Kent, 1343.

ROCKWELL, *Deacon*, b. Sandisfield, 1800? set. Mich. Kalamazoo Port., 313.

ROCKWOOD, Garrett, b. Conway, 1795; set. N. Y., O. Genesee Port., 625.

—— Reuben, set. N. Y., 1815? Midland, 234.

RODGERS, Frank A., b. Sandwich, 1849; set. Maine, 1859, Mich., 1880. Grand Rapids City, 368; Grand Rapids Hist., 788.

—— George H., set. Me., 1859. Grand Rapids City, 368.

ROE, Mehitable, b. 1787; m. Nathaniel Green of O. Newaygo, 369.

ROGERS, Chris. W., b. Petersham, 1847; set. Mo. Lenawee Hist. I, 472.

—— Dwight, b. Hardwick, 1818; set. Mich., 1832. Lenawee Hist. II, 247.

—— Edward T., b. Petersham, 1845; set. Mo. Lenawee Hist. I, 472.

—— Elona, b. Colerain, 1805; m. 1828 Alvin Cross of Mich. Washtenaw Hist., 449.

—— Isaac, set. N. Y., 1800? O. Jackson Hist., 925.

—— James, set. Mich.; d. 1846. Lenawee Illus., 412.

—— James, b. Ashfield, 1815? set. Mich., 1830? O. Lenawee Illus., 285; Lenawee Port., 915.

—— Jesse, b. Dana, 1808; set. Mich., 1850? Lenawee Hist. I, 472.

ROGERS, Margaret, b. Dartmouth, 1788; m. Benjamin Slade of N. Y. and Mich. Lenawee Hist., II, 275.

—— Mary, of Ipswich; m. Abiel Foster of N. H. (b. 1735). Berrien Port., 886.

—— Mary A., b. Hardwick, 1816; m. 1834 George Colvin of Mich. Lenawee Hist. I, 305.

—— Obadiah, b. Dana, 1792; set. Mich., 1832. Lenawee Hist. I, 167, 305; II, 247.

—— Samuel, b. near Boston, 1773; set. N. Y., 1797. Lenawee Hist. II, 330.

—— Thomas, of Colerain; set. N. Y., 1809, O., 1816. Washtenaw Hist., 449.

ROOD, Aaron, set. Vt., Mich., 1826; d. 1854. Genesee Port., 350.

—— Edward A., b. 1840; set. Mich., 1861. Berrien Hist., 438.

—— Ezra, set. Vt., Mich., 1823. Kent, 687.

—— Ezra, set. Vt., Mich., 1861. Berrien Hist., 438.

—— Josiah F., from Buckland. Berrien Hist., 438.

—— Moses; Revolutionary soldier; set. Vt. Genesee Port., 351.

ROOT, Daniel, set. N. Y., 1815, Mich., 1835. Jackson Hist., 836.

—— Joan, b. Stockbridge, 1780; m. 1803 Stephen Ingersoll of N. Y. and Mich. Lenawee Hist., II, 358; Lenawee Port., 743.

—— Mary, m. 1820? Silas Pierce of N. Y. Grand Rapids City, 356.

—— Pliny, b. Ludlow, 1785; set. N. Y., Mich. Jackson Hist., 1109.

—— Timothy, b. 1760? set. Mich. Jackson Hist., 1109.

—— William, b. Ludlow, 1816; set. N. Y., Mich., 1836. Jackson Hist., 149, 1109.

ROSE, Nathan, b. 1783; set. N. Y., 1790? Macomb Hist., 835.

—— Samuel, b. Granville, 1817; set. N. Y., 1827, Mich., 1836. Grand River, 439; Newaygo, 423.

ROSS, A. Hastings, b. Winchendon, 1831; set. O., Mich. St. Clair, 592.

Ross, Rowena, m. 1825? Orin Babcock of N. Y. Midland, 234.

—— Tamar, b. Worcester Co.; m. 1805? Ebenezer Brooks of Vt. Macomb Hist., 691.

Rounds, David C., b. Dartmouth, 1836; set. Mich., 1861. Gratiot, 238.

—— Richard A., b. Leyden; set. N. Y., Mich. Kent, 1302.

Rounseville, Benjamin, set. N. Y., 1800? Ingham Port., 833.

Rowland, Almira, m. 1830? Henry Harmon of N. Y. and Mich. Kalamazoo Port., 943.

Roys, J. E., b. 1824; set. Mich., 1855. Kent. 1269.

—— Myron, b. Sheffield, 1808; set. Mich., 1833. Kent, 261, 1422.

—— Norman, b. Sheffield, 1807; set. Mich., 1831. St. Joseph, 136.

Rude, Mary F., m. 1831 William Packard of Mich. Berrien Hist., facing 434.

Rundel, Warren, set. Conn., Pa., Mich., 1840? Oakland Port., 200.

Rundell, James, set. N. Y., 1830? Mich., 1840. Saginaw Port., 663.

Runyan, Silas, b. W. Stockbridge; set. N. Y., 1810? O. Gratiot, 381.

Rush, Justin, Revolutionary soldier; set. N. Y. Ionia Port., 350.

—— Orissa, b. 1800? m. Delonza Turner or N. Y. and Mich. Hillsdale Port., 539.

—— Samuel F., b. Cheshire; set. N. Y.; d. 1865. Hillsdale Port., 091.

Russ, Nathaniel, b. Salem; set. N. Y., 1830? Mich., 1836. Lenawee Hist. I, 261.

Russell, Ainsworth T., b. Townsend, 1811; set. Mich., 1861. Bay Hist., 205.

—— Elihu, of Franklin Co., set. N. Y., 1818. Ionia Hist., 319.

—— Esteven, b. Sunderland, 1817; set. N. Y., 1818, Mich., 1843. Ionia Hist., 320.

—— Hannah, b. 1815? m. John Brooks of O. Gratiot, 598.

—— Howland, set. N. Y., 1800? Genesee Port., 557.

Russell, John, set. N. Y., 1825? Mich., 1835. Jackson Hist., 955.

—— Mary R.. b. Nantucket; m. 1868 Isaac W. Wood of Mich. Kent, 1175.

—— Miriam, m. 1820? Ashley Smith of N. Y. Gratiot, 683.

—— Newton, b. 1801; set. N. Y. Hillsdale Port., 900.

—— William S., b. Sunderland, 1807; set. N. Y., Mich. Wayne Chron., 345.

Rust, Angeline, b. Northampton; m. 1825 Abel French of N. Y. Ionia Hist., 440.

—— Justin, see Rush, Justin.

Ryan, Maria L., b. Milford; m. 1880 John F. Skinner of Mich. Clinton Past., 320.

—— Will E., b. Adams, 1867; set. Mich. Grand Rapids City, 372; Grand Rapids Hist, 782.

Ryder, Polly, m. 1820? William O. Marshall of O. and Wis. Lenawee Port., 1088.

Ryther, Elkanah, b. 1795; set. Canada, Mich., 1838. Berrien Port., 247.

Sabin, Rhoda, m. 1825? Younglove C. Carpenter of N. Y. and Mich. St. Joseph, 85.

—— Ziba, b. 1784; set. N. Y. Allegan Hist., 291.

Sackett, Lemuel, Jr., b. Pittsfield, 1808; set. N. Y., 1822, Mich., 1829. Macomb Hist., 601; Macomb Past, 608.

Saddler, Seth C., b. Ashfield, 1809; set. N. Y., Mich., 1831. Genesee Hist., 231.

Sage, Eliza, m. 1840 Daniel Harris of N. Y. Ingham Port., 621.

Salmon, Caroline, m. 1825? Nathaniel Redington of O. and Mich. Ionia Port., 221.

Sampson, Caleb, b. 1781; set. Mich. Washtenaw Hist., 590.

—— Miss E. L., of Lakeville; m. 1859 James S. P. Hatheway of Mich. Macomb Hist., 908.

Samson, George W., b. 1781; set. N. Y. Berrien Port., 250.

SAMSON, Horatio G., b. Kingston, 1812; set. Mich., 1836. Berrien Port., 250.

SANDERSON, David, b. 1805? set. N. Y., 1806, O., 1834, Mich., 1850. Macomb Past, 268.

―― Elnathan, b. 1776; set. N. Y., 1806. Macomb Past, 268.

―― Pliny, set. N. Y., 1820? O., 1836, Mich. Clinton Port., 776.

―― William, b. Franklin Co., 1809; set. Mich., 1830. Washtenaw Hist., 1449.

―― Zimri, set. Mich., 1830. Washtenaw Port., 608.

SANDFORD, J. M., b. S. Westport, 1811; set. Mich., 1835. Jackson Hist., 869.

SANFORD, Frank, of Boston; bought land in Mich., 1837. Allegan Hist., 269.

SANGER, Chloe, b. 1797; m. John B. Brockelbank of N. Y. Lenawee Port., 573.

―― Laoidea, m. 1825? Henry Hubbard of Mass. and O. Ionia Port., 705.

SARGEANT, James F., b. Boston, 1829; set. Mich., 1836. Kent, 1118.

―― Nathaniel O., set. Mich., 1835. Grand Rapids Hist., 170; Grand Rapids Lowell, 102.

―― Thomas, from Boston; set. Mich., 1835? Grand Rapids Hist., 177.

―― Thomas S., b. Malden, 1831; set. Mich., 1836. Kent, 1118.

SARGENT, Ann, b. Templeton, 1771; m. Asa Woolson of Vt. Bay Gansser, 501.

―― Nancy, b. Pittsfield, 1836; m. 1855 Moses B. Marsh of Mich. Midland, 263.

SAUNDERS, James B., b. W. Harwich, 1844; set. Mich., 1857. Washtenaw Past, 79.

―― Thorndike P., b. Bedford, 1810; set. N. Y., Mich., 1857. Washtenaw Past, 79.

SAVAGE, John, b. Salem, 1788; set. N. Y., 1788, Mich., 1840. Cass Hist., 405; Cass Twent., 84.

SAVERY, George C., set. N. Y., 1840? Washtenaw Port., 359.

―― Isaac, set. N. Y., 1848. Washtenaw Port., 544.

SAVERY, Isaac P., b. 1838; set. N. Y., 1848, Mich., 1859. Washtenaw Port., 544.

SAWTELL, Levi, b. near Boston; set. N. Y., 1800? Lenawee Illus., 76.

SAWYER, Albert E., b. Charlemont, 1820; set. O., 1850, Mich. Osceola, 295.

―― Amanda P., b. Egremont, 1813; m. Camp Kelley of N. Y. and Mich. Hillsdale Port., 661.

―― Caleb, b. 1811; set. N. Y., Mich., 1834. Ingham Port., 639.

―― Holloway, b. Harvard, 1827; set. Mich., 1849. Monroe, appendix, 32.

―― Sarah, b. 1784; m. Richard Bryan of Mass. and Mich. Hillsdale Port., 410.

SCOTT, Jesse, b. Chester, 1818; set. Mich., 1831. Washtenaw Hist., 506, 735.

―― Joseph E., set. N. Y., Mich., 1845. Kalamazoo Port., 984.

―― Lemuel S., of Cheshire, b. 1790; set. Mich., 1831. Ionia Hist., 465; Washtenaw Hist., 590, 735.

―― Nathan B., b. Cheshire, 1825; set. Mich., 1830. Ionia Hist., 461.

―― Olive, m. 1825? Chauncy Crittendon of Mass., and N. Y. Kalamazoo Port., 825.

―― Samuel b. Berkshire Co.; set. N. Y., 1814. Newaygo, 277.

SCOVEL, Lois, b. Berkshire Co.; m. 1810? David S. Walker of N. Y. and Mich. Lenawee Hist. I, 518.

SCUDDEL, Eliza H., of Hyannis; m. 1871 N. Cordary of Mich. Washtenaw Hist., 1199.

SEARS, Achsah, m. 1810? George Ranney of N. Y. Hillsdale Port., 871.

―― Carrie, b. Greenwich, 1800; m. John G. Clark of N. Y. Ingham Port., 389.

―― Hannah M., b. W. Hawley, 1839; m. Benjamin Wing of Mich. Isabella, 498.

―― John, set. Me., 1800? Branch Port., 352.

―― Mary Ann, b. Ashfield, 1813; m. 1831 Abraham Moe of Mich. Lenawee Hist. II, 149.

SEARS, Peter, b. Ashfield, 1787; set. Mich., 1826 or 1827. Lenawee Hist. II, 149; Washtenaw Hist., 646; Washtenaw Past, 806; Washtenaw Port., 340.

—— Rhoda, b. Yarmouth, 1771; m. —— Smith of N. Y. Macomb Hist., 763.

—— Richard, b. 1775; set. Conn., N. Y.; d. 1829. Lenawee Hist. II, 271; Lenawee Port., 645.

——Roxana, m. 1810? Austin Lilly of Mass. and O. Kalamazoo Port., 327.

—— Solomon F., b. Ashfield, 1816; set. Mich., 1827. Washtenaw Hist., 506, 665; Washtenaw Port., 340.

—— *Mrs.* Sophia J., b. 1792; set. Mich., 1837; d. 1879. Washtenaw Hist., 488.

—— Thomas, b. Ashfield; set. N. Y., 1820? Mich., 1837. Washtenaw Hist., 818; Washtenaw Port., 228.

—— Thomas, b. Peru, 1827; set. Mich., 1837. Washtenaw Hist., 818.

—— William, b. Ashfield, 1818; set. N. Y., Va., Mich., 1857. Grand Rapids Lowell, 493.

SEAVER, William, of Lowell; set Mich., 1858. Allegan Hist., 366.

SECOY, Phebe, m. Samuel Sprague of O. Gratiot, 389.

SEEKELS, Jerusha, b. Ashfield; m. 1830? David Taylor of O. Genesee Hist., 391.

SEEKINS, Diadama, m. 1810? Daniel Smith of N. Y. Washtenaw Port., 389.

SEELEY, Minerva, of Berkshire Co.; m. 1820 Ira R Paddock of N. Y. and Mich. Branch Port., 454.

SERGEANT Gennett, b. 1822; m. Ethan H. Rice of Mich. Jackson Hist., 699.

—— James, b. Boston, 1831; set. Mich., 1836. Kent, 263.

——Nathaniel O., see Sargeant.

——Richard B., set. N. Y., 1815? Clinton Port., 752.

SESSIONS, George, b. S. Wilbraham, 1784; set. N. Y., Mich., 1833 or 1834. Washtenaw Hist., 646; Washtenaw Port., 451.

SESSIONS, Orrin F., set. Vt., 1820? Kent, 752.

SEVERANCE, Sarah J., b. Rockport, 1854; m. 1875 Owen F. Teeples of Mich., Sanilac, 434.

—— W. D., of Franklin Co., b. 1812; set Mich., 1835. Jackson Hist., 1029.

SEXTON Hannah, m. 1810? Dan Monroe of N. Y. Newaygo, 437.

——Martha, m. 1790? Ephraim Hutchisson of N. Y. Jackson Hist., 832.

SEYMOUR, Hannah, b. 1787; set. Mich. Washtenaw Hist., 590.

—— Lovica C. b. Hadley, 1814; m. 1834 Edwin Cook of N. Y. and Mich. Lenawee Port., 353.

SHACKLETON, Thomas, b. Lowell, 1841; set. Canada, 1843, Mich., 1873. Macomb Hist., 603.

SHADDUCK, Roxania, b. near Boston, 1800; m. 1800 Joseph Camburn of N. Y. and Mich. Lenawee Hist. I, 412.

SHATTUCK, Alfred, b. 1794; set. N. Y., Mich., 1832. Oakland Port., 438.

—— Charles A., b. Leyden, 1815; set. N. Y., Wis., Mich. Hillsdale Port., 923.

—— Mary, b. Colerain, 1795? m. Ira Donelson of Mich. Oakland Biog., 174.

—— Roland, set. N. Y., 1830? Clinton Port., 446.

—— Samuel Dwight, b. Chesterfield, 1811; set. N. Y., Mich., 1832. Macomb Hist., 834, 884, 896; Macomb Past, 245.

SHAW, Addison C., set. O., Mich., 1846. Branch Port., 395.

—— Brackley, b. Abington, 1790; set. N. Y., 1825, Mich., 1835. Lenawee Hist. I, 424; II. 437; Lenawee Port., 237.

—— Brackley, b. Plainfield, 1818; set. N. Y., 1825, Mich., 1835. Lenawee Hist. I, 424; Lenawee Port., 238.

—— Ebenezer, 1812 soldier; set. Canada. Ingham Port., 836.

—— Hannah, b. Middleboro, 1782; m. George W. Samson of N. Y. Berrien Port., 250.

Shaw, Humphrey, b. Westport, 1809; set. Mich., 1837. Saginew Port., 564.

—— James, set. O., 1840? Ionia Port., 717.

——Lyanda, b. Worthington, 1813; m. 1831 Alonzo Mitchell of Mich. Lenawee Port., 286.

—— Persis, m. 1825? Solomon Cowles of N. Y., Canada and Mich. Ionia Port., 346.

——Philip, b. 1770; 1812 soldier; set. N. Y., 1815? Mich., 1830. Oakland Biog., 668.

—— Philip, b. Dighton, 1781; set. N. Y., Mich., 1829. Oakland Hist., 322.

—— Sarah, of Lanesboro, m. 1832 David A. Noble of Mich. Monroe, 250.

——Silena M., m. 1833, Norton D. Warner of Mich. Lenawee Hist. J, 352.

Shearer, James M., b. Colerain, 1815 or 1817; set. Vt., Mich., 1849. Ingham Port., 810; St. Clair, 123.

—— Jonathan, b. Colerain, 1796; set. N. Y., 1822 or 1824, Mich., 1836. Ionia Hist., 394; St. Clair, 119; Wayne Chron., 79, 189.

——Lydia, b. Ashfield, 1818; set. Mich. St. Clair, 123.

—— Maria, m. 1847, D. G. Jones of N. Y. and Mich. St. Clair, 715.

Shedd, Sylvester, b. 1786; 1812 soldier; set. N. Y., Mich., 1836. Berrien Port., 549; Berrien Twent., 882.

Sheffield, Joseph H., b. Worcester, 1861; set. Mich., 1884. Muskegon Port., 165.

Shepard, James M., b. N. Brookfield, 1840; set. Mich., 1868. Berrien Port., 288. Cass Hist., 180; Cass Twent., 557.

—— Joseph, b. 1779; set. N. Y. Berrien Port., 673.

—— Mary A., m. 1800? Augustus Greenman of N. Y. Shiawassee, facing 284.

Shepherd, Dexter, see Cutler.

Sheridan, Owen, b. Middlesex, 1827; set. Wis., 1851, Mich., 1855. Upper P., 310.

Sherman, Abram, 1812 soldier; set. N. Y., 1820? Oakland Port., 556.

Sherman, Daniel, set. Mich., 1832. Shiawasee, 523.

—— Electa, of Lanesboro; m. 1803 Daniel Loomis of Mass. and N. Y. Lenawee Hist. I, 123.

——Elizabeth, m. 1830? John Swick of Mich. Hillsdale Port., 755.

—— Jarrah, set. N. Y., 1830? Jackson Port., 753.

—— Lydia, of Berkshire Co.; m. 1815? Caleb Beals of N. Y. and Mich. Lenawee Port., 214, 844.

——Mary, b. Grafton, 1725? m. 1748 John Cooper, of Hardwick. Branch Port., 614.

—— P. L., b. New Bedford, 1844; set. Mich., 1879. Bay Hist., 274.

—— Timothy, of Lanesboro; set. O., 1812. Lenawee Hist. I, 123.

Sherwood, Lucinda, m. 1825? Rufus Herrick of N. Y. and Mich. Ingham Port., 619.

Shipton, Charles, b. Sternville, 1860; set. Mich., 1868. Detroit, 1390.

Short, Hopy, b. 1768; m. James Green of N. Y.. Oakland Port., 839.

—— Lucinda, m. 1800? Isaac Bishop of N. Y. Macomb Hist., 646.

—— Naomi, m. 1800? John Norton of N. Y. and Mich; d. 1825? Kent, 1342; Oakland Biog., 164; Oakland Hist., 151.

Shumway, Levi, b. Belchertown, 1788; set. N. Y., 1804, Mich., 1829. Branch Hist., 246; Branch Port., 622; Lenawee Hist. I, 270.

—— Sally, b. 1787; m. Amariah Bemis of Conn. Oakland Port., 349.

Shurtleff, Selah, of Montgomery; set. O., d. 1861. Branch Port., 403, 540.

Shurwin, A. S., Revolutionary soldier; set. O. Muskegon Port., 347.

Sibley, Alvah, b. Berkshire, 1796; set. N. Y., 1817, Mich., 1835. Macomb Hist., 710.

——John, set. N. Y., 1810? Clinton Past., 288.

——Solomon, b. Sutton, 1769; set. O., 1796, Mich. Detroit, 1031; Wayne Land., 364.

SIKES, Orrento Montague, b. Westhampton, 1815; set. Mich., 1837. Berrien Hist., 485.

——Zenas, b. Westhampton; set. Mich., 1837. Berrien Hist., 478.

SILCOX, *Mrs.* E., set. Mich., 1854. Wayne Chron., 84.

SILLIMAN, Amanda A. m. 1850? John Doud of O. Newaygo, 223.

SIMMONS, Ephraim, set. N. Y., 1800? Clinton Port., 524.

—— I., set. Mich., 1824. Wayne Chron., 75.

——Joshua, b. Dighton, 1801; set. N. Y., 1801, Mich., 1824 or 1825. Oakland Biog., 411; Oakland Hist., 332; Oakland Port., 208, 602.

SIMONS, Marion, of Salem; b. 1850? m. Robert W. Lonsdale of Mich. Mecosta, 497.

SINES, Isaac, b. Berkshire, 1798; set. Mich., 1824. Washtenaw Hist., 506.

SIZER, Adelia S., Sheffield, 1830; m. 1849 Henry A. Angell of Mich. Lenawee Illus., 341; Lenawee Port., 393.

—— Charles F., b. Chester, 1833; set. Mich., 1859. Lenawee Illus., 87.

—— Emma I., b. Lee, 1853; m. 1875 Walter S. Westerman of Mich. Lenawee Illus., 86.

SKINNER, Elias, b. Shelburne; set. N. Y. Genesee Hist., 351.

—— Hannah, m. 1830? Stillman Montague of N. Y. Branch Twent., 717.

——Harriet, of Williamstown; b. 1795? m. Austin E. Wing of Mich. Monroe, 151.

—— Mary H., b. Roxbury, 1807; m. 1824 Ebenezer Davis of Mass., N. Y. and Mich. Lenawee Hist. II, 131.

SLADE, Benjamin, b. Dartmouth, 1782; set. N. Y., Mich., 1835. Lenawee Hist. II, 275.

—— Lavina D., b. Chelsea; m. 1855 John Whittemore of Mass. and Mich. Kent, 1167.

—— Phebe, b. Fall River; m. 1804 John Hoxie of N. Y. and Mich. Lenawee Port., 1217.

SLADE, Sarah, b. Uxbridge, m. 1850? John Foss of Conn. and R. I. Bay Gansser, 698.

SLATER, Leonard, b. Worcester, 1802; set. Mich., 1826 or 1827. Grand Rapids Hist., 78; Grand Rapids Lowell, 51; Kalamazoo Hist., 286; Kent, 192, 800.

SLAYTON, Reuben, b. 1769; set. N. Y. Lenawee Port., 431.

——Russell, b. Worcester, 1798; set. N. Y., 1820, Mich., 1845 or 1846. Grand Rapids City, 1015; Kent, 773.

SLOAN, James, b. Townsend; set. Vt., 1800? Lenawee Hist. II, 241.

—— Thomas, set. N. Y., 1810? Gratiot, 274.

SLOCUM, Benjamin, b. 1786; set. N. Y., 1810, Mich., 1825. Lenawee Hist., II, 142.

—— Smith, b. Berkshire Co., 1787; set. N. Y., 1816. Hillsdale Hist., 199.

SLOSSON, Ozias J., b. Great Barrington, 1805; set. N. Y., Mich., 1856. Osceola, 223.

SMALLEY, Rufus, set. N. Y., 1790? Vt. Jackson Port., 232.

SMEAD, Elizabeth, b. 1817; m. 1842 Ebenezer Fisk of Mich. Lenawee Port., 335.

——Lavina, m. 1833 John A. Hawks of Mich. Lenawee Port., 255.

——Rufus, b. Montague or Sheburne, 1757; set. N. Y., 1800? Mich., 1834. Lenawee Hist., I, 337; Lenawee Illus., 124; Lenawee Port., 255, 335, 434.

SMEDLEY, Lois, m. 1830? John B. Clark of Mich. Clinton Port., 651.

—— Sallie, m. 1830? Silas O. Hunter of N. Y. Muskegon Port., 267.

SMITH, —— b. Ashfield, Apr. 6, 1770; set. N. Y., 1812. Macomb Hist., 762.

—— ——b. Adams, 1783; m. John Tibbits of N. Y. and Mich. Branch Port., 629.

—— Achsah, b. Chicopee; m. 1800? Levi Chapin of N. Y. and Mich. Ingham Hist., 317.

—— Alice, b. Salem; m. James Marble of Ind. Berrien Port., 707.

SMITH, Asa, set. Mich., 1854. Macomb Hist., 712.

—— Asa L., b. Boston, 1792; set. Mich., 1825? Washtenaw Hist., 894, 1040.

—— Ashley, set. N. Y., 1828. Gratiot, 683.

——Austin, of Hampden Co., bought land in Mich., 1814. Allegan Hist., 293.

—— Chipman, b. Ashfield, 1817; set. Mich., 1875. Washtenaw Hist., 1271.

—— Clarissa, b. 1802; m. 1827 James B. Arms of Mich. Washtenaw Hist., 1451.

—— Daniel, b. 1790? set. N. Y., 1810? Washtenaw Port., 389.

—— David B., b. Worcester Co., 1836; set. Mich., 1842. Saginaw Hist., 831.

—— Dean Uriel, b. Buckland; set. N. Y., 1820? Macomb Hist., 883.

—— Dollie, of Shrewsbury; m. 1787 William Hobart of Mass. and N. Y. Jackson Port., 604.

—— Eaton, set. N. Y., 1815? Mich., 1840? O. Jackson Port., 222.

—— Edward, b. Walpole, 1830; set. Mich., 1842. Saginaw Port., 706.

—— Edward C., of Hadley; set. N. Y., 1844; d. 1847. Oakland Biog., 426.

—— Elijah, b. Ware, 1772; set. Vt., N. Y., Mich. Kalamazoo Hist., 423.

——Elisha, b. Amherst; set. Mich., 1836. St. Clair, 683.

—— Elizabeth, m. 1856 John B. Dumont of Mich. Kalamazoo Port., 728.

—— Emeline P., m. 1857 George W. Carlton, of Mich. St. Clair, 671.

—— Ephraim, Revolutionary soldier, set. Conn., 1800? N. Y. Clinton Port., 809.

—— Eugene, b. Amherst, 1821; set. Mich., 1836. St. Clair, 683.

SMITH, Eunice, m. 1800? Joshua Parmalee of N. Y. Hillsdale Port., 766.

—— Ezekiel, set. Vt., 1788, N. Y. Lansing, 160.

—— George H., of N. Amherst; set. Mich., 1837. Calhoun, 137; Jackson Port., 451.

—— Gilbert, set. N. Y., 1845? Midland, 288.

—— Hannah, b. N. Adams, 1783; m. Gideon Ramsdell of Mass and N. Y. Lenawee Hist. I, 254; Lenawee Port., 637.

——Henry, b. Worcester, 1798; set. N. Y., 1803, Mich., 1833. Lenawee Illus., 272.

——*Henry O., b. Hatfield, 1817; set Mich., 1852. Macomb Hist., 672

—— Jabez, b. 1766; set. Canada, 1800? Jackson Hist., 1019.

—— Jane, b. 1767; m. Nathan Ball of Vt. and N. Y. Lenawee Port., 986.

—— Laura, b. 1805? m. Jeremiah Holmes of N. Y. Midland, 208.

—— Levi Lincoln, b. Whately, 1826; set. N. Y., Mich., 1866. Gratiot, 683.

——Lorenza S., m. 1859 John McCurdy of Mich. Jackson Port., 451.

—— Lyman B., set. Mich., 1836. Lake Huron, 143.

—— Martin, set. N. Y., 1830? Kalamazoo Port., 449.

—— Mary, m. 1825? Jonathan White of N. Y., Ill. and O. Genesee Port., 464.

—— Mary, m. 1850? Augustus Lilley of Mich. Kalamazoo Port., 954.

—— Mathias, b. Martha's Vineyard; soldier in French and Indian war; set. Me. Berrien Port., 466, 528.

SMITH, Nathaniel, set. N. Y., Mich., 1790? Lenawee Port., 1120.

—— Nicholas, of Stockbridge; set. N. Y. 1789. Shiawassee, 529.

—— Obed, b. Hawley, 1796; set. N. Y., 1814, Ill., 1838, Mich., 1843. Lake Huron, 209.

—— Oliver M., of Northfield; set. N. Y., Vt. Jackson Hist., 727.

—— Phebe, b. Adams, 1772; m. Darius Comstock of Mass., N. Y. and Mich. Lenawee Hist. I, 370.

—— Reuben R., set. Mich., 1835. Macomb Past, 105.

——Ruth, m. 1825? Aruna Fox of O. Clinton Port., 864.

—— Sallie, b. 1790; m. Sylvester Shedd of Mich. Berrien Port., 549; Berrien Twent., 882.

—— Samuel, b. Acton; set. Mich., 1829. Branch Hist., 224.

—— Samuel, set. N. Y., 1835? Kent, 1035.

—— Samuel E., of Colerain; set. Mich., 1835. Hillsdale Hist., 151.

—— Seth, b. Dighton, 1825; set. N. Y., Mich., 1863. Macomb Hist., 712.

—— Stephen, set. N. Y., 1800? Jackson Hist., 928.

—— Thomas, set. O., 1830? Kalamazoo Port., 739.

—— Wanton, b. Berkshire Co., 1776; set. N. Y., 1783. Lenawee Illus., 217; Lenawee Port., 579.

—— William, b. Dalton, 1794 ;set. N. Y., 1820? Mich., 1837. Lenawee Hist. II, 289.

—— William, b. Worcester Co., 1800; set. Mich., 1842. Saginaw Hist., 831; Saginaw Port., 684, 706.

—— William, Jr., b. Worcester Co., 1838; set. Mich., 1842. Saginaw Port., 684.

—— William C., b. Dalton; set N. Y., Mich., 1837 Hillsdale Port., 877.

SNOW, Alonzo, b. 1810 set. N. Y. 1820, Mich., 1832. Oakland Port., 736.

—— Ansel, b. Bridgewater, 1784; set. Mich., 1837. Kalamazoo Hist., 415; Kalamazoo Port., 866.

SMITH, Elizabeth, b. Boston; m. 1841 Lewis C. Gesler of Mich. Ionia Port., 319.

—— Sparrow, set. O., 1817. Detroit, 1269; Wayne Land., 820.

—— William W. b. Millbury, 1837; set. Mich., 1860. Jackson Hist., 728.

SOULE, John, b. 1787 or 1788; set. N. Y., 1810? Mich., 1825. Macomb Hist., between 672 and 710, also 840.

—— Marcia, m. 1835? David Crapo of O. and Mich.. Ionia Port., 736.

SOUTHWICK, David, set. N. Y., 1800. Kalamazoo Port., 738.

SOUTHWORTH, James B., b. Hancock, 1816; set. N. Y., 1822, Mich., 1849. Branch Twent., 841.

—— Norman, of Hancock; set. N. Y., 1822, Mich., 1850? Branch Twent., 805, 841.

—— Sarah I., b. Hancock, 1824; m. 1845 Arteman H. Legg of N. Y. and Mich. Branch Twent., 804.

SPAFFORD, Thomas L., b. Dalton, 1797; set. N. Y., 1813, Mich., 1836. Washtenaw Hist., 1351.

SPARKS, Austin, b. Sheffield, 1798; set. N. Y. Hillsdale Port., 775.

—— Mary, m. 1830? Lewman Fox of N. Y. Kalamazoo Port., 514.

SPAULDING, Charles A., b. Middlebury, 1839; set. Mich., 1845. Branch Port., 289.

—— Ephraim, b. Townsend, 1801; set. Vt., Mich., 1845. Branch Port., 290.

SPEAR, Sally, b. 1810? m. James Benjamin of N. Y. Genesee Port., 801.

SPENCER, Elias T., b. Middlefield, 1815; set. O., 1840? Muskegon Port., 556.

—— Grove, b. 1803; set. Mich., 1835? d. 1887. Washtenaw Hist., 1231; Washtenaw Port., 475.

—— Ralph H., b. Tyringham, 1854; set. Mich., 1879. Grand Rapids Hist., 222; Grand Rapids Lowell, 713.

SPERRY, Elizabeth, m. 1820? Ebenezer Andrews of N. Y. Ionia Port., 718.

—— Pamelia., m. 1815? Patrick Gibbins of Mass. Jackson Hist., 1141.

—— S. H. b. Berkshire Co., 1816; set. Mich., 1845. Jackson Hist., 906.

STEVENS, George, b. Worcester, 1831; set. Mich., 1839. Hillsdale Hist., 229.

—— Israel, set. N. Y., 1820? Lenawee Port., 661.

—— Joseph, b. 1790; set. Mich., 1830? Clinton Past, 204.

—— Mary Ann, b. 1819; m. George Peters of N. Y. Newaygo, 418, 475.

—— Ransom F., b. Lee, 1820; set. O., 1831, Mich. Kent, 629.

—— Samuel, b. Worcester Co., 1793; set. Mich. 1838. Hillsdale Hist., 229.

——Samuel, set. N. Y., 1830? Muskegon Port., 317.

—— Silas, b. Southwick, 1755; set. N. Y. Berrien Port., 406.

—— Warren, b. Cheshire, 1809; set. N. Y., Mich., 1829. Hillsdale Port., 264.

—— William W., b. Worcester Co., 1836; set. O., 1840? Mich., 1854. Clinton Port., 662.

STEWARD,, Jabez, b. Paxton, 1770; set. N. Y., 1810. Hillsdale Hist., 197.

STEWART, Anna, b. 1785? m. John C. Bell of O. Gratiot, 682.

—— Harvey, set. N. Y., Mich., 1811. St. Clair, 717.

—— Ira, set. N. Y., Mich., 1830? Lenawee Port., 1111.

STICKNEY, Lemuel, b. 1761; Revolutionary soldier; set. N. Y. Macomb Hist., 853.

STILES, Mercy, b. 1784, m. 1820? Stephen ball of N. Y. and Mich. Ionia Hist., 261, 262; Ionia Port., 390.

—— Samuel, Revolutionary soldier; set. N. Y., 1790? Jackson Port., 585.

STIMPSON, John, set. N. Y., 1800? d. 1831. Jackson Hist., 1127.

STIMSON, Benjamin G., b. Dedham, 1816; set. Mich., 1837. Wayne Chron., 387.

—— Ephraim ,set. N. Y., 1820? d. 1832. Kalamazoo Port., 329.

——Robert, set. N. Y., 1797. Genesee Hist., 260.

STITT, Henry, b. Berkshire Co., 1833; set. O., Mich., 1862. Gratiot, 512.

—— John, b. Berkshire Co.; set. O., 1835, Mich., 1864. Gratiot, 442, 512.

STOCKING, Billious, b. 1779; set. N. Y., 1800? Grand Rapids Lowell, 390; Kent, 1137.

STOCKWELL, Lovina, b. 1770; m. Oliver C. Derby of N. Y. Ingham Hist., facing 214.

—— Parley, b. 1803; set. Mich. Branch Twent., 253.

STOELL, Sarah, m. 1820? Nathaniel Kellogg of N. Y. Jackson Hist., 657.

STOKER, Minnie, m. 1883 Francis McMann of Mich. Saginaw Port., 228.

STONE, Alvah G., b. Charlton, 1852; set. Mich., 1877. Lenawee Illus., 406.

—— Clement W., b. Gloucester, 1840? set. Mich., Washtenaw Past, 181.

—— David, b. 1793; set. N. Y., Mich., 1836. Macomb Hist., 805.

——Elias, set. Mich., 1780? Macomb Hist., 804.

——Isaiah, b. 1785; set. Vt., N. Y.., 1800, N. Y., O., 1835. Lenawee Hist. II, 418; Lenawee Port., 239

—— Martha, m. 1st, 1800? Nicholas Cook of Mass; m. 2d —— —— of O. Hillsdale Port., 634.

—— Nabby, b. Framingham; m. 1820? Samuel Murdock of N. Y. Washtenaw Hist., 868.

—— Nathan, set. Vt., 1805? Jackson Hist., 891.

—— Solomon, set. N. Y., Mich., 1845? Macomb Past, 460.

—— Solon, b. 1801; set. N. Y., 1830? Mich. Clinton Port., 873.

——William B., b. Boston; set. Vt., 1850? Oakland Biog., 333.

—— William W., b. 1821; set. N. Y., Mich., 1855. Muskegon Port., 155.

STOW, —— set. N. Y., Mich.; d. 1835. Clinton Port., 335.

STOWE, Elbridge G. b. Conway, 1821; set Mich., 1844. Kent, 1320.

STOWELL, Jesse, b. Boston; set. N. Y., 1810? Jackson Port., 275.

—— Josiah, b. Petersham, 1797; set. Vt., 1800? Lenawee Port., 1072.

—— Luther, b. 1772; set. Vt. 1800? Lenawee Port., 1072.

STOWELL, Silas W., b. Littleton, 1802; set. N. Y., Mich., 1834. Jackson Hist., 151; Jackson Port., 275.

STRATTON, Mary T., of Gill; m. 1884 Ransom Nutting of Mass. and Mich. Kalamazoo Port., 786.

STREETER, Sereno W., b. 1811; set. O. Northern P., 354.

—— Thankful, b. Chester, 1795; m. Robert H. Baird of O. Kalamazoo Port., 702.

STRONG, Abigail L., of Northampton; b. 1821; m. 1845? Adin C. Evans of O. Northern M., 327.

—— Asahel of Northampton; set. O. Northern M., 328.

—— Asahel B., b. Westhampton, 1826; set. O., Mich., 1849. Hillsdale Port., 571.

—— Jared, b. Northampton, 1801; set. Mich., 1846. Kent, 715.

—— Olive, of Northampton; m. Abner Clark of O. Berrien Port., 582.

—— Phineas, b. Southampton; set. N. Y., 1830? Kent, 1140.

STUART, Charles, of Martha's Vineyard; set. N. Y., 1805. Kalamazoo Port., 205.

—— Ebenezer, set. N. Y., 1810? d. 1817. Macomb Hist., 805.

—— James, set. N. Y. Genesee Port., 622.

STUDLEY, Elbridge G., set. N. Y., 1840? Grand Rapids Hist., 1086.

STYLES, Mercy, see STILES.

—— Pamelia, b. 1791; m. Peter Downs of Mich. Allegan Hist., 463.

SUMNER, Lucina, m. 1780? William Carpenter of N. H. and N. Y. Lenawee Illus., 121.

—— Ruth, b. 1791; m. 1822 John Towar of N. Y. and Mich. Lansing, 434.

SUTTON, Amsey, set. N. Y., 1830, Mich., 1837. Macomb Hist., 713.

SWAIN, Joseph G., b. New Bedford; set. N. Y., 1830? Mich., 1846. Branch Twent., 441.

—— Richard, b. Nantasket? 1773; set. N. Y., 1796. Detroit, 1232.

SWAN, Mrs. Betsey, wife of Abel Swan, later wife of John Bean; b. Heath, March, 1793. Sanilac, 249.

SWEETSER, Luke, of Hampshire Co., bought land in Mich., 1836. Allegan Hist., 270.

SYKES, Alanson, set. N. Y., Mich., 1837. Kalamazoo Port., 895.

SYMES, J. T., b. Berkshire Co., 1821; set. O., Mich., 1855. Saginaw Hist., 913.

TABER, Benjamin, b. 1775; set. N. Y., Mich. Hillsdale Port., 245.

—— Earl, Revolutionary soldier; set. N. Y., 1799. Oakland Port., 577.

TAFT, Cynthia, b. Chesterfield, 1790; m. Silas Wilcox of N. Y. and Mich. Lenawee Hist. II, 190.

—— Levi B., b. Billingham, 1821, set. Mich., 1834. Oakland Hist., 47; Oakland Port., 225.

—— Lydia, m. 1790? Royal Wheelock of N. Y. Washtenaw Port., 609.

—— Mary Ann, b. Worcester Co., 1829; m. Danford Parker of Mich. Ingham Port., 754.

—— Moses, b. Mendon, 1792; set. Mich., 1834. St. Joseph, 220.

TAGGART, —— b. Roxbury? set. N. H. Branch Port., 316.

—— John, Jr., b. Roxbury, 1750; set. N. H. Branch Hist., 330.

TALBOT, Samuel, set. N. Y., 1800? Kalamazoo Port., 765.

TALMADGE, Joseph I., b. Williamstown, 1807; set. Mich., 1834. Lenawee Hist. I, 251.

TAPLIN, Elliott, set. Vt. Saginaw Port., 234.

TARBELL, Betsey, m. 1820? Asquar Aldrich of Mich. Gratiot, 389.

TASKER, Reuben C., b. New Bedford, 1836; set. Mich., 1881. Saginaw Port., 942.

TATEUM, William A., graduate of Wesleyan University; set. Mich., 1887. Grand Rapids City, 432.

TAYLOR, Alanson, set. O., 1835? Newaggo, 224.

TAYLOR, Almira M., b. 1829; m. 1857 B. F. Chamberlain of Mich. Washtenaw Hist., 697.

—— Betsey, m. 1800? Amos Gray of Vt. Washtenaw Hist., 853.

—— Chloe, b. Springfield, 1781; m. 1803 Seth Otis of N. Y. Washtenaw Hist., 1029.

—— David, b. Ashfield; set. O.; d. 1840? Genesee Hist., 391.

—— Elbridge G., b. 1826; set. Mich. 1844. Washtenaw Port., 201.

—— James, Sr., b. Buckland, 1791; set. N. Y., Mich., 1836. Ionia Hist., 402.

—— John, b. Westfield, 1762; set. N. Y., 1802, Mich., 1832. Macomb Hist., 763.

—— John, b. Deerfield, 1792; set. N. Y., 1810? Mich., 1832. Macomb Hist., 763.

—— Joseph, b. Harvard? 1790?; set. Vt. 1810? Kent, 792; Newaygo, 363.

—— Mary A., of Westfield; m. 1828 Nathan Dickinson of Mass. and Mich. Macomb Past, 337.

—— Obed, b. 1799; set. Mich., 1832. Washtenaw Hist., 697.

—— Sylvester, b. Berkshire Co., 1814; set. N. Y., 1816, O., 1829, Mich., 1854. Ionia Hist., 171.

TEMPLETON, Sarah, m. Isaac Butterfield of N. Y. and Mich. Kent, 963.

TENNEY, Weston, set. N. Y., 1820? Newaygo, 302.

TERRY, Polly, m. 1820? Joseph Chaddock of N. Y. Muskegon Port., 368.

THACHER, Isaac E., b. N. Wrentham, 1833; set. Mich., 1855. Ionia Port., 642.

—— Israel, b. 1810; set. N. Y., Mich. Hillsdale Port., 654.

—— Martha M., b. N. Wrentham, 1829; m. 1854 Nelson E. Smith of Mass., Penn. and Ill. Ionia Port., 790.

—— Moses, b. Princeton, 1795; set. Penn., 1803; N. Y., Ill., Mich. Ionia Port., 643, 790.

—— Tyler, b. Princeton, 1801; set. Cal., 1851. Ionia Port., 644.

THAYER, Betsey, b. Taunton, 1778; m. 1818 William Freeman of Mass. and Mich. Lenawee Hist. I, 245; Lenawee Port., 668.

—— Dolly, m. 1825? Willard Richards of N. Y. and Mich. Genesee Port., 927.

—— Hosea, b. Plainfield or Springfield, 1784; set. N. Y., 1800? Lenawee Hist., I, 357; Lenawee Port., 579.

—— John, b. Randolph, 1787; set. Me., 1820? Ionia Hist., 165.

—— Nathan, b. Milford, 1765? set. N. Y., Mich., 1824. Washtenaw Hist., 1049.

—— Nathaniel, set. Vt., 1820? Grand Rapids Lowell, 380.

THOMAS, David, of Rowe; set. Mich., 1841. Hillsdale Hist., 257; Hillsdale Port., 221.

—— Sophia, b. 1781; m. 1808? Frederick Wright of Mass., N. Y. and Mich. Jackson Hist., 1020; Jackson Port., 593.

—— Victor H., b. Berkshire Co., 1837; set. N. Y., 1842, Mich., 1857. Berrien Twent., 767.

—— Zimri D., b. Rowe, 1809; set. N. Y., 1820? Mich., 1852 or 53. Hillsdale Port., 683; Kalamazoo Port., 219.

THOMPSON, Caleb S., b. Northboro, 1805; set. N. Y., Mich., 1829. Genesee Hist., 249.

—— Cyrus, set. N. Y., 1800? Jackson Hist., 817; Jackson Port., 335.

—— Horace, b. Uxbridge, 1809; set. Mich., 1831. Cass Hist., 144, 307.

—— Lewis S., b. Peru, 1827; set. N. Y., Mich. Genesee Port., 740.

—— Lovina, b. Worcester Co., 1782; m. 1799 John Barber of N. Y. Lenawee Hist. II, 191.

—— Lyman, set. N. Y., Mich., 1840? Genesee Port., 740.

—— Margaret, b. Monson; m. 1853, James C. Bennett of Mich. Kalamazoo Port., 794.

—— Oren C., b. Stockbridge, 1806; set. Mich., 1831. Wayne Chron., 159.

—— Sally, b. Berkshire Co.; m. Elisha Branch of O. Ingham Hist., 347.

THORN, *Mrs.* Sampson, b. Falmouth, Aug. 6, 1813; set. Mich., 1838. Jackson Hist., 152.

THORNTON, Isaac, set. O., 1835? Midland, 299.

THORP, Susannah, b. Springfield; m. 1810? Timothy Wood of Mass. and N. Y. Saginaw Hist., 940.

THORPE, Hannah, m. 1820? Justus Alvord of N. Y. and O. Isabella, 382.

TIBBITTS, John, b. Adams, 1783; set. N. Y., Mich. Branch Port., 630.

TICKNOR, Deborah, m. Alfred Bingham of Vt. Saginaw Port., 468.

TIFFANY, Gideon of Norton; set. N. H. 1780? Lenawee Hist. I, 523.

—— Oliver, set. N. Y., 1820? Mich., 1836. Jackson Port., 310.

—— Polly, m. 1810? Mason Whipple of N. Y. and Mich. Washtenaw Hist., 819; Washtenaw Port., 250.

—— Sylvester, b. Norton; set. Canada, 1792, N. Y. Lenawee Hist. I, 523.

TILLOTSON, Leonard, set. O., 1815. Clinton Port., 558.

TILTON, Caleb, of Conway; set. Mich., 1832. Calhoun, 162.

—— John, of Berkshire Co.; set. Mich.; d. 1849. Calhoun, 162.

—— Joseph, b. Sudbury, 1779; set. N. H., 1800? Mich. 1833. Lenawee Hist. I, 72.

—— Lucy J., m. 1855 Martin N. Hine of Mich. Kent, 1219.

TIMOTHY, Clarissa A., m. 1840? David P. Allen, of N. Y. and Mich. Saginaw Port., 684.

—— Elkana, set. N. Y., 1820? Saginaw Port., 684.

TINNEY, Olive, b. 1793; m. Benjamin Tobey of N. Y. and Mich. Lenawee Port., 68.

—— Sally, b. Lee, 1790; m. 1815, Ezra Howes of N. Y. and Mich. Lenawee Hist. II, 151.

TOBEY, Benjamin, b. Conway, 1779; set. N. Y., 1820? Mich., 1844. Lenawee Hist. I, 147; Lenawee Port., 681.

TOMS, Ira, set. N. Y., Canada., Mich., 1824. Oakland Hist., 288.

TOOMBS, Louisa, b. 1811; m. 1843 Josiah Childs of Mich. Washtenaw Port., 545.

TORREY, Ann, m. 1825? Ezra Newton of N. Y. and Mich. Ionia Port., 732.

—— George, b. Salem, 1801; set. Mich., 1833. Kalamazoo Hist., 284, 489.

—— Miles, set. N. Y., Mich., 1845. Lansing, 542.

—— Norman, b. Williamstown, 1807; set. Mich., 1830. Lenawee Port., 575.

TORRY, Ruth, b. Williamstown, 1770; m. Stephen Frazier of Mass. and N. Y. Lenawee Port., 948.

TOWER, Clarissa, m. 1800? Elkana Timothy of N. Y. Saginaw Port., 684.

—— Deborah, m. 1807, Ansel Ford of Mass. and O. Lenawee Port., 1137.

—— Osmond, b. Cummington, 1811; set. Mich., 1834 or 1835. Clinton Port., 768; Ionia Hist., 160; Kent, 263.

TOWN, Betsey, m. 1812? Festus Persons of N. Y. Newaygo, 382.

—— Nathan, b. Berkshire Co., 1792; set. N. Y., Canada, 1820? Mich., 1838. Lenawee Hist. I, 269; Lenawee Illus., 446; Lenawee Port., 874.

—— Stephen, set. N. Y., Mich., 1845. Jackson Hist., 739.

TOWNSEND, Abiel, set. Mich., 1836. Ionia Port., 268.

—— Isaac, b. New Salem, 1750? set N. Y., 1800 Branch Port., 491.

—— James, b. Berkshire Co., 1842; set. Mich., 1845. Jackson Hist., 907.

—— Josiah, set. N. Y., 1850? Gratiot, 180.

—— Martin, 1812 soldier; set. N. Y. Branch Port., 491.

—— Tartullus, of Berkshire Co.; set. Mich., 1845. Jackson Hist., 907.

—— Thomas, Revolutionary soldier; set. N. H., d. 1814. Genesee Port., 954.

TOWNSON, Calvin, b. 1776; set. N. Y. Jackson Port., 352.

TRACY, Addison, b. Pittsfield, 1796; set. O., 1840? Mich., 1864. Grand Rapids City, 292; Kent. 790.

—— Hannah, of Lenox; m. 1785? Isaac Grant of Vt. and N. Y. Osceola, 191.

TRACY, James, set. N. Y., 1810. Jackson Hist., 873.

—Sarah, m. 1810? Ira L. Watkins of Mich. Jackson Hist., 873.

—Thomas, b. Berkshire Co., 1790; set. N. Y., Ill., 1832, Mich., 1853. Kalamazoo Port., 530.

TRAIN, Samuel, b. 1833; set. O. Newaygo, 246.

—Sylvester, set. Vt., 1830? Mich., 1840. Grand Rapids City, 236; Kent, 1229.

TRASK, Annie, b. Leicester, 1790; m. John Wood of N. Y. and Mich. Ingham Port., 415.

—Luther H., b. Millbury, 1807; set. Mich., 1835. Kalamazoo Port., 239.

—Salmon, set. Mich., 1835. Bean Creek. 49.

TREMAIN, Justus, b. Berkshire Co., 1798; set. N. Y., Mich., 1833. Monroe, 505.

TROWBRIDGE, Luther, b. Framingham; Revolutionary soldier; set. N. Y., 1785? Detroit, 1034; Wayne Chron., 178.

TRUMBULL, Orrin S., b. 1821; set. Mich., 1845. Kent, 774.

TRYON, Rodolphus, b. Deerfield, 1809; set. N. Y., Mich., 1836. Ingham Hist., facing 214.

— Sebina, set. N. Y., 1810? Clinton Port., 700.

— Zebina, b. 1785; set. N. Y. Ingham Hist., facing 214.

TUBBS, Seth, set. N. Y., 1800; d. 1859. Shiawassee, 247.

TUCKER, Luther L., b. Windsor; set. Mich., 1836. Hillsdale Hist., 129.

— Mary, b. Charlton, 1770? m. Abel Foster of Mass. and R. I. Lenawee Hist. I, 92.

TUCKERMAN, Benjamin, set. N. Y., 1795? Allegan Hist., 390.

TUFFS, Rebecca, b. Malden, 1797; m. James H. Young of Mass. and Mich. Washtenaw Port., 469.

TUFTS, Aaron, b. 1794; set. N. Y. Lenawee Port., 565.

TUFTS, Aaron, b. 1803; set. N. Y., 1821. Lenawee Hist. I, 417; Lenawee Illus., 274.

TULLER, Artemidorus, b. Egremont, 1783; set. N. Y., O., Mich. Hillsdale Port., 451.

TURNER, Anna, m. 1825? Joseph S. Blaisdell of Vt. and Mich. Kent, 1212.

— Carmi, set. O., 1800? Lenawee Port., 370.

—Delonza, b. 1798; set. N. Y. Mich., 1836. Hillsdale Port., 539.

— Ezra, 1812 soldier; set. N. Y., 1815? Muskegon Port., 452.

— Mary, b. 1810? m. Cornelius D. Seager of O. Lenawee Port., 370.

—Mary R., b. Pittsfield, 1818; m. 1848 Moses A. McNaughton of Mich. Jackson Port., 509.

— Nathaniel, b. 1780; set. N. Y., Mich., 1835. Branch Hist., 323.

— Stiles, set. N. Y., Mich., 1831. Ingham Port., 522.

TURRELL, Deborah, b. Pelham, 1804; m. Horace Turner of Mich. Hillsdale Port., 611.

—Noah, b. Bridgewater; set. N. Y., 1812. Hillsdale Port., 612.

TUTEN, R. P., b. E. Cambridge, 1845; set. N. H., Mich., 1875. Northern P., 91.

TUTTLE, Annie, b. Franklin Co.; d. 1834; m. Zedock Hale of Vt. Kalamazoo Port., 447.

— Nelson, b. 1800; set. O., 1830? Ionia Port., 414.

TWITCHELL, Chloe O., b. Mendon, 1808; m. E. A. Roby of Wis. and Mich. Kent, 1343.

TYLER, Frank C., b. Stoneham, 1855; set. Mich., 1857. Muskegon Hist., 95.

—Sarah H., of Greenfield; m. 1837 Preston Mitchell of Mich. Calhoun, 78.

— Susan, m. 1800? Asabel Cogswell of N. Y. Saginaw Hist., 755.

UNDERWOOD, Daniel K., b. Enfield, 1803; set. Mich., 1836. Lenawee Hist. II, 360; Lenawee Illus., 137.

UNDERWOOD, E. E., of Otis; b. 1806; set. N. Y., 1814, Mich., 1832. Jackson Hist., 933.

——Edmund, b. 1803; set. O., 1835? Mich., 1870? Clinton Port., 525.

——Samuel, set. N. Y., 1814; Mich., 1832. Jackson Hist., 933.

UPHAM, Joshua C., set. Vt., O., 1836. Kalamazoo Port., 221.

UPTON, Elias, b. Heath, 1790? 1812 soldier; set. Mich., 1856 or 1857. Clinton Past, 421, 486; Clinton Port., 869.

——Frank W., b. Charlemont, 1849; set. Mich., 1856. Clinton Past, 420.

——Hart L., b. Heath, 1827; set. N. Y., Mich., 1856. Clinton Port., 869.

——Henry, set. Mich., 1829. Newaygo, 252.

——James, b. Heath, 1821; set. N. H., Mich. Shiawassee, 518.

——James, set. Mich., 1850? Clinton Past, 486.

——Josiah, b. Heath, 1824; set. Mich., 1856. Clinton Past, 420, 421.

——Mary, m. 1st, 1800? Richard Floyd of Vt.; m. 2d, Joseph Fuller, of N. Y. Hillsdale Port., 529.

——Sarah, b. Charlemont, 1819; m. 1846 Justin W. Beckwith of Mass. and Mich. Clinton Port., 820.

URE, Margaret E., m. 1854 Francis L. O. Banks of Mich. Midland, 241.

VADER, Eliza, m. 1820? Jefferson Louden of N. Y. and Mich. Lenawee Port., 993.

VALENTINE, Augusta M. of Cambridgeport; m. 1848 Ezra T. Nelson of Mich. Grand Rapids Lowell, 464; Kent, 1089.

VAN DUSEN, S. A., b. Berkshire Co., 1838; set. N. Y., Mich., 1861. Bay Hist., 151.

VANSICKLE, John W., b. Hunterdon? 1787; set. Mich. 1831. Washtenaw Hist., 630.

VAUGHAN, David C., b. New Salem; set. N. Y., 1825. Jackson Port., 265.

——Sewell S., b. Franklin Co., 1820; set. N. Y., 1825, Mich., 1836. Jackson Hist., 744; Jackson Port., 266.

VHAY, John, b. New Bedford, 1848; set. Mich. Wayne Land., appendix, 279.

VILAS, Aaron, b. Worcester Co., 1770; set. Vt., Canada. Genesee Port., 812.

VINCENT, Edwin H., b. Florida, 1850; set. Mich. Berrien Port., 306.

——Isaac M., b. Franklin Co., 1822; set. Mich., 1865. Berrien Port., 306.

——Sarah, b. Coleraine, 1814; m. 1844 Robert Gragg of Mich. Lenawee Hist. I, 181.

VINTON, David, Jr., b. Hampshire Co., 1828; set. O., Ind., Mich., 1870. Traverse, 91.

——Hannah, b. 1810? m. Samuel W. Herrington of N. Y., Penn. and Mich. Genesee Port., 861.

VOSE, Lucy, m. Joseph Shepard of N. Y. Berrien Port., 673.

VROMAN, Mrs. Eliza, b. Salem, Apr. 25, 1811; set. Mich., 1852. Jackson Hist., 153.

WADE, Ebenezer F., b. Franklin Co., 1810; set. Mich., 1843 St. Clair, 124.

——John P., b. Scituate Harbor, 1822; set. Mich., 1844. Allegan Twent., 147; Kalamazoo Port., 363.

——Jonathan, set. Canada, 1815? Newaygo, 296.

——Uriah, b. 1796; set. N. Y., 1800, Mich., 1835. Jackson Hist., 842.

WADSWORTH, Minerva, m. 1830? Silas Churchill of N. Y. Sanilac, 390.

WAIT, Asenath, m. 1825 Jacob Hosner of N. Y. and Mich. Oakland Port., 633.

WAITE, Elihu, b. 1796; set. N. Y., Mich. Genesee Port., 552.

—— Waldo F., b. 1825; set. Mich., 1850. Northern M., 193.

WALES, Mary, b. Milford, 1833; m. Simon Woodbury of O. Clinton Past, 389.

WALKER, Mrs. Arethusa (wife of Joel, of Mich.) b. Greenfield, 1818. Hillsdale Port., 486.

—— Daniel, set. Vt., 1800? Lenawee Port., 613.

—— David S., b. Berkshire Co.; set. N. Y., 1810? Mich. Lenawee Hist. I, 518.

—— Edward, set. N. Y.; d. 1828. Gratiot, 698.

—— Eliakim, b. Taunton, 1801; set. Canada, 1805, Mich., 1835. Washtenaw Hist., 631.

—— Emma L., of Northboro; m. 1855 George F. Warren of Mass. and Mich. Saginaw Port., 288.

—— Enos, Revolutionary soldier; set. Vt., 1780? Jackson Port., 787.

—— George E., b. Berkshire Co., 1824; set. Mich., 1835. Ingham Port., 454.

—— Jonathan, b. Harwich, 1790; set. Mich., 1863. Muskegon Hist., 38.

—— Myron H., b. Westboro, 1855; set. Mich., 1870. Grand Rapids City, 448; Grand Rapids Hist., 756.

—— Rebecca, b. 1821; m. 1840? Erasmus Brown of N. Y. and Mich. Lansing, 492.

——Silas, of Westboro, b. Holden, 1811; set. Mich., 1870. Grand Rapids City, 488; Grand Rapids Hist., 756.

—— Tisdal, set. N. Y., 1800? Lenawee Hist. II, 336.

WALLACE, George, b. Townsend, 1808; set. N. Y., 1820? Mich., 1837 or 1838. Clinton Port., 259; Saginaw Hist., 914; Saginaw Port., 812.

WALTON, Mrs. Jane B., b. 1809; set. Mich., 1838. Cass Twent., 89.

WARD, Sally, m. 1815? John Soule of N. Y. and Mich. Macomb Hist., 673.

——Trowbridge, b. Worthington, 1816; set. O., 1833, Mich., 1864. Hillsdale Port., 357.

WARE, Catherine A., of Ware; m. 1835 Jacob M. Howard of Mich. Wayne Chron., 176.

——Phebe, of Shelburne Falls; m. 1790 Jeduthan Cross of Mass. and N. Y. Lenawee Hist. I, 324.

WARN, Abram, b. 1798; set. N. Y., 1815? Northern P., 70.

WARNER, James, set. N. Y., 1795? Clinton Port., 428.

—— John, b. Conway, 1781; set. N. Y.? Wayne Land., 850.

——Oliver, set. N. Y., 1810? d. 1825 Washtenaw Hist., 1273.

—— Stephen, b. Cummington, 1779; set. Mich., 1831. Lenawee Hist. I, 351.

—— William W., b. Hampden Co., 1840. Allegan Twent., 101.

WARREN, George F., b. Ashby, 1831; set. Mich., 1859? Saginaw Port., 288.

—— Philip, b. Norfolk Co., 1783; set. Mich. Hillsdale Port., 232.

—— Rachel, b. Cheshire, 1777; m. 1810 Jabez Steward of N. Y. Hillsdale Hist., 193.

—— Robert, S., b. Pittsfield, 1824; set. N. Y., 1840? Berrien Twent., 724.

——Thankful, b. Boston; m. 1805? John Dawson of N. Y. Clinton Port., 308.

WARRENER, Eli, set. N. Y., O., 1852, Mich., 1864. Clinton Port., 687.

WATERMAN, Alanson H., b. 1817; set. N. Y., Penn., O., Mich., 1864. Mecosta, 350.

—— Oliver, set. N. Y., 1820? Penn; d. 1868. Mecosta, 350.

WATERS, Jonathan, b. 1784; set. Mich. Washtenaw Hist., 591.

WATKINS Alanson, set. Mich., 1870. Branch Twent., 543.

—— Dollie, b. Berkshire Co., 1785? m. Jesse Goodwin of N. Y. Jackson Port., 854.

—— Ephraim, b. Berkshire Co., 1788; set. N. Y., Hillsdale Port., 446, 589.

WATKINS, Esther, m. 1810? Reuben Slayton of Mass. and N. Y. Lenawee Port., 431.

—— Esther, m. Titus R. Read of N. Y. and Mich. Berrien Port., 349.

—— Gilbert N. Revolutionary soldier; set. N. Y.; d. 1827. Cass Hist., 176.

—— Hannah, m. 1808? Elnathan Wing of N. Y. Clinton Port., 774.

—— Levi, b. Partridgefield, 1785; set. N. Y., 1793, Mich., 1832. St. Joseph, 179.

WATSON, A. J., of Boston; set. Mich., 1876. Berrien Hist., 148.

—— John W., of Worcester Co., bought land in Mich., 1834. Allegan Hist., 218, 221.

—— Susan, b. 1788; m. James Livermore of Me. and Mich. Ingham Port., 198.

—— Willliam, set. Mich., 1834. Jackson Port., 243.

WATT, Charles A., b. Pittsfield, 1859; set. Mich., 1869. Grand Rapids Hist., 788.

—— Clara W., b. Litchfield, 1861; m. Harmon Cowens of Mich. Grand Rapids City, 116.

WATTERMAN, William P., b. Shutesbury, 1828; set. Mich., 1866. Jackson Hist., 818.

WATTLES, Eunice, m. 1825? Jeremiah Van Wormer, of N. Y. and Mich. Jackson Hist., 841.

WEATHERBY, William, Sr., b. near Boston, 1769; set. Vt., 1798, N. Y., 1823, Mich., 1831. Lenawee Hist. I, 136.; Lenawee Illus., 117; Lenawee Port., 1020.

WEAVER, Daniel, set. N. Y., Mich., 1855. Newaygo, 201.

WEBB, Loomis, b. 1803; set. N. Y., 1851. Clinton Past, 164.

—— Lucy, m. 1805? Jesse Holcomb of N. Y. Ionia Port., 783.

—— Newton L., b. Otis, 1840; set. Mich., 1872. Clinton Past, 164

WEBSTER, Edwin D., b. Franklin Co., 1828; set. Mich., 1834. Clinton Port., 596.

—— John, b. Berkshire Co.; set. N. Y, 1800. Clinton Port., 754.

WEBSTER, Lyman, set. Mich.; d. 1856. Gratiot, 499.

—— Lyman, set. Mich., 1834, Cal., Australia. Clinton Port., 596, 970.

—— Stewart H., b. Berkshire Co.; set. N. Y., Mich., 1835. Genesee Hist., 186.

WELLMAN, Eustis J., b. near Boston, 1823; set Vt., N. H., N. Y., Mich., 1844. Grand Rapids City, 1074.

—— Isaac, b. Mansfield, 1790; set. Vt., 1849, N. Y., Mich. Grand Rapids City, 1074.

WELLS, Charles C., b. Deerfield, 1808; set. Mich., 1833. Lenawee Hist. II, 290.

—— David, set. Vt., 1810? Washtenaw Hist., 1353.

—— Nancy K., b. N. Adams; m. 1839 Leonard G. Hall of N. Y. and Mich. Lenawee Port., 918.

—— Oziah, set. N. Y., 1815, N. J. Ingham Hist., 491.

—— Phoebe, b. 1779; m. 1810? Joshua Lapham of Mass. and Mich. Oakland Port., 789.

WENTWORTH, Lora A., b. Windsor? m. 1829 Melzar Bird of N. Y. and Mich. Ingham Port., 770.

—— Sion, b. Sharon, 1769; set. Maine, 1795? Bay Gansser, 555.

WESSON, Leonard, set. Mich., 1840? Midland, 363.

—— Leonard, b. Millbury, 1818; set. Mich. Genesee Port., 734.

—— William B., b. Hardwick, 1820; set. Mich. 1833. Detroit, 1074; Wayne Chron., 354.

WEST, Lyman, set. O., 1840? Mich. 1867. Clinton Past, 238.

—— Nathan, set. N. Y., O., 1800? Lenawee Hist. II, 491; Lenawee Port., 199.

—— Nathan B., b. Lee, 1816; set. Mich. Kalamazoo Port., 557.

—— Timothy N., set. Mich., 1836. Kalamazoo Port., 557.

WESTON, Jacob, set. Mich., 1836. Washtenaw Hist., 715.

—— Samuel, set. Me., 1770? d. 1776? Muskegon Hist., 134.

WESTOVER, James, b. 1810? set. Ind. Genesee Port., 579.

—— Luther, b. Berkshire Co., 1817; set. Canada, 1845, Mich., 1865. Bay Hist., 122.

WETHERBEE, William, set. N. Y., Mich., 1830? Berrien Port., 410.

WETHERELL, Noah, 1812 soldier; set. N. Y., 1810? Osceola, 279.

WHEAT, Benjamin, b. Conway, 1720? set. N. Y. Branch Port., 612.

—— Benjamin, b. 1790? set. N. Y.; d. 1817. Branch Hist., 193; Branch Port., 612.

WHEATON, Robert, set. N. Y., 1795? Lenawee Hist. II, 395.

—— Wilbur, b., 1787; set. N. Y., Mich., 1835. Lenawee Hist. II, 395.

WHEELER, Aaron, b. 1770; set. N. Y., 1800? Washtenaw Hist., 663.

—— Benjamin, Revolutionary soldier; set., N. Y. Oakland Port., 768.

—— Cyrus, b. Berkshire Co., 1791; set. N. Y. Kalamazoo Port., 310.

—— Katy, of Shrewsbury; m. 1777 Stephen Clapp of N. Y. Lenawee Hist. I, 492.

—— Mary, m. 1835? Joseph Harris of Mich. Washtenaw Port., 355.

—— Reuben, of Gardner; set. Mich., 1840. Lenawee Port., 844.

WHEELOCK, Royal, b., 1766; set. N. Y., 1790? Washtenaw Port., 609.

WHIPPLE, Abigail J., b. Pelham, 1815; m. 1836 George W. Chapman of Mass. and Mich. Saginaw Hist., 815.

—— Adella E., of Douglas; m. 1872 Walter M. Adams of Mass. and Mich. Detroit, 1394.

—— Jerusha, b. 1806; m. William Crane of O. and Mich. Hillsdale Port., 720.

—— Mason, set. N. Y., 1815, Mich. 1833; d. 1842. Washtenaw Hist., 819.

WHITAKER, Flavilla, b. Springfield, 1805; m. George W. Palmer of Mich. Newaygo, 376.

WHITCOMB, Charles H., b. Ashby, 1844; set. Mich., 1873. Berrien Twent., 602.

WHITE, Abisha, of Douglas; set. N. Y., 1800? Hillsdale Hist., 250.

—— Amanda, of Ashfield; m. 1823 William M. Ferry of Mich. Grand Rapids Lowell, appendix, 23; Ottawa Hist., 38.

—— Azuba, b. Douglas, 1807; m. Azariah Mallory of N. Y. and Mich. Hillsdale Hist., 250; Kent. 1222.

—— Benjamin, b. 1775; set. N. Y., 1800? Kent, 1384.

—— Bryant, set. N. Y., Ind. Hillsdale Port., 755.

—— Calvin C., b. Grafton, 1803; set. Mich., 1832. Allegan Twent., 572.

—— Cynthia, m. 1790? Moses Baker of N. Y. and Mich. Lenawee Illus., 148.

—— Erastus, b. 1828; set. Vt., 1850? Clinton Port., 527.

—— J. D., set. N. Y., 1830? Mich., 1850. Washtenaw Hist., 1055.

—— John, b. 1790; set. Mich., Ill. Northern M., 304.

—— John, b. Blanford, 1800; set. N. Y., 1820? Saginaw Port., 824.

—— Jonas, b. Salton, 1795; set. O. Kalamazoo Port., 819.

—— Joseph H., b. 1821; set. O., Mich., 1851. Kalamazoo Port., 819.

—— Laura C., b. Berkshire Co.; m. 1825? John Stitt of O. and Mich. Gratiot, 442, 512.

—— Leonard, set, N. Y., Mich., 1843. Kent, 602.

—— Levi G., b. Plainfield, 1821; set. O., 1825, Mich., 1865. Gratiot, 543.

—— Lucy m. 1810? Eseck Burlingame of N. Y. Calhoun, 133.

—— Maria, m. 1815? Caleb Bates of O. and Mich. Hillsdale Port., 875.

—— Marvel A., b. Worcester Co., 1821; set. N. Y., Mich., 1846. Oakland Port., 780.

—— Mary A. (or W.), b. Ashfield, 1813; set. Mich., 1835. Grand Rapids Lowell, appendix, 69; Ottawa Hist., 52.

—— Samuel, b. Granby, 1798; set. Canada, N. Y., Mich., 1833. Branch Port., 494.

—— Thomas W., b. Ashfield, 1805; set. Mich., 1833? Grand Rapids City, 100; Kent. 261.

WHITE, Wilson, b. 1770; set. N. Y. Jackson Port., 351.

WHITING, Bernice, m. William Park of N. Y. Saginaw Port., 636.

—— John, set. N. Y., 1815? St. Clair, 684.

—— William, set. N. Y., 1800? Saginaw Port., 636.

WHITMAN, Mahitable, b. 1817? m. Norton Gilbert of O. and Mich. Kent, 614.

WHITMARSH, Alvah, b. Cummington, 1796; set. N. Y., 1834, Ill. Lenawee Port., 1135.

—— Horace, of Cummington, set. Mich., 1832? Lenawee Hist. I, 352.

—— Nahum, of Cummington, set. Mich., 1832? Lenawee Hist. I, 352.

—— Samuel P., b. Springfield, 1831; set. N. Y., 1834, Ill., Cal., Mich., 1867. Lenawee Port., 1135.

WHITMORE, Ada, m. 1845? George Hull of Ind. Osceola, 275.

—— Daniel, set. N. Y., O., 1825? Mass., N. J. Lenawee Hist. II, 251.

WHITNEY, Ami, b. 1781; set. N. Y., 1792. Hillsdale Port., 192.

—— David, Jr., b. Westford, 1830; set. Mich., 1856 or 1861. Wayne Chron., 444; Wayne Land., appendix, 203.

—— Deborah, b. Goshen, 1794; m. Ephraim Watkins of N. Y. Hillsdale Port., 446, 589.

—— Edson L., b. Gardner, 1861; set. Mich., 1894. Northern M., 442.

—— Isaac, set. N. Y., 1800? d. 1817. Macomb Hist., 776.

—— J. H., set. Mich., 1870? Washtenaw Hist., 1237.

—— J. W., b. 1816; set. Mich., 1854. Saginaw Port., 646.

—— Joel, b. Conway; set. N. Y., 1785? Lenawee Port., 824.

—— John, 1812 soldier; set. Vt., 1820? Saginaw Hist., 750.

—— John, of Hancock; set. N. Y., Mecosta, 374.

—— John W., set. Mich., 1850? Osceola, 257.

WHITNEY, Jonathan, set. N. Y., 1792; d. 1794. Hillsdale Port., 192.

—— Mary, m. 1820? Samuel Brinton of Conn. and Mich. Branch Twent., 447.

—— Nathan B., set. Ill., 1850? St. Joseph, 85.

—— Richard H., b. 1808; set. Mich., 1831. Lenawee Hist. II, 393.

—— Willard S., b. Hancock, 1821; set. N. Y., 1835, Mich., 1868. Mecosta, 374.

—— William H., set. Mich., 1831. Lenawee Illus., 468.

WHITON, Sophia, b. Montague, 1799; m. 1824, Reuben Nims of Vt. and Mich. Macomb Hist., 833; Macomb Past, 219.

WHITTAKER, Nancy, b. Williamstown, 1788; m. William W. Johnson of N. Y. Isabella, 401.

—— S. A., of Lawrence; set. Mich., 1835. Hillsdale Hist., 220.

WHITTEMORE, Betsey, m. 1825? William Farrar of N. Y. and Mich. Genesee Port., 898.

—— John, b. Salem, 1771; set. Vt., 1790? Lake Huron, 135.

—— John, b. Malden, 1824; set. N. Y., 1826, Mich., 1866. Kent. 1167.

WHITWOOD, Deodatus C., b. W. Stockbridge, 1813; set. Mich., 1836. Detroit, 1234.

WIGHT, Buckminster, b. Sturbridge, 1791; set. Mich., 1832. Wayne Chron., 166.

—— Henry A., b. Sturbridge, 1821; set. Mich., 1832. Wayne Chron., 170.

—— Stanley G., b. Sturbridge, 1825; set. Mich., 1832. Wayne Chron., 170.

WILBER, Laura A., b. Wrentham, 1815; m. Jehial M. Rush of N. Y. Hillsdale Port., 189.

WILBUR, John, b. Adams, 1797; set. Mich., 1835. Jackson Hist., 154.

—— Smith, b. N. Adams, 1785 or 1789; set. N. Y., O., 1834. Branch Port., 318; Hillsdale Port., 824.

WILCOX, Charles, set. N. Y., d. 1816. Branch Port., 449.

—— Harry, b. 1799; set. N. Y., Mich. Jackson Hist., 162.

WILCOX, Jennie E., b. Stockbridge; m. 1849 George E. Rice. Jackson Port., 727.

—— John, of Plymouth, set. N. Y., 1805. Berrien Port., 419.

—— Oliver, set. N. Y., O.; d. 1827. Berrien Port., 419.

——Orrin, set. N. Y., Mich., 1852. Genesee Port., 457.

WILDE, George E., b. Duxbury, 1850; set Mich., 1884? Northern P., 206.

WILDER, Clark W., set. N. Y., 1810? Kalamazoo Port., 324.

—— Oshea, b. Gardner, 1782 or 1784; set. N. Y., Mich., 1831. Calhoun, 134; Homer, 25, 45.

WILKINS Esther, m. 1840? George C. Hayward of N. Y. Newaygo, 228.

WILKINSON, James E., b. Essex Co., 1857; set. N. Y., Mich., 1888. Muskegon Port., 419.

WILLARD, Lucy, b. Dalton or Worcester, 1780; m. 1807? Erastus Day of Canada, N. Y., and Mich., Macomb Hist., 695, 791.

—— Luther B., b. Cambridge, 1818; set. N. Y., 1832, Mich., 1835. Wayne Chron., 233.

——Sallie, m. 1815? Joshua C. Upham of Vt. and O. Kalamazoo Port., 221

——Samuel, b. Lancaster, 1793; set. N. Y., 1794, Mich., 1837. Cass Hist., 337.

WILLIAMS, Alfred L., b. Concord, 1808; set. Mich., 1815. St. Clair, 122; Shiawassee, 159.

—— Alpheus, of Concord, set. Mich., 1815. Saginaw Hist., 194.

—— Alpheus, of Concord, set. Mich., 1815. Saginaw Hist., 194.

—— Alpheus F., b. Concord, 1812; set. Mich., Cal. Shiawassee, 159.

—— Benjamin O., b. Concord, 1810; set. Mich., 1815. St. Clair, 120; Shiawassee, 159.

——Caroline, L., b. Concord, 1806; m. Rufus W. Stevens of Mich. Shiawassee, 159.

—— Celia, b. Northbridge, 1856; m. —— Taylor. Isabella, 341.

WILLIAMS, Elisha, set. N. Y., 1820? Mich., 1836. Branch Twent., 469.

——Elizabeth, m. 1820? William Dewey of Vt. and Mich. Jackson Port., 495.

——Ephraim, S. (or J.), b. Concord, 1802; set. Mich., 1815. St. Clair, 124; Shiawassee, 159.

—— Erastus, b. Stockbridge; set. N .Y.; d. 1873. Kalamazoo Port., 217.

—— Gardner D., b. Concord, 1804; set. Mich., 1815. Saginaw Hist., 209; Shiawassee, 159.

—— Harriet L., b. Concord, 1814; m. George W. Rogers of Mich. and Cal. Shiawassee, 159.

—— Harvey, b. Concord, 1774; set. Mich., 1809. Saginaw Hist., 194.

——Henry, b. Leverett, 1786; set. Vt., 1810? N. Y., 1827. Ionia Port., 215.

—— Jacob A., set. N. Y. Berrien Port., 703.

—— John, set. N. Y., 1838. Clinton Port., 504.

—— John D., b. Boston, 1819; set. N. Y., 1838; Mich., 1848. Clinton Port., 504.

—— Joseph R., b. Taunton, 1800; graduate of Harvard 1831; set. Mich., 1839. St. Joseph, 125.

—— Lucy, m. J. Hoadley of N. Y. Berrien Port., 520.

—— Mary, m. 1826 Fellows Gates of Canada and Mich. Ionia Port., 434.

—— Mary Ann, b. Concord, 1807; m. Schuyler Hodges of Mich. Shiawassee, 159.

—— Oliver, b. Roxbury, 1774; set. Mich., 1808 or 1815. Oakland Hist., 300; Shiawassee, 158.

—— Paul W., set. Mich., 1860? Isabella, 341.

—— Riley, b. Westfield, 1766; set. Vt. Lenawee Hist. I, 288.

WILLIAMSON, Britton, set. Mich., 1840? Mecosta, 194.

WILLIARD, Julia, b. Berkshire Co., 1815; m. 1st, Stephen L. Gilbert of O.; m. 2d, Marcus Van of Mich. Hillsdale Port., 753.

WILLIS, Lucretia, m. 1830? John Seaman of N. Y. and Mich. Newaygo, 214.

WILLIS, Richard Storrs, b. Boston, 1819; set. Mich. Detroit, 1104; Wayne Land., 858.

WILMARTH, Susan, b. Stockbridge; m. 1815? Charles De Land of N. Y. and Mich. Saginaw Port., 625.

WILMER, Nancy, b. Stockbridge, 1795? m. Ethan Brown of N. Y. Mecosta, 528.

WILMOUTH, Arbelia, b. 1795; m. Ansel Snow of Mass. and Mich. Kalamazoo Hist., 415; Kalamazoo Port., 866.

WILSON, Charles S., b. Springfield, 1819; set. Mich., 1838. Allegan Twent., 572.

—— Daniel, b. Berkshire Co., 1810; set. Mich., 1836. Branch Hist., facing 312.

—— David, b. Bellingham, 1766; set. Conn., 1776. Lenawee Hist. I, 398.

—— Martin, b. Norwich, 1794; set. Mich., 1838. St. Clair, 122.

—— Rebecca, b. Adams, 1799; m. 1822 Asa Hill of Mass., N. Y. and Mich. Lenawee Hist. II, 317, 375.

—— Reuben, b. Berkshire Co., 1772; set. N. Y., Mich., 1835. Branch Hist., facing 312; Branch Port., 188.

—— Samuel, set. Vt., N. Y., Mich., 1838. Genesee Port., 655.

—— William J., b. Boston, 1866; set. Mich., 1871. Ionia Port., 564.

WINCHELL, Dennis, m. 1830? William Homes of N. Y. and Mich. Newaygo, 458.

WINCHESTER, Lucy, b. Petersham, 1807; m. Levi Babbitt of N. Y. and Mich. Jackson Port., 620.

—— Phebe, b Middlesex Co.; m. 1800? Jesse Stowell of Mass. and N. Y. Jackson Port., 275.

WING, Austin E., b. Conway, 1792; set. O., Mich., 1815? Monroe, 151.

—— Benjamin, b. Hardwick, 1774; set. N. Y., 1815? Mich., 1832. Washtenaw Hist., 870.

—— Benjamin, b. Hawley, 1832; set. Mo., 1869, Mich., 1875. Isabelle, 498.

—— Elijah, b. 1775; set. N. Y., 1814 Lenawee Hist. II, 265.

—— Elnathan, set. N. Y., 1810? Clinton Port., 774.

WING, Walden, b. Washington, 1814; set. N. Y., 1826; Mich., 1838. Lenawee Hist. II, 265; Lenawee Port., 947.

WINSHIP, Nehemiah, b. Lexington; set. N. Y., 1790? Genesee Port., 355.

WINSLOW, George W., b. Colerain, 1809; set. Mich., 1835. St. Clair, 119.

—— Sarah, m. 1830? Daniel McLaren of N. Y. and Mich. Washtenaw Hist., 816.

WITHERELL, James, b. Mansfield, 1759; set. Conn., 1783, Vt., 1788, Mich., 1808 or 1810. Detroit, 1132; Wayne Chron., 125, 275; Wayne Land., 287.

WITHINGTON, William H., b. Dorchester, 1835; set. Mich., 1857. Jackson Hist., 757; Jackson Port., 791.

WIXSON, Solomon, set. N. Y. 1790? d. 1812. Branch Port., 295.

WOLCOTT, Axa, m. 1810? Elijah Daniels of N. Y. Ingham Port., 733.

—— Jason B., b. Berkshire Co., 1787; set. N. Y., O., Mich. Hillsdale Port., 942.

WONSEY, Henry, set. Mich., 1825. St. Clair, 708.

WOOD, Abner B., b., 1784; set. N. Y., Mich., 1836. Ingham Port., 741.

—— Andrew, b. Middlebury, 1783; set. N. Y., 1793. Macomb Hist., 765.

—— Charles M., b. W. Brookfield, 1826; set. N. Y., Mich., 1845. Ingham Port., 415.

—— Cynthia, b. Cheshire, 1783; m. 1807, Henry Bowen, 2d, of Mass. and N. Y. Lenawee Hist. II, 195.

—— Isaac W., b. Westboro, 1844; set. Mich., 1872. Kent, 1175.

—— Jedediah, set. N. Y., 1803? Hillsdale Port., 404.

—— Joel, set. N. Y., 1824? O., 1847, Mich., 1882. Clinton Port., between 754 and 774.

—— Jonas B., set. N. Y., 1820? Muskegon Port., 514.

—— Levi, of Pelham; Revolutionary soldier; set. N. Y., 1803. Hillsdale Port., 404.

—— Louisa, m. 1810? Spencer Marsh of N. Y. Jackson Hist., 834.

WOOD Mehitable, m. 1815? Aaron Dunham of N. Y. and O. Lenawee Port., 992.

—— Susan B., b. Westfield, 1814; m. 1834 John Benson of Mich. Saginaw Hist., 940.

—— Timothy, b. Springfield; set. N. Y.? 1830? Saginaw Hist., 940.

WOODARD, Jonas, b. Dana; set. Mich., 1831. Kalamazoo Hist., 429.

WOODBURY, Abigail, b. Beverly, 1776; m. Ebenezer Fiske. Branch Port., 341.

—— George B., b. Sutton or Worcester, 1816; set. N. Y., Mich. 1837 or 1840. Grand River, 441; Muskegon Hist., 77; Muskegon Port., 124.

—— Jeremiah P., b. 1805; set. N. Y., Mich., 1836. Kalamazoo Port., 233.

—— Lydia, b. Salem; m. 1817 Curtis Brigham of Mass. and Mich. Kalamazoo Port., 361.

WOODCOCK, David F., set. N. Y., Mich. Berrien Port., 509.

WOODMANSEE, George, set. Mich? Gratiot, 608.

WOODRUFF, Harriet A., m. Albert C. Noble of N. Y. and Mich. Ingham Port., 859.

WOODS, David, b. Shutesbury, 1777; set. Vt., 1800? N. Y., 1837. Jackson Port., 380.

WOODWARD, F. E., b. Millbury, 1813; set. Mich., 1839. St. Clair, 122.

WOODWORTH, John, b. 1775; set. N. Y. Lenawee Hist. II, 191.

WOOLCOTT, Samuel, set. O., Mich. Berrien Port., 729.

—— Warren, set. O., Mich.; d. 1877. Berrien Port., 729.

WOOLSON, Asa b. Lunenburg, 1767; set. Vt. Bay Gansser, 501.

WORDEN, Clark, set. Mich., 1825. St. Clair, 725.

WORTH, Richard, b. Nantucket; set. N. Y., 1780? Lenawee Port., 838.

WORTHINGTON, Henry, b. Agawam Corners, 1814; set. O., Mich., 1840. Berrien Twent., 429.

—— Henry, b. Springfield, 1815; set. Mich. Cass Twent., 89.

WRIGHT B. W., b. Plympton, 1838; set. Mich., 1855. Houghton, 286; Northern P., 198; Upper P., 451.

—— Clarinda, m. 1825? Zebedee Phillips of N. Y. Ingham Port., 495.

——David, b. Northfield; set. N. Y., 1800? Kent, 793.

—— Deodatus E., b. Williamstown, 1812; set. N. Y., Mich., 1836 or 1837. Gratiot, 623; Jackson Hist., 1020; Jackson Port., 593; Northern M., 373.

—— Emma H., of New Marlboro;; m. 1884 James W. Woodworth of Mich. Clinton Port., 884.

—— Ermina, m. 1815? Samuel Livermore of Mass. Saginaw Port., 481.

—— Frederick, b. Berkshire Co., 1785; set. N. Y., 1814 or 1824; Mich., 1836. Jackson Hist., 1020; Jackson Port., 593; Northern M., 373.

—— Jason K., set. Penn., 1840? Northern P., 207.

—— Joseph S., set. N. Y., 1835? Mich., 1870. Jackson Hist., 824.

—— Marcia, b. Wilbraham, 1791; m. Obed Edwards of O. Monroe, 476.

—— Philander, b. Northampton, 1805; set. Wis. Kent, 638.

—— Sarah or Sally, b. Deerfield, 1795 or 1796; m. 1816 Joseph Woodman of N. Y., and Mich. Ionia Port., 352; Kent, 1406; Wayne Chron., 133.

—— Solomon, graduate of Williams college; set. Mich., 1837. Grand River, 165.

—— William, set. N. H., N. Y., 1815. Genesee Port., 897.

WYLLYS, Rufus, b. 1805; set. O., Ill., Mich., 1851. Hillsdale Port., 258.

WYMAN, Jonathan, b. Concord, 1769 or 1774; set. N. H., N. Y., 1804. Lenawee Hist. I, 290; Lenawee Port., 797.

—— Thomas, set. N. Y., 1825? Oakland Biog., 165.

YAW, Lydia, b. Berkshire Co., 1836; m. Daniel Harris of Mich. Berrien Port., 376.

YAW, Theodore, b. N. Adams; set. Mich., 1852. Berrien Twent., 796.

YOUNG, Henry, b. Martha's Vineyard; set. N. Y., 1800? Northern P., 439.

——James H., b. Boston, 1798; set. Mich., 1830. Washtenaw Hist., 1411; Washtenaw Port., 468.

YOUNG, Joseph, set. N. Y., 1815? Shiwassee, 530.

YOUNGS, Curtis S., b. Lanesboro; set. N. Y., 1825? Mich., 1836. Branch Twent., 861.

It will be noted that few cross references have been used. Names are spelled in every case exactly as found in the records, with references made from one form of name to another only when both forms seem to be employed by the same individual.

It is assumed that the searcher will know the various spellings of a family name; such as Waterman and Watterman, Whitmore and Whittemore, Willis and Wyllys, etc. We know of no better guide to such variations than the Index to vols. 1—50 of the New England historical and genealogical register.

When this work was undertaken, every effort was made to find and index all the Michigan county histories in existence. Inquiries were made of the large libraries of Michigan and the libraires outside that seemed likely to have any considerable number of these books; and every work of this character possessed or known by these institutions was located and indexed. Still it is not strange that other works have come to our attention (a few of them published since our search).

The following have been noted and are listed in the same form as those on pages 1—5. It is needless to say they have not been indexed.

It may be added that the Library of Congress has made large additions to its collection of Michigan material and now possesses 70 of the works, indexed, lacking only *Jackson Port., Lake Huron, and Lansing.*

Alcona. History of Alcona Co. by Charles P. Reynolds, 1877. (No copy located).

Alpena. Centennial history of Alpena County . . . By David D. Oliver. Alpena, Mich, Argus printing house, 1903. 186p. (L. C.)

Genesee Biog. Biographical history of Genesee County. Indianapolis, B. F. Bowen & Co. [1908?]. 401p. (L. C.)

Grand Traverse. History of Grand Traverse and Leelanaw counties. By Sprague & Smith. B. F. Bowen & Co., 1903. 806p. (No copy located)

Gratiot Hist. Gratiot County, Michigan. Historical, biographical, statistical . . . Willard D. Tucker, Saginaw, Mich., Press of Seeman & Peters, 1913. 1353p. (L. C.)

Jackson DeLand. DeLand's history of Jackson County . . . by Col. Charles V. DeLand. [Logansport? Ind], B. F. Bowen, 1903. 1123p. (L. C.)

Leelanaw County, see GRAND TRAVERSE.

Lenawee Memoirs. Memoirs of Lenawee County . . . Richard I. Bonner. Madison, Wis., Western historical association, 1909. 2v. (L. C.)

Manistee Cent. Centennial history of Manistee County, containing addresses by Hon. John C. Blanchard and Hon. B. M. Cutcheon. (No copy located)

Manistee Hist. History of Manistee, Mason and Oceana counties. [Chicago, H. R. Page & co., 1882] 78, 154, 88p. (L. C.)

(Each county has special title page.)

Mason County, see *Manistee.*

Northern M. Bowen. Northern Michigan. Chicago, B. F. Bowen & co. 1905. (No copy located)

Northern M. Powers. A history of northern Michigan and its people by Percy F. Powers. Chicago, Lewis publishing company, 1912. 3v. (L. C.)

Northern P. Sawyer. History of the Northern peninsula. By Alvah L. Sawyer. 1911. (No copy located)

Oceana County see *Manistee.*

St. Joseph Biog. Biographies of St. Joseph County. Chapman bros., 1889. 609p. (No copy located)

St. Joseph Cutler. History of St. Joseph County . . . H. G. Cutler. Chicago and New York. Lewis publishing company, 1911. 2v. (L. C.

Wexford. History of Wexford County by John H. Wheeler. [Logansport, Ind.] B. F. Bowen, 1903. 557p. (L. C.)